D1570997

Imagining
the
World

Imagining the World

Mythical Belief versus Reality in Global Encounters

O. R. DATHORNE

BERGIN & GARVEY
Westport, Connecticut • London

Library of Congress Cataloging-in-Publication Data

Dathorne, O. R.
    Imagining the world : mythical belief versus reality in global
encounters / O. R. Dathorne.
        p.   cm.
    Includes bibliographical references and index.
    ISBN 0–89789–364–6 (alk. paper)
    1. Discoveries in geography. 2. Voyages and travels.
3. Geographical myths. I. Title.
    G95.D38 1994
    910.4—dc20   93–9016

British Library Cataloguing in Publication Data is available.

Library of Congress Catalog Card Number: 93–9016
ISBN: 0–89789–364–6

First published in 1994

Bergin & Garvey, 88 Post Road West, Westport, CT 06881
An imprint of Greenwood Publishing Group, Inc.

Printed in the United States of America

The paper used in this book complies with the
Permanent Paper Standard issued by the National
Information Standards Organization (Z39.48–1984).

10   9   8   7   6   5   4   3   2   1

For

Hilde Ostermaier Dathorne

who has made this book possible

Contents

Acknowledgments

First, I wish to thank the University of Kentucky and particularly the Department of English for affording me the time and opportunity to research, write and rewrite this book. Having taught in various parts of the world, and indeed, for the past quarter of a century in the United States, I am constantly surprised and always grateful to exist in a climate free from the small wars that constantly plague academia. I know this because I am myself a veteran.

Second, I must thank my graduate students at the University of Kentucky who first put up with the various courses I aired under this rubric, and who very often in discussion were able to constantly challenge my conclusions. Additionally, Emily Carpenter has proved a real boon, in assisting me with many of the tasks needed to see this work to completion. For her services, I am further indebted to the University of Kentucky for grant support.

Third, another long-suffering group of unknowing participants are the members of the Association of Caribbean Studies. For the past few years at our annual conferences in the Dominican Republic, Dakar, Jamaica, and Egypt, they have interacted with me on Columbus and the conquistadors, on Africa and Afrocentrism, on Arabism, on the New World and the non-European. Our deliberations helped me to formulate what at first were only fleeting ideas in my own mind.

Fourth, Jan Carew, author and fellow countryman, has been a friend of longstanding. My wife swears that he knows everything; so often when the standard sources failed, I would call on him, and we would talk endlessly. I always came away gratified and challenged; hopefully, perhaps, even a little less sure.

Fifth, the dedication speaks for itself; it is no mere formality. My wife makes it possible for me to work, free from the everyday hassles which she takes on. I remain most grateful to her for her unselfishness and generosity.

Finally, I owe a special thanks to Dr. Lynn Flint of Greenwood, who helped persuade me that the work was worth finishing, and who made herself always available. I hope that she will feel that the final result made her patience worthwhile and, perhaps, in some small way justified her expectation.

In the final analysis, I have to bear the burdens of whatever notions are expressed here, and which may not at times satisfy the whimsies of the expert. I was not seeking to research one narrow area to death; instead I was trying to convey my own vital surprise at what I had found, namely that here in this so-called New World, we have inherited the fables of Africa and Europe and, perhaps, in no small measure, this constantly prevents us from truly perceiving one another. It is my wish that, in some small way, this book will help us dare to imagine not the older worlds but a newer one, with limitless possibilities. Someone once accused me of being an optimist. Perhaps this is what I have to be, despite serious misgivings.

Imagining
the
World

Chapter 1 _____

Europe Invents a
New World

Europeans did not merely "discover" the so-called New World — they invented it. An examination of the European past can help identify the persistent archetypes that arose there and later reemerged in New World encounters. In addition to Arab and Greek scientific reasoning, the Bible offered an obvious backdrop against which fifteenth-century exploration occurred. Beyond that, two elemental themes are worth considering — first, the journey as archetypal quest, a concept rooted in the European past, and, second, mystical beliefs lingering on in postmedieval Europe. When Europe encountered another world, it simply passed on its own beliefs.

Christopher Columbus' four New World encounters were symbolic of the European encounter generally, for he actively demonstrated that his journey was redemptive. Had he not suffered and been brought back to Spain in chains? Was he not the living embodiment of the hero figure?

This motif — the journey and its transforming values — was part of what most people understood in the postmedieval world. After all, they had inherited the archetypal journey not only as theory but also as immediate fact. For instance, pilgrimages to the Holy Cities were fairly commonplace. As devotees embarked on these personal journeys of faith, they sought to make contact with the physical artifacts of Christ's presence on earth. Similarly, the Crusades, which had been organized with active church support since 1095, lasted until well into the thirteenth century; these also introduced the opportunity for redemption, as Christians pitted themselves against the heathen Muslims.

One major difference exists between the pilgrimage and the Crusade. The former was personal and individual, whereas the latter was group-oriented. Thus, the pilgrimage achieved its ends if there were small acquisitions from the biblical past; the Crusade sought to create its effect through the domination of another people.

Both pilgrimage and crusade were present in fifteenth- and sixteenth-century exploration. The "pilgrim" was the solitary explorer who sought to "discover" not himself but something outside himself — new peoples, new lands. The "crusader" was the explorer as spokesperson, acting for a king or the Church and seeking to convert large groups of "savages" to a new way of life.

Pilgrim and crusader elements transform the epic journeys of the *Odyssey* and the *Aeneid*, and certain aspects of these showed up in the medieval experience. The "pilgrim" element is apparent in that both Ulysses and Aeneas undergo "other-worldly" experiences, in the most literal sense. As Ulysses wanders, he encounters one-eyed Cyclops and cannibals; as Aeneas journeys, he visits the "underworld," and he meets Centaurs, half-human, half-horse, as well as the six-headed Scylla, who has consumed six of his companions.

All of these themes return in the encounters of travel literature, as the "pilgrim" and "crusader" link up with classical heroes. The opening of the *Odyssey*, "about the man of many turns, who many/ways wandered," and the first few lines of the *Aeneid*, concerning "the man, Aeneas, who, after many years of wandering came to Italy," illustrate a pertinent point. To "wander" or to sing of the self is itself partly the key to self-discovery. The texts do not advocate a life-style centered around hearth and home. Instead, "wandering" brings change and alteration, thereby restoring wholeness to the group and the individual.

Against this backdrop, the sixteenth-century explorer as archetypal voyager demonstrates four aspects of medieval life that must be considered — the visual, the verbal, the viewed, and the visionary. These aspects all exist in the texts of earlier travelers, in what they related about their world and in how they view their world. The "visual" refers to the way in which they perceived the worlds to which they journeyed, particularly in terms of the illustrations and maps that often accompanied travel publications. The "verbal" often takes second place to the visual, in that verbal accounts are more often than not passed on orally from one literature person to a host of nonliterates. With each telling, the account changes, but there remains an overall perspective, derived partly from illustrations and maps and partly from the recounting of travel tales. This process contributes to remaking a new type of legend. The "viewed" is more difficult to ascertain, for it concerns itself not so much with a speaker/reader response but with a perception of what the original writer observed. For instance, when do the biblical and Greek legends distort the "viewed" into the "reviewed"? When is the "seen" really part of an "unseen" that is located only in the primary reporter's mind? The "visionary" is the most exciting, in that it draws from the total experience and places a spiritual value judgment on it. One cannot pretend that such a response is anything but ethnocentric, but it does provide an understanding of new people and places that goes beyond itemizing the fantastic. Visual, verbal, viewed, and visionary approaches represent aspects of activity and response in the postmedieval period. There are clear signposts in them all, as well as perceptions from differing angles.

The journey is as old as that of Adam and Christ. Adam's expulsion from Eden begins his travail, during which he undergoes the experiences that humanize him. Christ's epic journey more easily resembles Joseph Campbell's formula — his departure is from a heavenly kingdom, his initiation is the crucifixion, and his return comes about through resurrection and ascension.

One begins with the Bible, because in the medieval world of Europe, Christianity was an accepted norm. Columbus stated this over and over again in his log-book and letters but even more so in *Libro de las profecías*; this he put together with scriptural quotations after the débacle of his second voyage of 1493. Columbus made the point that his journey was inspired by God and that he was "Christo ferens" (Christ bearer), as his signature attested. Columbus noted to their Catholic Majesties: "The Lord purposed that there should be something clearly miraculous in this matter of the voyage to the Indies." He cited Isaiah 49 with particular relish: "Give ear, ye islands, and hearken, ye people from afar." He placed the word "Note" beside his reference to Isaiah 60: "For the islands wait for me, and the ships of the sea in the beginning: that I may bring thy sons from afar." The Bible is a major source for us to understand the cultural climate. It exalts humans as "righteous ones whose line is gone out through all the world" in Psalm 19. In *Libro de las profecías*, this psalm is cited three times, along with numerous references to standard and apocalyptic scripture.[1]

Greek thought was also most influential. Aristotle was said to have stated that one could cross the ocean from Spain to the Indies in just a few days; Strabo confirmed that this feat had been attempted by mariners of his own time. Revival of learning, with Arab and Italian assistance, recirculated Ptolemy's books, especially his *Guide to Geography*,[2] which influenced Europeans for over a thousand years.

Pierre d'Ailly's *Tractatus de Imagine Mundi* (*Imago Mundi*)[3] (c. 1410) and Paolo Toscanelli's letters to Columbus both had influences on the man and his view of the world. A copy of Toscanelli's letter to a Portuguese canon offers insight into intellectual ideas in Europe in 1492.[4] For

Toscanelli, Marco Polo was right: From Lisbon to Cipango (Japan) or from Lisbon to Quinsay (Hangchow), there were only a few thousand miles. D'Ailly quoted Aristotle on the proximity of Spain to the Indies. Pope Pius II's *Historia Rerum Ubique Gestarum* (1477)[5] was also most influential. The first European globe, commissioned by the Nuremberg town council and created by Martin Behaim in 1492, showed just how near the Far East was in relation to Europe. Apart from the mythical sea islands, there was no land area for the Americas.

In addition, we should note certain transformations that took place, particularly as visions of "worldly treasures" changed fifteenth-century exploration from pilgrimage and Crusade into "discovery." At first, the visual version, through maps and illustrations, presented a very basic view of the world. Later, "words" began to make the encounter assume new aspects, including the "viewed," when Europeans seemed to be acting out of their cosmic sense of being right. With the "visionary" concept, we enter into the world where European mythology and spiritual beliefs were directed toward non-European people.

VISUAL ACCOUNTS

At the visual level, two aspects are most important — namely, illustrations and maps. Illustrations still tend to popularize both books and maps. The problem is that, very often like the books and maps themselves, the early visual accounts frequently ignored credibility. Map illustrations, painted in graphic form, often depicted the end of the world and the acceptance of the faithful into Christ's bosom. They also helped to imprint in people's minds, especially for those many who were unable to read, a rather startling view of the world. For example there were two distorted figures representing Gog and Magog.

Around the edges of many medieval maps, the "monstrous races" were depicted in all their abnormality — the Ciapod, who used his one enormous foot to shelter himself from the sun; the Essidenes, whose fare consisted of their dead parents; the manticore, part-human, part-lion; and the ostrich, who fed on iron. The biblical scenes of the Last Judgment and of Lot's wife being turned into a pillar of salt reinforced a belief in the monstrosities. On Columbus' second voyage, he named them Caribs or cannibals "que son habitadas de gente que comen carne humana."[6] As Kirkpatrick Sale has noted, Columbus, like "any knowledgeable man [of his time] would have expected to meet them in such a place as the Indies."[7]

The "cannibals" gave their name to the entire region, not because of their dietary preferences but because of European imaginings. They gave legitimacy to Columbus' second voyage by confirming the mythology of cartographical illustrations. The real problem is that depictions of man-eating Caribs continued to project the image of monstrosity, so beloved of earlier travelers, onto the original inhabitants of the entire continent. Theodore de Bry's illustration for the fourteen-volume series *Historia Americae* (c. 1594) helped to circulate further the myth of man-eating Caribs. There they are depicted consuming large human bones, roasting human flesh in a huge open fire, and licking their fingers in obvious delight. Women, men, and children are all part of this scene.

A map is itself a "legend," but an especially important one in an illiterate society. Maps projected a European world view on the rest of the world. There were climatic diagrams that presented a quadripartite arrangement of the world. At the center was the Ocean River and north and south parallel lines that divided up the world into "torrid," "temperate," and "frigid" zones. Other kinds of diagrams offered a T-O categorization of the world, with the continents forming the "T" and the encircling ocean the "O." At the top (east) lay Asia, to the left (north) was Europe, and to the right (south) was Africa. Diagonally, the Don and Nile rivers divided Asia from Europe and Africa, while the Mediterranean separated Europe from Africa. Around the entire circumference ran the "Ocean River" or, as the Arabs termed it, "the Sea of Darkness."

From the outset, these *mappae-mundi*, as they were known, focused on the problem of rendering Asia and Africa as continents distinctly apart from Europe, with their borders on the unknown and frightening Ocean Sea. They made the possibility of the journey even more difficult, since they emphasized the perilous nature of the unknown. Macrobius (c. 399–423 A.D.), Orosius (c. 383–post 417), and Isidore of Seville (c. 560–636) popularized the *mappae-mundi* in ways that sketched their own fears. Their depictions lasted well into the fifteenth century.[8]

The visual images of the *mappae-mundi* were first ignored by the church fathers. Cosmographic depictions were not significant for Christians. "What can Christians learn from science?" Saint Damien had asked, but both Saint Jerome (340–420) and Saint Paulinus (353–431) found maps useful. By the fourteenth century, Fra Paolino Veneto could endorse the *mappae-mundi*, stating:

I think that it is not just difficult but impossible without a world map to make an image of, or even for the mind to grasp, what is said of the children and grandchildren of Noah and the Four Kingdoms and other nations and regions, both in divine and human writings. There is needed moreover a twofold map, [composed] of painting and writing.[9]

Fra Veneto was making two important points. First, the church by then had acquiesced to map-making; second, for the map to be useful, it had to incorporate both a visual and a verbal text.

Once the map had established its features, even with the blessing of the church, it placed invariable limits on the extent of the world. In a way, the visual representation fit in quite well with the medieval Christian view of the world — that the world was possibly coming to an end by the year 2000 A.D. Christian influence indicated another mythical direction for these maps. At the center, the navel of the world, was Jerusalem, toward which pilgrims would wend their way. The T-O format could thus be presented as a cross at the center of the world, reinforcing the universal symbolism of Christ's crucifixion.[10]

Hereford Cathedral contained an example *par excellence* of a point at which geography and religion were one. Dated from 1290, this cathedral mural, both illustration and map, utilized biblical beliefs that warned of the imminent destruction of the world. The map portion resembled an illustration located in Hughes de Saint-Victor's *Descriptio Mappae Mundi*,[11] composed between 1128 and 1129. The map depicted how fact and nonfact had both become part of medieval belief. At the left outer circumference, the biblical tribes of Gog and Magog were shown; to the right lay the mythical kingdom of "prester," or Prester John.[12]

Any would-be traveler therefore had a plan, even a route map, such as the one made by Matthew Paris.[13] The world had been made to conform to premedieval and Christian interpretation. The attention of anyone who looked at a T-O map would thus be focused on Jerusalem, legitimizing the pursuits of the "pilgrim" and "crusader" through the illustration. The map had moved from being a crude representation of widely held belief to being carefully executed art that sought to correct old opinion and dispense new ideology.

Portolani, or sailing charts, tended to be more accurate, but they were restricted in large measure to the Mediterranean, with a plethora of coastal detail and little information about inland areas. Although these would have been used primarily by sailors, they still confirmed a sense of place, emphasizing the known as opposed to the unknown, the charted as opposed to the uncharted. Some writers have seen the *portolani* as limited transformations of the Greek cartographical *periplus* into a chart, in response to scientific knowledge.[14]

What was visually perceived and rendered as a chart, a map, an illustration, and later an atlas was used to define relationships with both "other" people and "other" lands. With the aid of the map, a journey could be begun, later arrangements for mapping the area could be made, and information could be passed on. In the sixteenth century, maps, therefore often contained the collective knowledge of a nation. As such, they were jealously guarded. Sailors were often sworn to secrecy, and frequently children were employed to help draw maps, in an effort to prevent adults from learning their secrets. After all, no one should be able to acquire the route to the transforming journey easily.[15]

Yet maps continued to display "legends." Abraham Cresques, who probably drew the famous Catalan atlas of 1375, was a much sought-after mapmaker. He adorned his atlas with the tall stories of his time, like the pearl divers of the Indian Ocean who were specially protected from sharks. Cresques' atlas is in eight parts. In it, Prester John's place is taken by the equally exotic (but real) African Emperor, Mansa Musa of Mali.

Mapmakers not only described the world, but presented, through the visual images, a European projection of it based on speculation and hearsay. In a way, mapmakers were afraid to break with the past. Fra Mauro, for instance, produced "El Mappamundo" for King Alfonso of Portugal in 1459.[16] This map was a radical departure, in that the world is no longer contained nor the journey outward circumscribed by the forbidding outer ring of the Ocean Sea. Instead, Fra Mauro opened up a route to the fabled Indies. Now, according to his visual representation, one could sail round the circular ocean to Africa and China. The mapmaker had thus anticipated the voyager.

VERBAL ACCOUNTS

The focus of verbal belief is, of course, what the pictures tell. Fundamental to the verbal response are, first, the Bible; second, the classics; third, scientific belief; and fourth, accepted mythology. Visual and verbal representations complement each other, pass through stages of pre-Christian versions and then Christian synthesizing, and finally lead to a concept of the "viewed" — what is actually seen as a result of the total experience.

The quest for the Holy Grail can be interpreted as the larger "journey" against which fifteenth- and sixteenth-century exploration may be observed in its verbal sense. Put differently, although Ulysses, Aeneas, and even Beowulf seemingly have a religious motif to complement their sense of being "wanderers," the quest of Arthurian knights has become Christianized. The Anglo-Saxon hero of *Beowulf* endures anguish, but for no reason other than the fact that his lord has died. He moans, "Everything is full of hardship in the kingdom of earth."[17] More pertinent, because it combines the "journey" with the symbolic sea, is "The Seafarer," who cries out, "I heard naught there save the sea booming, the ice-cold billow, at times the song of the swan.[18] The protagonists of both "The Wanderer" and "The Seafarer" seek solace in Christian faith. Likewise, later accounts of Celtic myths, which had been full of horns of plenty and cauldrons that restore life, substitute the silver Holy Grail as a Christian boon.

Jerusalem had been conquered in 1099, and, although the Fall of Acre in 1291 effectively terminated the Crusades, their effect continued to be significant in Europe. Columbus, for instance, constantly implored his sovereign to devote himself to the reconquest and to permit Columbus to do so as well. He cited Psalm 14, verse 7: "Oh that the salvation of Israel were come out of Zion." Columbus then added, "I pledge myself, in the name of God, to bring Him there in safety."[19]

Earlier Christians had anticipated Columbian exploration. St. Isidore of Seville had written his explanation of the world in the sixth century.[20] Helena Flavia Augusta (died 337 A.D.), the mother of Constantine I and reputedly the discoverer of Christ's cross, had visited Jerusalem some three centuries before. Richard Hakluyt wrote that she was both beautiful and learned, speaking Greek and Latin fluently.[21] In the eighth century, Bishop Arculf and Bishop Willibald also journeyed there, and, in the ninth century, in 827 A.D., Bertrand the Wise left an account of his own voyage. They all visited religious cities, sometimes witnessed miracles, and observed holy relics.[22] The accounts speak of the marvels that derived from holy pilgrimage; in Syria, Bishop Willibald, in the company of a Black man and his wife, was mysteriously saved from a lion:

And on their way they were met by a lion, which threatened them with much fearful roaring; but the black encouraged them, and told them to go forwards; and when they approached it, the lion, as God willed, hurried off in another direction, and they soon heard him roaring in the distance.[23]

These are the earlier versions of the "wonders" and "marvels" that explorers would later encounter in the fifteenth and sixteenth centuries. The accounts use the "visual" representation of Jerusalem on the *mappae mundi* as the *raison d'être* for travel. Along the way, one learns incidentally about surrounding areas. What is emphasized is "otherness," the differences between the self-righteous "us" and the pagan "them."

When writers feel more comfortable with the verbal mode and rely on fewer maps and illustrations, verbal exaggeration may replace cornucopia as superlative effusions. Thus, Henry Maundrell, much later, in 1697, observed a marble fountain "of greater beauty than is usually seen in Turkey" and an orange garden "gilded with fruit, hanging thicker upon them than ever I saw apples in England."[24] Columbus spared no adjectives when he described his first landfall: "In this island the trees were so dense that it was marvellous, and there were such varieties of trees, unknown to anyone, as was astonishing. Some of them were with fruit, some were in flower, so that everything was green."[25] These words recall the loss of Eden and the search for the Heavenly Kingdom, afterward to be partially located in El Dorado in the New World.

Seeking and acquiring gold are sanctioned in the Bible. Additionally, gold had preoccupied Europeans since the twelfth century, when the philosophy of alchemy (actually, the "art" of a synthetic system from the Chinese, Indians, Arabs, and ancient Romans) was totally distorted. Much of the search focused on attempts to transmute "base" metals into gold. The search for wealth derived, therefore, from this, as well as from biblical references such as in 1 Kings 10:11 where "Huram's fleet, which has brought gold from Ophir, also brought from there a large amount of juniper wood and jewels." Thus, Solomon's wisdom takes on greater luster when he becomes an archetypal "Gilded Man." Columbus and those who followed him sought Ophir as an obvious goal. The Gilded Man is a personification who indicates the reason for the journey, substituting his form for gold, pearls, silver, spices, and so on. Furthermore, the Gilded Man assumes the role of a social boon, in that the pursuit of him and the acquisition of his wealth not only bring honor to the seeker but also endow the nation with wealth.

There was, of course, a very pragmatic reason for Europeans to venture out, namely that Muslims had locked off routes to the gold of Africa, the silk of China, and the spices of the Moluccas. Columbus, like other explorers, knew his Bible, and, for him, the verse from 2 Chronicles 8:18 linked the quest of gold with the sea: "And Huram sent him [Solomon] by the hands of his servants' ships, and servants that had knowledge of the sea; they went with the servants of Solomon to Ophir, and took thence four hundred and fifty talents of gold and brought them to King Solomon." Columbus cited Flavius Josephus' *Antiquities of the Jews* (93 A.D.) as his authority that Ophir is "now called the Gold Country, which is India."[26] In his 1503 letter, Columbus argued that, just as God had pointed out the gold's location to David and Solomon, so God had also shown him the regions of the New World full of wealth.

El Dorado itself was first found by the Spanish in Colombia. The story went that, every morning, the emperor bathed with gold dust, afterward ritually cleansing himself in Lake Guatavita. In token of his royal majesty, his subjects also tossed golden objects and jewels into the lake.[27] Writing about the fabled city, Pedro de Castañeda stated:

In the year 1530 Nuño de Guzman, who was President of New Spain, had in his possession an Indian, a native of the valley or valleys of Oxitipar, who was called Tejo by the Spaniards. This Indian said he was the son of a trader who was dead, but that when he was a little boy his father had gone into the back country with fine feathers to trade for ornaments, and that when he came back he brought a large amount of gold and silver, of which there is a good deal in that country. He went with him once or twice, and saw some very large villages, which he compared to Mexico and its environs. He had seen seven large towns which had streets of silver workers. It took forty days to go there from his country, through a wilderness in which nothing grew except some very small plants about a span high. The way they went was through one country between two seas, following the northern direction.[28]

Likewise, in *De Orbe Novo*, Peter Martyr recounted how Vasco de Núñez was told of enormous supplies of gold that lay on "the other side of the watershed [where] the whole south slope of the mountain chain is very rich in gold mines."[29]

From the beginning, several devices have been common to the El Dorado narrative. First, El Dorado is a mirror, giving back to Europeans the legendary goal they sought most. Nearly always, the account is at least once removed — here, Tejo recalls what his father had told him and, in turn, tells the story, after a time lapse, to the president of the judicial and administrative board governing the province of New Spain. In turn, the administrator passes on the account; his position lends authority to the story.[30]

Second, the location of El Dorado is made intentionally vague, with strong mythic and biblical overtones, as in the reference to "seven large towns," most likely the legendary "Island of Seven Cities" or the "Seven Golden Cities of Cibola."[31] This story, along with St. Brendan's Isle, Hy-Brasil, and Antilla (for which Columbus searched on his first voyage) represented European fantasies of what lay to the west. It is important to note that what was *not* found (but should have been, according to the visual authorities of maps), was simply named — Cibola, Brazil, the Antilles, the Caribbean.[32]

Third, the account of Tejo's city indicates an important, even archetypal journey "though a wilderness, . . . through one country between the two seas," reminding us of some of the legendary heroes to whom we have alluded. In order to prove the hero's mettle, the epic journey must be fraught with danger and isolation. The landscape must be hostile, for only in this way can the hero overcome his fear and triumph over internal and external obstacles. Tejo aptly gauged the nature of the *personae* of these new adventurers, and his tale is embellished with the sort of details they would recognize as authetic.[33]

Note that Sir Walter Raleigh's account follows a similar "plot" outline.[34] Writing, in 1595, Raleigh remarked that "the first that ever saw Manoa [El Dorado] was Juan Martín, master of the munition to Ordaz," adding that Martín spent seven months there after being set adrift as a punishment. When Martín finally left, he was accompanied by several locals "all laden with gold which he [the Emperor] gave to Martín at his departure."

Raleigh's version, perhaps unwittingly, incorporates the same techniques as Castañeda's; the account is again once removed, for Raleigh has not experienced it personally, but rather was informed about it: "I have been assured by such of the Spaniards as have seen Manoa." At one point, to distance himself as the messenger even further from the message, Raleigh used quotation marks to cite the authority of Don Antonio Berrio, the governor of Trinidad. Furthermore, Raleigh pointed out that the sole witness, Juan Martín de Albujar was dead. As in the former account, the location is vague: Juan Martín enters the fabled city blindfolded and is "not suffered to wander in the country anywhere." Furthermore, the archetypal voyage is again stressed. The terrain is unfamiliar: "he travelled all that day till night through the city, and the next day from sun rising to sun setting ere he came to the palace of the Inca." This is a journey-within-a-journey (Martín's within Raleigh's), lending it even more authority, since Martín still has to undertake the voyage home. It is significant that he is robbed of most of his gold, but he can tell, on his death-bed after his final confession, how "certain servants of the Emperor, having prepared gold made into fine powder, blow it through hollow canes upon their naked bodies."

Several attempts were made to find El Dorado, now meaning both the Gilded Man and the Golden City, for the legend had given new meaning to the quest. In 1539, Gonzalo Pizarro traveled over the mountains from Quito; between 1541 and 1542, Francisco de Orellana sailed down the Napo and Amazon rivers; and, between 1569 and 1571, Gonzalo Jiménez de Quesada searched the region east of Bogotá. But gold was the cure for not only Spanish ailments, as Hernando Cortés explained to the curious natives. Portuguese explorers were still seeking El Dorado as late as 1603; Péro Coelho de Sousa explored the northern area of Pernambuco, and Raleigh investigated the Orinoco in 1595. Even the Germans sought gold in Peru. El Dorado, Cibola, Quivira, and City of the Caesars were all secular versions of Paradise.[35]

In the New World, there were several locations for the City of Gold. In large measure, it depended on the areas of national sovereignty. Thus, Portuguese explorers sought it in Brazil, Spanish explorers in New Spain, and English explorers in Guiana. Raleigh, writing of the Emperor's treasures, noted: "All the vessels of his house, table and kitchen were of gold and silver rare. . . . He had in his wardrobe hollow statues of gold which seemed giants. . . . He had also ropes, budgets, chests and troughs of gold and silver."[36] Note that, while the language of excess is again used for emphasis to strengthen the claim, Raleigh, like other reporters of the exotic account, felt free to locate El Dorado anywhere, since it emanated from the mind. King Midas himself became manifest in the New World.

Spaniards, Portuguese, English, and Germans were seeking the magic of El Dorado, Cibola, Quivira, and the City of the Caesars as logical extensions of European myth in the New World. In 1528, Alvar Núñez Cabeza de Vaca located his fabled city in the southwestern United States, and he has put his account in the context of an epic "adventure": "I have related the journey. The *arrival at*, and the *departure from*, the country and *return to* this realm" (my italics).[37] What sustains the reader in this account is the search for an elusive goal, in a territory that is new and unmapped. Cabeza de Vaca faced internal dissension, the unfamiliarity of a hostile landscape, and the threat of sudden death. A pilgrim/crusader shadows the narrative flow. Cabeza de Vaca makes constant references to God's mercy, and he even proselytizes. This activity does not prevent him, however, from wounding, killing, and kidnapping as he goes on his way.

What makes Cabeza de Vaca's account, *La Relación* (1542), particularly intriguing is that it presents us with an interesting technique — the only example that survives from this time. First, he rendered his own account, in a stream-of-consciousness manner, in which God and landscape, Native American and Spaniard, the "I" narrator and the shadow of the "I" ("The Negro" — Estevanico), all merge. True, some Native Americans are still presented as stereotypes (naked and lazy), but this description is balanced by Europeans, who find themselves "half dead" and "as naked as we had been born."[38] In a way, Cabeza de Vaca and his party subvert the travel narrative.

Clearly, order has broken down. Cabeza de Vaca and his party trek through isolated landscapes, in which they are always hungry and alone. This stark contrast emphasizes the appealing nature of the boon. The point of the experience becomes not just "gold" or "discovery," but rather self-fulfillment in which human triumph is never certain but always possible.

Interestingly, the text of *La Relación* is accompanied by a "joint report" made by other members of the expedition. We are therefore afforded a second opportunity to review the identical events. The facts are the same, but the "joint report" is more formal and bureaucratic, at times placing the account of Cabeza de Vaca in the larger perspective of European myth. We are told: "Compare this with the wanderings of Ulysses, the voyage of Jason, or the labors of Hercules." The report argues for the elevation of Cabeza de Vaca's text over and above mere fiction: "Even if you place Perseus and his Medusa with them, they could not have walked the steps those Christians walked."[39]

The "joint report" presents the opportunity to philosophize about El Dorado, summed up succinctly in "Oh, damned gold!" Crucially, the journey does not result in tangible goals. Some members of the expedition outstay their welcome among the indigenous people. In cryptic fashion, the report sums up that "[T]he other two Spaniards went further down the coast and there they died of hunger." Their activities are reduced to the most elemental — a search for food and water — as they wend their nomadic way across the land. No anguish is too humiliating, and as we try to reconcile the two texts, we discover that this account is actually the fifteenth-century *Everyman* and the later *Pilgrim's Progress* (1678) retold in the New World:

They suffered that same thirst, when bringing water on their backs for the Indians, their masters, and even for their neighbors. Everyone ordered around the Spaniards, and they feared everyone. Moreover, all treated them poorly by deed and by words. The children cut away at their beards everyday, as a diversion.[40]

Quests for spices, gold, silver, and, later, fur are voyages back to a real understanding of how the individual can truly grow closer to the cosmos, as the alchemists had preached. As a result of their experience, Cabeza de Vaca and his party change. Now they seem more at peace with the native population, no longer battling them but learning how to live with them. Through humility and understanding, the "Christians" in this account may not learn to respect another religion, but they do at least learn to live with a new understanding of themselves and their role on the continent. This was not a lesson that any of the European powers understood. Had they done so, the story of the search for the New World gold and spices might well have become an account of the search for "another" yet equal human — the "Indian" on whom Cabeza de Vaca had to rely, if he were to save himself.

VIEWED ACCOUNTS

A viewed response involves what emerges from the experience of "education," which permits post-medieval people to understand the cosmographic concepts of their universe. Especially as interpreted by Paolo dal Pozzo Toscanelli (1377–1482) and Pierre d'Ailly (1350–1420), these viewpoints were influenced by the classics, especially Plato and Pliny. The mythological view (already partly noted in maps and charts) further contributed to the accretion of ideas about a distinct new world view. This was the cultural version of the world that Columbus and Cortés, the Pizarros and Juan Ponce de León, Pedro Álvares Cabral and John Cabot took with them in their encounters.

The Greeks had imposed an earth-centered universe on Europe. Even though the heavens were mystical, they could be explained in rational terms. Ptolemy elaborated on this idea, arguing that the stars and planets rotated round each other. The Ptolemaic universe, with its concept of "wheels within wheels," was accepted for fourteen centuries until Nicolaus Copernicus and Galileo Galilei put forward alternatives.[41]

Ptolemy did his major research at the famous library in Alexandria between 127 and 145 A.D. He was known both as an astrologer and astronomer, and Arab translators utilized his important work that was subsequently known as the *Almagest*. His work was taken up as Church dogma, although the system proved somewhat unwieldy. Additionally, his *Guide to Geography* aided in the construction of maps, listing various places in the three known continents. Columbus used the *Guide* to shore up his beliefs that the continent of Asia stretched so far eastward that it could easily be reached from western Europe.

Ptolemy was, of course, partly the product of his own "visual" world and imprisoned by his own mythology. For him, the source of the Nile was in the Mountains of the Moon, and the Indian Ocean was a large lake. Constantine gathered all this information — indeed, the knowledge of Egypt, Italy, and Greece — and reintroduced it to the Christian world. An edition of Ptolemy's work was brought out in 1486. But, as J.R.S. Phillips has shown, despite the fact that Ptolemy's maps had been drawn with coordinates very much like latitude and longitude, "many of his co-ordinates were incorrect in themselves, while a further co-application was introduced because of his underestimate of a geographical degree."[42] Carl Sagan has noted that Ptolemy is "a reminder that intellectual capacity is no guarantee against being dead wrong."[43]

Nevertheless, after the fall of Toledo in 1105, when its libraries revealed the vast extent of Arab scholarly diligence, Ptolemy had still more impact on the West; Gerard of Cremona went there in the middle of the twelfth century to rediscover Ptolemy. The year 1477 has been given as the most likely date for the reprint of his *Geography*. In 1507, Martin Waldseemüller, the German cartographer, reproduced Ptolemy's portrait in a wall map.

From Ptolemy, Europeans obtained a specific but flexible view of the world, its size and proximity, its shape and the position of places with reference to others. Nonetheless, on his third voyage, Columbus commented: "I have always read that the world, land and water, was spherical, and authoritative comments and the experiments which Ptolemy and all the others have recorded concerning this matter, so describe it."[44] He later added, drawing from his own experience and that of d'Ailly's *Imago Mundi*: "this other hemisphere is as the half of a very round pear, which has a raised stalk, as I have said, or like a woman's nipple on a round ball. Of this half, neither Ptolemy nor the others who wrote of the world had knowledge."[45] The reason was that Columbus had found Paradise. Thus, even though Columbus often mentioned Ptolemy, if only to disagree with him, the Ptolemaic view of the universe was his starting point. After all, the impetus for Portuguese navigation was stated in the chronicle of Diego Gomes, a close associate of Prince Henry, as follows: "The Prince wishes to know about the western ocean, and whether there were islands or continents beyond those that Ptolemy described."[46]

D'Ailly was a chancellor at the University of Paris. Columbus made several annotations in his copy of *Imago Mundi*. Since d'Ailly himself was indebted to earlier medieval geographers and cosmologists, "Columbus' vision was thus deeply rooted in the cosmology of the Middle Ages." As the editors of the *Libro* have noted, "The sharp discontinuity by which many historians and biographers separate him from his medieval roots is a fiction."[47]

In addition to the Bible and *Imago Mundi*, Columbus probably read or received two important letters from one of the leading intellectuals of his day — Paolo Toscanelli — as two later biographers — Columbus' son Ferdinand[48] and Bartolomé de las Casas[49] mentioned. In the first, according to las Casas, Toscanelli stated that the map (the visual) enclosed with his letter (the verbal) clearly showed the area "in which all the West is shown, from Ireland to the south as far as the end of Guinea, with all the islands which lie on this route." Most importantly, for Columbus' conception of the world, the letter continued: "You must not wonder if I call the place where spices grow, West, because it is commonly said that they grow in the East; but whoever will navigate to the West will always find the said places in he West, and whoever will go by land to the East will always find the said places East."[50]

This passage places the visual and verbal contexts of the Columbian proto-journey in an interesting light. Clearly, the letter suggests that the point of arrival will be the same, whatever the route chosen. In other words, the experiences of travelers, whether as pilgrims, crusaders, or explorers, actually involve a particular discovery, in that they all endure alienation and aloneness; nevertheless, through the cyclical nature of the experience, they can begin to understand the meaning of life itself.

Toscanelli's first letter is full of references to "spices and jewels and precious stones," as well as to "a Prince who is called the Great Khan, whose name means in our language king of kings"[51] (*Rey de los Reyes*, the Spanish), with its strong biblical reference. Toscanelli's words are poetic and imbued with a heightened sense of wonder. The letter is at once a map in words, a visual representation of language, and words about a map, a verbal depiction of pictures. "The straight lines which are shown lengthwise in the said chart" or "I showed in the said chart many places in the regions of India,"[52] are Toscanelli's words to express transitions between the verbal and the visual.

Rife with prophetic hints (not only for Columbus, who sought spices, gold, precious stones, and the Great Khan), the text contains a "closed" meaning in its clear references to the other-worldly, pilgrim-like nature of the projected voyage: "The name of this city in our language means city of Heaven: wonderful things are told of this city in regard to the magnificence and the workmanship and of the revenues."[53] To drive home his point regarding other-worldliness (the *otro mundo*), which Columbus finally acknowledged, Toscanelli concluded with references to "Antilla," the "Seven Cities," and the Gilded City: "Know that the temples and royal houses are covered with pure gold; therefore because of the route being unknown, all these things are concealed."[54] El Dorado was found before it was discovered.

Dated June 25, 1474, this letter is the most succinct statement regarding the world in which Columbus and the conquistadors lived. Partly bolstered by the Bible, Aristotle, Greek and Latin learning, and the new evolving sciences, it nevertheless retained its own kind of truth.

The Latin version also combined scholarship with maritime and geographical knowledge (with an underlying spiritual meaning), elevating the voyage to a quest. Myth and reality are close:

Sed ab insula antilia vobis nota ad insulam nobilisimam çippangu sunt decem spacia est enim illa insula fertilissima aur[o] margaritis $ gemmis, & aur[o] solido cooperiunt tenpla domos regias ita quod per ygnota itinera non magn[a] maris spacia transeundum.[55]

[But from the Island of Antilla known to you, to the most noble Island of Cipango [Japan] are ten spaces: for this island is most rich in gold, pearls and precious stones, and they cover the temples and palaces with solid gold: so that the spaces to be traversed on the sea by unknown journeys are not great.]

Again, in the Italian version, the bare statements point to facts such as a port "where every year 100 great ships are loaded and unloaded with pepper," spices, and great kingdoms and cities. Yet there are also references to the *Re de' Re* and the desire of the people of Cathay to be christianized.[56]

It is not known whether Columbus read this letter, in any one of the languages, that was addressed to Fernam Martins, canon at Lisbon. But the letter does represent the views and opinions, as well as the underlying concerns, of intellectuals of his age. These people suspected that they were on the brink of departure. Would they be able to understand how the quest for gold approximated the search for God?

Fred Kravath has shown the extent to which medieval cosmography was dependent on Greek and Roman ideas of the world.[57] Capella (third century A.D.), for instance, a North African from Carthage, used the works of Eratosthenes, Archimedes, and Aristotle to help him calculate the earth's circumference. Macrobius (c. 395–423 A.D.) was widely read, including his curious beliefs about the nature of the world. Kravath has maintained that although Columbus never mentioned Macrobius, he could well have believed that the earth was divided into four large islands and that the two northern islands presented no navigational problems. Kravath has offered the link between the visual, the verbal, and the viewed, arguing that Macrobius' map was the precursor of those "which later would become adorned with monsters . . . and illustrations for fantastic legends."[58] The explanation that accompanied the reproduction of the map, again published in 1483, stated that, of the "islands" (continents), "only one, the Eurasian-African, was inhabited."[59]

In no small measure, this later belief could account for the treatment of indigenous New World inhabitants as "nonpeople." Clearly, if the continent were not habitable, then the people who lived there were nonpersons. On his very first voyage, Columbus noted that the inhabitants were not like "negroes in Guinea," that "their hair is flowing, and they are not born where there is intense force from the rays of the sun."[60] Clearly then the "new" people were not Europeans, Africans, or Asians. A serious debate then began questioning Native American "humanity." This debate preoccupied Spanish intellectuals until 1550, when Juan Ginés de Sepúlveda, opposing Bartolomé de las Casas, was able to argue plausibly that "they are as inferior to the Spaniards as children to adults, women to men, as the wild and cruel to the most meek . . . as monkeys to men."[61]

In passing, we should note that Indian philosophers, Aryabhata (c. 476 A.D.) and Brahmagupta (c. 628 A.D.), as well as Chinese philosophers, Hoching-Tien (mid-fifth century A.D.) and Y-Hang (c. 721 A.D.), were all relatively outside the influence of Ptolemy and Aristotle and were themselves unknown in the West. This was a pity, for their calculations of distance more closely approximated present-day reckonings. Y-Hang, for instance, used a scientific method, dispatching two sets of recorders to measure the sun's altitude and the polar star. According to some scholars, they all had a more humane view of the world.[62]

For purposes of the journey outward, therefore, faulty cosmography gave early adventurers the wrong notions of a smaller world. Still, they had inherited this as the cultural baggage that they would take on their journeys, and their accounts reveal the ways in which their misconceptions affected the people and landscapes with which they came into contact.

VISIONARY RESPONSES

Visionary elements involve the intentional attempt at projecting European notions into cosmic terms. Again, the reference points are the Bible and the classics, but now a different goal emerges. Paradise may be found and located. Dante, after all, had situated it in his *Divine Comedy*, and, for fifteenth- and sixteenth-century explorers, Paradise was real, in a very physical sense.

The flip side of the search for Paradise was the encounter with "monsters" or the monstrous races. Recall that early maps and charts had depicted them visually, described them verbally, and, in many instances, authenticated their presence with reference to the Bible. For example, Peter Martyr, in *De Orbe Novo*, related how Spaniards encountered in Mexico "a region among the northern mountains exclusively inhabited by women,"[63] who behaved in an abnormal way. Martyr also confirmed the presence of giants, wild men living in trees, harpies, mermaids, and sea serpents.

Likewise, the nature of the adventure should not surprise us. Journeys to seek unknown worlds were no different from those we would term "literature," but they contain the same components of "good" hero and "bad" villains. The danger is that, in real circumstances, the perceiver is demonizing the perceived, altering objective history, not so much at will but as necessitated by the indifferent problems of a concocted mythology.

We can empathize, at least on one level, in the German/Anglo-Saxon epic of the encounter of Beowulf with Grendel and Grendel's mother. We do so because Anglo-Saxon is Beowulf's language and because we view him as an "anglicized" hero fighting against the evil of the world. There is no story told from the monsters' perspective. Against the background of the "civilized" court, with whose rituals we can easily empathize, Grendel enters, bent on destruction. Beowulf is a sea-hero who comes to Hrothgar's hall, Heorot, to restore order.

Here, too, monsters, which explorers will encounter in the New World as the Caribs, are cannibals. In *Beowulf*, Grendel, the monster, having taken hold of a warrior, tore him to pieces, drank his blood, and swallowed him.[64] Beowulf, by contrast, had earlier declared that he would depend on God. The epic is definitely one sided, much as the encounter in the New World would be. Grendel and his mother are embodiments of the nonhuman. As such, they incur both Beowulf's anger and, finally, the anger of God.

At one level, and this is also to be noted in New World exploration, there is a particular tendency to distort, disfigure, and dehumanize women. In *Beowulf*, apart from the shadowy figure of Hrothgar's wife, the only other major woman present is Grendel's mother, "monstrous among women-kind, [who] brooded over her misery."[65] Interestingly, she is associated with Cain, the traditional "other." Therefore, as woman, outsider, and monster, she is triply damned.

Three-hundred years later, not much had changed in European literature. In the thirteenth century, the influence came from Muslim Spain via France, but the effect was the same. Courtly love invented King Arthur and the splendor of Camelot, but the scene is not much different from the mead-hall in *Beowulf*. In *Sir Gawain and the Green*

Knight, the intruder is a giant knight of a different color, green. After being decapitated, he picks up his head and rides off. Although the poem later follows the pattern of most other verse in the Arthurian cycle, it is important to note the bleakness of the forest, so much like Grendel's fen, the temptation by the lady of the castle, and Sir Gawain's wound. About the bleak forest, Gawain wonders even as he calls on Heaven: "'This prayer-house is ugly, overgrown with herbs.'"[66] Even though the "stranger" is finally explained, he is still feared throughout the poem.

A good example of the medieval fear of the great unknown occurs in "The Owl and the Nightingale," another Middle English poem, probably from the thirteenth century. The solemn owl and the happy nightingale debate, and the nightingale, defending herself, asks why she should sing to people who will never have happiness. There live men "wilde and unisele" (wild and miserable), lacking in "sibbe" (kinship) and living like wild animals out of hell.[67] "There" is somewhere else, the wild and barbaric North.

First, it must be noted how the literary texts (and examples exist throughout Europe) reveal certain presuppositions. One assumption is that the perceived has nothing to record. Cortés had no hesitation in murdering Emperor Quauhtemotzin, King Cohuanacox of Texcoco, two other kings, and a king's brother. Beyond that, he ensured that their version of history, "representing the hanging of these prisoners by their feet to prolong their sufferings,"[68] was destroyed. This issue is obviously one of profound importance. The story of "conquest," or "discovery" is ethnocentric, told from one perspective. In this way, the "plot" and "structure" associated with medieval legendary narration, such as we have just discussed, were replicated in the history of New World settlement.

Second, the epic, while not uniquely intrinsic to European thought patterns, formed a basic archetype that fifteenth- and sixteenth-century journeys tended to parallel. A major problem occurs when the basic structure of the epic demands that a clearly identifiable "good" be contrasted with an obviously demonstrated "evil." This involves us in a quandary that is hard to justify.

Third, "otherness" belongs to Grendel's mother and the Green Knight. They are strange; they inhabit areas where nonhumans live; and they are clearly identifiable with an unstated "evil." In the New World, this demanded both their conquest and extermination. Since even las Casas had to concede that Indians were barbarians, the best he could assert in favor of Cortés was that he had thought Tenochtitlán "worthy of admiration because of its buildings, which are like those of Venice."[69]

Tragically, neither Cortés nor Hernando de Soto, despite their barbarism, were to be confused with barbarians: they were seen as civilizers, bringing westernization to unwilling Indians.

As already noted, depictions of strange beings were represented visually on *mappae mundi*, as well as in churches. In addition, they were used to illustrate books, the most important being Marco Polo's *Il Milione* and Sir John Mandeville's *Travels*. From the start of the journey, therefore, pilgrims and crusaders were already aware of the abnormal problems that would beset them and for which, more than ever, they would have to depend on God's guidance.

Sebastian Münster's *Cosmographica*, published in Basel in 1550, depicted monsters in woodcuts.[70] His book was popular, had several subsequent editions, and was accompanied by a textual rendering of the various monsters. There were fish the size of mountains, usually encountered near Iceland; there was the physeter, mentioned by the ancient Greeks, which could suck in a ship and blow it out again; there were large serpents and sea monsters, creatures that could eat and disgorge just as quickly. In the northern forests, there was a superabundance of pelt. Strange accounts were verified such as the sea monster resembling a pig, which was sighted in 1537. There were large crabs, strange rhinoceri, and braying pelicans. The annotation concludes that:

Just as the torrid zone of Africa has its own peculiar and wonderful creatures which can barely exist without the heat of that climate, so the Creator has given to the cold northern region its own creatures which cannot bear the heat of the sun. This was done in order that the glory of God might be known throughout the world.[71]

In reality, these creatures were expressions of the same fear of the world as were the monstrous races for Europeans. They represented the vast unknown and the perils of venturing out. Against this background early travel became even more laudable, since all the voyager possessed was a firm fate in divine power.

Monstrous races were part of the combined biblical and mythical world of the medieval imagination. As noted, abnormal people decorated maps, were located in specific places of the earth, and provided an "otherness" to European normality. Regarding early travel, Peter Jackson and David Morgan have pointed out:

These distant parts were peopled, in Western fantasy, not only by fellow-Christians but by a variety of exotic races. Some were monsters and freaks culled from Classical authors like Herodotus and Pliny: they included a people with dogs' heads (the Cynocephali), a people with no heads at all whose faces were located in their chests, and those with only one leg who propelled themselves by hopping. In the fourth century marvels of this kind were incorporated in a work masquerading as a life of Alexander the Great, whose author has since become known as Pseudo-Callisthenes. But his labours were paralleled by those of other writers, such as Solinus (third century) and Isidore of Seville (d. 636), both of whom are cited by [William of] Rubruck himself when vainly enquiring as to the whereabouts of these monsters at the Great Khan's court. In addition, the corpus of legends about Alexander came to include the story of a great barrier that the conqueror had built in order to keep certain barbarian races from over-running the civilized world. By the thirteenth century such "enclosed" peoples were commonly identified with the race Gog and Magog of Revelations XX, 7–8.[72]

John Friedman has listed most of the Plinian monsters. These include Amazons (single-breasted women); Amyetyrae (people with protruding lips); Androgini (who possessed both male and female genitals and lived in Africa); Anthropophagi (cannibals, who were particularly fond of consuming their parents); Blemmyae (who have heads between their shoulders); Cyclops (one-eyed giants); Ethiopians (men blackened by the sun who live in the mountains); Giants; hairy men and women; Mononculi (one-eyed) and Panoti (all ears); Pygmies in India and Africa, with cattle "proportionate in size"; Sciopods (huge one-legged people, who used their enormous feet to protect themselves from the sun); Sciritoe (flat-faced men); speechless men and Troglodytes (also lacking in speech, who lived in caves); and Wife-givers (who willingly shared their wives with strangers).[73]

Aspects of all that the monstrous races represented would be diligently found by explorers in the New World. Authorities for their existence also appear in the works of Homer, Virgil, and particularly, in Pliny's *Natural History*. Homer provided the Lotus Eaters (The Astomi or Apple-Smellers in medieval lore), and Polyphemus offered an example of the race of giants. Virgil and Homer both legitimized one-eyed giants (Cyclops) in the popular imagination, and the biblical Goliath may also have bolstered the belief. But the original monsters were to be found in Pliny.

Pliny's *Natural History*, written around 77 A.D., may be considered both a key source and the authority for according other-worldly status on non-European peoples, places, and animals. Pliny cited Aristotle as his authority for the Amazons. Other people were also distinctly odd: There were "families in the same part of Africa that practise sorcery, whose praises cause meadows to dry up, trees to wither and infants to perish."[74]

Some could "bewitch with a glance" and "kill those they stare at."[75] Women, "incapable of drowning" had "a double pupil in one eye and the likeness of a horse in the other." Even "among ourselves Cicero states that the glance of all women who have double pupils is injurious everywhere." Women in India "bear children only once in their lifetime." One woman gave birth to an elephant while a maidservant bore a snake. Often women (a case was cited in Africa) change into men. But, when a woman retains her sex and becomes pregnant, "if the child is a male, the mother has an easier delivery." In India, a tribe of women "conceive at the age of five and do not live more than eight years."[76]

Apart from women, otherness was conferred on all non-Europeans. In Africa, the "Atlas" tribe had fallen below the level of human civilization, never addressed each other by name, cursed the rising sun and never dreamed. "The Cave-dwellers" were "entirely devoid of intercourse by speech" and "Garamantes live with their women promiscuously."[77]

Pliny also mentioned the "Tergedus" or "dog-faced baboons" and was not surprised that Ethiopia produced "animal and human monstrosities." There were African people "without noses," others who "have no upper lip and others no tongues." Some had "the mouth closed up," lacked nostrils and possessed "only a single orifice through which it breathes and sucks in drink by means of oat straws." Furthermore, "some of the tribes communicate by means of nods and gestures instead of speech."[78] "On the African side, of the Red Sea," Pliny added, there were the Dochi "who never wear any clothes" and the Mesanches who "are ashamed of their black colour." Again, "on the African side," exist the Ptoemphani "who have a dog for a king" and divine his commands through his movements.[79]

Pliny reported that cannibalism was rampant, away from Italy and Sicily. Cyclops and Laestrygones "beyond the Alps habitually practise human sacrifice" as did another group, the Arimaspi, who possessed only "one eye in the centre of the forehead." In the Himalayas dwelt people who had their feet turned backward behind their legs. People in far away Albania were "bald from childhood" and possessed the eyesight of an owl. He cited Aristotle to confirm that androgynous people existed "who perform the function of either sex alternately" and "their left breast is that of a man and their right breast that of a woman."[80]

Foreign places for Pliny — he especially cited India and Ethiopia — "teem with marvels." In these parts, dogs and trees were enormous as were the people. There were mountain people who had dogs' heads and barked; the Monocoli "who have only one leg" and the Sciopod who "lie on their backs on the ground and protect themselves with the shadow of their feet."[81]

Moving westward, Pliny described "a people without necks, having their eyes in their shoulders." Near the source of the Ganges, Pliny cited, on authority, a people with "no mouth and a body hairy all over." They exist on the scent of roots, flowers and wild apples and can be killed by any strange odor.

Among the distant peoples, there were some who lived for an inordinately long time:

The Indian race of Cyrni according to Isigonous live to 140; and he holds that the same is true of the long-lived Ethiopians, the Chinese. . . . Crates of Pergamum tells of Indians who exceed a hundred years. . . . Ctesias says that . . . the Panda dwelling in the mountain valleys, live two hundred years.

Near them, "men are born with a hairy tail," and, "in the deserts of Africa ghosts of men suddenly meet the traveller and vanish in a moment."[82]

Most of these observations appear in Book VII, but scattered throughout *Natural History* are disturbing descriptions that profoundly influenced sixteenth-century thinking. For instance, Columbus quoted Pliny on his third voyage, stating that "the sea and land together form a sphere but that the ocean forms the greatest mass,"[83] so we know that he was familiar with Pliny. In fact, Columbus owned an edition translated into Italian by Cristofor Landino and printed in Venice in 1489.[84] The work remained a classic and was rendered into English in 1601 by Philemon Holland. One of Pliny's modern editors, Paul Turner, has noted that the title of the work might have appealed to Raleigh, who began writing his *Historie of the World* three years after the English version of Pliny was published.[85]

For our purposes, we should note that Pliny had a long-lasting effect on the concept of "otherness." The non-European world, as shown in the direct quotes, was largely excluded from being considered human. Africa and India were made the focal points of human abnormality. And, since Columbus was sailing to the "Indies" on his proto-voyage, much of this kind of cultural baggage, obtained in whatever form, went with him. Columbus and the other adventurers were not fools and did not believe everything that Pliny wrote. But, in the absence of practical knowledge, text and illustrations accompanying maps of the real world often seemed to demonstrate that these ideas were actual.

Since women played a very limited role in early European contact with the New World, many of Pliny's assertions, especially about their sexual appetites, were left standing. Indeed, as we note from the accounts, indigenous Native American women suffered especially from the

European mythology. They were clearly desirable to sex-starved sailors who had been months at sea, but they were accorded little individuality and no significance. They became the objects of sexual gratification and lust. Their revenge — and current research casts doubt as to origins — was probably to inflict Spanish sailors with syphilis.

Equally serious as gender-based distortion was Pliny's ethnic prejudice. Although Portuguese exploration to the New World had been preceded by African coastal voyages, this did not really help to make Europeans more tolerant of differences. In addition, considering the cultural legacy that Jews, Moors, and Muslims had given to Spain, one remains at a loss to comprehend how Iberians could have been so apparently unaffected.

Pliny's fantastic monstrosities became part of accepted belief in the Middle Ages and afterward. As such, they formed a mental picture of the unknown world, an image that would allow Europeans to inflict their distortions on the New World. Pliny's monsters were inherited by the sophisticated and the narrow-minded alike as part of a European fantasy world. With sixteenth-century adventurism, the perceivers were predisposed to find the very monsters they had left behind. As contemporary bestiaries show, the early European explorers saw the New World as a barren and wild landscape. For medieval man, the external world remained frightening; hence, departure on a voyage to the Americas became even more perilous. A late fourteenth-century account, based on Isidore, described "men that have their feet against our feet," referring to the legendary Antipodes, who walked upside down. This belief would long persist in the popular mind.[86] Additionally, the monster, the other-worldly, came to be identified first with Africans and later with Native Americans, who, as Samuel Purchas suggested, were not even conscious of a basic human recognition of themselves for "they saw no living creatures but parrots among them." This, Purchas says, explains their deification of the Spaniards.[87]

In *The Tempest*, Trinculo sees Caliban (cannibal) the monster/Indian. As Stephen Greenblatt has remarked, "The discoverer sees only a fragment and then imagines the rest in the act of appropriation."[88] Not unnaturally, Raleigh "discovered" similar abnormalities in Guiana, indicating that he had heard tales about men whose heads were between their shoulders.

Peter Martyr, in *Decades of the World* (1516), accepted Columbus' invention of the fierce, man-eating Caribs, because it fit in with the accepted European belief.[89] They were "cruel to strangers," like the fabled Donestre who, as Friedman has noted, "kill the traveler and then mourn over his head."[90] The Caribs, Martyr continued, "are those new anthropophagi who live on human flesh, Caribs or cannibals as they are called."[91] Again, the point is clear: Martyr was not really describing the Caribs but reaching back to a legendary European past that was being imposed on the New World. These were, of course, the old Anthropophagi who, according to Pliny, drank out of human skulls.

The "Caribs" existed outside the norms of language, since they did not understand Spanish, comprehending neither the symbols of cross and flag nor the language of the proclamation declaring them subjects of Spain. As such, they were also Pliny's speechless men of Ethiopia, who communicated only by gestures. Indeed, as with Prospero's concept of "language," Europeans viewed non-European speakers as those who could not and did not subscribe to human norms. Such a portrayal dated back centuries for, after all, the Greeks had first used the term "bah bah" (barbarian) for those unable to communicate with them. Later, the word was extended to those outside the pale of the Roman empire and, still later, to non-Christians. Caribs were thrice condemned as non-Greek, non-Roman, and non-Christian — in short, non-people.

Of course, this viewpoint was definitely race-centered, but our purpose here is not to castigate, but to show how cultural predispositions made "conquest" and "discovery" into concepts that alienated conqueror from conquered, discoverer from discovered. The myth is infectious, for it involves not only Europeans but also native American peoples and later Africans in their attempts at self-realization. Curiously, these groups have borrowed and believe in aspects of this mythology.

Maximilian Transilvane, secretary to Emperor Charles V, asked, "Who will believe that men are found with only one leg? Or men of a cubit in height, and other such like, being monsters rather than men?"[92] The question seems almost quaint, but it is quite serious, for he was commenting on Ferdinand Magellan's round-the-world voyage. His conclusion was also ironic, for he noted that the Spaniards and Portuguese "did write of such monsters."[93] Columbus echoed a similar sentiment in his widely circulated letter of the first voyage: "In these islands I have so far found no human monstrosities."[94] But he had — he termed them "Caribs."

A little earlier in the same letter, Columbus mentioned casually, almost in a kind of mental parenthesis, that on the western coast of Cuba, "the people are born with tails." Yet, a few lines further on, he repeated, "I have found no monsters, so I have no report of any." He then added another curious note about a group with "this custom of wearing their hair long like women," probably an illusion to Pliny's Androgini. The men there, Columbus went on, "have intercourse with the women of 'Mantio' [Martinique]" where "these women engage in no feminine occupation, but use bows and arrows of cane,"[95] clearly the Amazons of the past. These were an opposite version of the Astomi (who lived by smelling apples and were hairy in all parts), the bearded ladies and hairy men and women.[96]

"Giants" were encountered in Mexico and Brazil. In fact, Cortés sent the bones of giants back to Charles V. Giants originated in what Friedman has termed "the apocryphal letter of Alexander to Aristotle on the Wonders of India."[97] As noted, the Bible also documented their existence. Therefore, the Magellan expedition encountered a giant. He was transformed and large but mute, inarticulate, and monstrous, "with a large visage painted with diverse colors." European wit could overcome giants, however, and two were captured as specimens — "The Captain named these people Patagons."[98] As such, incapable of speech like the people of Ethiopia, according to Pliny, they could not establish a meaningful relationship with the newcomers.

Indigenous peoples therefore had to become the very opposite of the "Christians," both because conquest must be justified and because they helped define an important goal for the journey. The theme of spreading the Christian message occurred in earlier travel literature and was especially relevant against a background of perceived "Saracen" hostility. Foreign people had to be conquered, subjugated, enslaved as the Slavs had been, made to pay tribute. The conquered were controlled, and the "controller" exerted an influence that could coopt language, apportion new names, exact a tribute in labor, and dominate totally. This was the pattern of European history that would be imposed on the New World.

As indicated, an anticipation of monsters and marvels prepared the adventurer for the Great Beyond. Not everything was frightening, however, and, as the *Iliad* and *Odyssey* showed, adventure could be inspiring and stimulate oral enquiry. Still, the ancients had put serious restrictions on the world, for beyond the Pillars of Hercules, there was nothing. The ancient prescriptions were never totally challenged. Ferdinand Columbus cited part of Seneca's *Medea*, but equally relevant are the lines that precede Ferdinand's citation, which I have roughly translated below:

> *Nunc iam cessit pontus et omnes*
> *patitur leges; non Palladia*
> *compacta manu regumque ferens*
> *inclita remos quaeritur Argo;*

quaelibet altum cumba pererrat.
terminus omnis motus et urbes
muros terra posuere nova,
nil qua fuerat sede reliquit
pervius orbis:
Indus gelidum potat Araxen,
Albin Persae Rhenumque bibunt.
venient annis saecula seris,
quibus Oceanus vincula rerum
laxet et ingens pateat tellus
Tethysque novos detegat orbes
nec sit terris ultima Thule.[99]

[Now already the ocean has ceased to obstruct us, and all things obey law. Not even Argo, made by the hand of Pallas, and manned by princes, is needed. All limitations are removed, and cities now have walls in new lands. The world, now traversible, has left nothing to obstruct [human] passage. The Indian drinks from the cold Araxes; the Persian tastes the waters of the Elbe and the Rhine. A time will come in the years that follow when the ocean will loosen the chain of things and the whole huge earth shall be open. Then Tethys shall reveal new worlds and Thule shall no longer be the limitations of land.]

References to Jason's Argonauts and Seneca's prophetic words appealed to both Ferdinand and his father. Columbus was to be the chosen instrument to "loosen the chain of things." On his fourth journey, Columbus combined Seneca and the divine will of God, writing "of the barriers of the Ocean Sea, which were closed with such mighty chains, He gave thee the keys."[100] His son commented that "it is considered certain that this prophecy was fulfilled in the person of the Admiral."[101]

Classical writers were often used to back up the legitimacy of Columbus' encounter. For instance, Ferdinand made the case that Plato had foretold the story of Atlantis. Certainly in this sense, the early encounters had a sense of justification by hindsight. Salvador de Madariaga has argued that Columbus was in Thule in 1477, "smitten with his inner belief in his destiny."[102]

For the ancient world, Atlantis lay just beyond the Pillars of Hercules. The Middle Ages inherited the legend as it had been stated in Plato's *Timaeus* and *Critias*. In the former, the relevant part for our purpose relates how gallant Athenians defeated warriors from Atlantis. The *Critias* continues the account; here authenticity is achieved by planting words into the mouth of Critias (c. 480 B.C.– c. 403 B.C.). In the *Timaeus*, Critias says:

For at that time the Atlantic sea was navigable and had an island before that mouth which is called by you the Pillars of Hercules. But this island was greater than both Libya and all Asia together, and afforded an easy passage to other neighboring islands, as it was likewise easy to pass from these islands to all the continent which borders on this Atlantic Sea.[103]

We are told that the existence of Atlantis was verifiable. Marcellus, who wrote a history of Ethiopia, confirmed that "there were seven islands" and "three others of an immense magnitude."

The *Critias* is a fragment, but the Platonic dialogue continues the exploration of the *Timaeus*. Again, the area of Atlantis lies "beyond the Pillars of Hercules," and is "larger than Libya and Asia." According to Critias, Atlantis dates from the beginning of time itself, and he anticipated the excitement of the early explorers attempting to render the New World in words:

Neptune, indeed, being allotted the Atlantic island, settled his offspring by a mortal woman in a certain part of the island, of the following description. Towards the sea, but in the middle of the island, there was a plain, which is said to have been the most beautiful of all plains, and distinguished by the fertility of the soil.[104]

The point that Critias was making is that Atlantis is the domain of mortal humans, and that, above all, man supplements the majesty of nature. Not unnaturally, the crowning glory — of man and earth, and of man and god — was perfected in the temple, where "[a]ll the external parts . . . except the summit, were covered in silver; for that was covered in gold."[105] This the explorers could certainly understand.

This Atlantis is actually an ideal place, predating prelapsarian Eden and anticipating Paradise. There was a perfect harmony in the lives of Atlantans who "were obedient to the laws and benignly affected toward a divine nature, to which they were allied."[106] Of course, this ends, but the fragment of *The Critias* that survives does not account for this early version of postlapserian human tragedy.

Atlantis became part of the European public record. It turned up again and again, not just in popular crackpot theories like that of Ignatius Donnelly (who set out to prove its physical existence in the New World),[107] but also in the manner in which New World explorers identified aspects of the New World — its bounty, its innocence, its warlike nature, its grandeur. All these could easily be associated with Atlantis. Atlantis implied the possibility of a new world and a historical (albeit legendary) justification for its existence. It represented the basic goal of the journey, the earth on which the adventurer would stand, once he had overcome the monsters. After all, Ferdinand Columbus himself, writing about Atlantis, cited Seneca, who had alluded to the Jason legend, and Ferdinand placed it within the larger legendary context of the globally acceptable Marco Polo.[108] The parallel patterns could not have escaped Columbus, his son, or their contemporaries. Jason goes in search of the Golden Fleece and, with the help of Medea, steals it from Colchis. The explorers were going in search of spices and gold; they too might have to steal it from Carib chiefs like Guacanagari or, with the assistance of indigenous female helpmates (Cortés' Malinche, John Smith's Pocahontas, etc.), bring back the fleece.

Jason is a seaman, and he has to suffer much in archetypal encounters. He endures storms and hostility. He is noble and religious, slaying enemies and dragons with the brave ruthlessness of his later embodiments — Ulysses and various medieval heroes. The story had fascinated the Greeks, and, indeed, Seneca's *Medea* was itself based on a drama by Euripides. Many references can be found to the perfect land, "the seed of the blest God's line/ In a land unravaged, peace-enfolden."[109] The later seaman/adventurer likewise goes in search of worlds of the European imagination, and he locates them in the New World future. Madariaga has termed this the "prophetic sense," a tendency "to find a hint of things to come."[110] This reference is to Ferdinand Columbus, but the view point can also be found in families and nations, especially in terms of a sense of purpose in attaining conquest.

Jason's voyage, like that of the great epic heroes, is not an "encounter"; it is a voyage of "discovery." Told from the viewpoint of the conquerors, magic and wonder (later on, guns and horses, for the conquistadors) are employed on their behalf. They exhibit physical prowess, as they battle human and elemental forces of disorder. They murder and desecrate, all in the name of an ethnocentric principle — the glorification of self, nation, and divinity.

Columbus made almost 437 marginal comments on a translation of Plutarch, exceeded only by the 898 he made in his copy of d'Ailly's *Imago Mundi*.[111] The account of Lycurgus must have had some appeal. That voyage of "discovery" involved knowledge. Lycurgus sailed from Crete to Asia, Plutarch wrote, in order to compare the civilizations. He made his acquaintance there with the works of Homer, and "eagerly copied and compiled them in order to take them home with him." As such, Plutarch argued, "Lycurgus was the very first to make them really known."[112]

Lycurgus visited Egypt and probably Iberia. After a journey to Delphi, he was in a position to institute reforms at home. Agriculture increased, and inequality almost disappeared as "he withdrew all gold and silver money from currency."[113] Lycurgus' travels had endowed him with the wisdom to make reforms. Even the Delphic oracle, as Herodotus noted, saw him as a god-fearing man, and, indeed, as a god:

> Hither to my rich temple have you come, Lycurgus,
> Dear to Zeus and to all gods that dwell in Olympus.
> I know not whether to declare you human or divine —
> Yet I incline to believe, Lycurgus, that you are a god.[114]

Such a process of deification took place for Columbus, Cortés, Pizarro, and many of the other early adventurers. It is almost a given that those who seek God as pilgrim/warriors end up as gods themselves. On Columbus' very first voyage, on Sunday, October 14, 1492, the indigenous people cried out, "Come and see the men who have come from heaven."[115] At another stage, on his third voyage, Columbus wrote, "God made me the messenger of the new heaven and our new earth."[116] Cortés conquered Mexico because he was seen as the reincarnation of Quetzlcoatl. Thus, the journey became what Samuel Eliot Morison has called in the *Great Explorers*, "a divine mission."[117] He has pointed out that Columbus' curious signature indicates his pervasive religious devotion and self-image as the Christ Bearer. This was the real meaning of Virgil's "*novus ordo seclorum*" (Eclogues IV: 5) and the reason that the phrase appears on the U.S. dollar bill. Presumably, the ancient classical world had predicted and sanctioned the New World.

When Agatharchides of Cnidus compiled *On the Erythraean Sea*, around 1 A.D., it became an important source of geographical information, albeit gravely mistaken. Agatharchides also noted the "other-worldly" images of his time. He too encountered "barbarians" who "live completely naked and possess their women and children in common like herds of animals." For many of the non-Greeks (Agatharchides had written about South Arabia, Ethiopia, and East Africa), life was languid and made up of song, dance, and sexual pleasure. He stressed nonconformity to Greek mores, and so the Root-Eaters, Fibre-Eaters, Elephant-Eaters, Locust-Eaters, and so on are all portrayed as very backward.

All the world is seen from the perspective of the European perceiver. Alternate life-styles are condemned or made to look silly. Herodotus' "long-lived Aethiopians," later ignored by Eratosthenes, were revived by

Agatharchides. They reappear yet again in the search for eternal youth, symbolized by the Fountain of Youth, to which Ponce de León and others devoted considerable effort and dedication.

At the end of *On the Erythraean Sea*, Agatharchides concluded with a perplexing note: "We have carefully recorded in five books the situation concerning the tribes located in the south as they were in our time. *But we have entirely given up the idea of writing an account of the islands in the sea which were discovered later* (my italics).[118] Since, as one of his editors asserted, Greek knowledge of "islands" (even of two island groups in the Indian Ocean, the Maldives and Laccadives) was not demonstrated until the Roman period, Agatharchides' reference is not at all clear. What the work does show, however, despite its lack of empathy, is what Mary B. Campbell has described as a sense of the unknown. Agatharchides has left us with the perplexing possibility that Atlantis still existed.

Friedman concluded his valuable study, *The Monstrous Races in Medieval Art*, by showing how the models of invented monstrosity passed on to New World inhabitants. He found that Pliny's races of men were condensed into one, the new handy category of "Wild Man" — naked, hairy, savage, violent, and lacking in morality. At times, the Wild Man could be domesticated, and, in one illustration, Wild Man and Wild Woman support the shield of Charles V. The phantoms of European nightmares were thus exported to the New World where they could then be "discovered."

Not only Columbus, but other explorers looked for the [monstrous] races in the Americas. In 1522 Cortez sent back to Charles V some bones supposed to be those of Plinian Giants, and Diego Velasquez told Cortez to seek the Panoti [people whose ears served as blankets] and Cynocephali [people with the heads of dogs] on his travels.[119]

Indeed, as Friedman has admitted, some of Pliny's monsters were readily and easily found. To these should be added the range of oddities from the Bible, Classical Greek and Latin texts, *mappae mundi*, and general folk belief.

One specific example stands out, both in terms of gender alienation and myth linkage. The legend of Amazon women warriors apparently goes back as far as 4 B.C. to Sarmatian women who lived in seclusion and who could not wed until they had killed an enemy in warfare. The legendary Jason fought them as did the historical Alexander. Hercules led an expedition to obtain Queen Hippolyte's girdle, and Theseus married one. Usually, Amazons and Greeks were seen in conflict. Quite obviously, the Greek ideal exalted the male, and women who removed one breast to facilitate their agility with the bow did not conform to Greek ideals.

Later, in the period with which we are most concerned, several travelers encountered Amazons in remote places. Marco Polo situated them in Socotra, where there were two fabulous islands called Male and Female. Leonardo Olschki, one of Marco Polo's biographers, has attempted to explain the presence of the Amazons in historical terms, arguing that Socotra was a Greek island that had probably inherited Greek beliefs.

That inveterate imitator, Sir John Mandeville, gave this account, shifting the territory of the Amazons from the borders of Scythia on the Black Sea to another region: "Next to Chaldea is the land of the Amazon, which we call the Maiden Land or the Land of Women; no man lives there, only women. This is not because, as some say, no man can live there, but because the women will not allow men to rule the kingdom."[120] The Amazons' lovers live close by. The women are cruel monsters, however, according to Mandeville, since they often kill their sons. In the Moseley collection of Mandeville's travels, the Amazons appear in the Egerton, Paris, and Bodleian texts.[121] Their existence was obviously considered true and important.

In a recent book, William Blake Tyrrell has considered the Amazons as part of the social mythmaking of the Greek people, designed, he has argued, to express gender polarity and consequent male fear.[122] To maintain the patriarchy, validate marriage, and keep female sexuality in check, the myth (in both verbal and visual form) became a coercive and controlling effort that was even used to justify Athenia expansionism. This type of social control was maintained in the Middle Ages by demonizing women as witches.

Francisco de Orellana, who had taken part in Pizarro's conquest of Peru, set out in April 1541. In the process of exploring a major South American river, he encountered not just the customary hoard of precious gold, but also cinnamon. What is of particular interest — and this shows how "naming" establishes a vested proprietorial interest in the myth — is that he met and fought with tribes of women warriors. At long last, Amazons had been found, and the area and river were thus named after them.

In this context, then, the myth of the Amazons, partly as an expression of masculine power and, later, as a justification for brutality, was bound to appeal to conquistadors. They were men without women, isolated, living against a backdrop of men and women who were alien to them.

They were at the very center of power, again at a time of expansionist inclinations, and it is understandable that the myth would resurface. Myth may often be used to rearrange phenomena — or to prove them.

Cynocephali (medieval dog-headed people) attired in animal skins were sighted by Magellan in Argentina. To name them, he used the Spanish word "Patagon," after a dog-headed monster in a sixteenth-centiury Spanish romance, *Amadís de Gaula*. The land of the Patagon became *"Patagonia, tierra maldita"* (Patagonia, accursed land). Antonio Pigafetta, who sailed around the world with Magellan in 1519–1522, wrote this about the encounter.

One day suddenly we saw a naked man of giant stature on the shore of the harbor, dancing, singing, and throwing dust on his head. When the giant was in the Captain General's presence, he marveled greatly, and made signs with one finger raised upward, believing that we had come from the sky. He was so tall that we reached up to his waist, and he was well proportioned.[123]

Morison has commented that he was "painted all over and partially dressed in guanaco skins. His feet, shod with guanaco-hide buckskins stuffed with straw looked enormous, which caused Magellan to name him *patagón*."[124]

Pigafetta was Italian and, very likely, most familiar with medieval superstitions. He combined a number of postmedieval attitudes in his account. First, the person who appeared was "naked," "dancing and singing," and, most importantly, a giant.[125] Many of the races derided by Pliny and Agatharchides were naked. True, the prelapsarian bliss of Adam and Eve had also required such a state, but nakedness had come to stand for a lack of refinement. Only after Jean-Jacques Rousseau would considerations of innocence and bliss support a different interpretation. When Pigafetta pointed to the dancing and singing, we are reminded of the blissful creatures who spend their days in this way. Moreover, a giant, might likely exhibit some of the characteristics of races with excessive hair. His gesturing itself suggests that he could be one of Pliny's speechless men of Ethiopia.

Second, the giant performed the familiar act, like Caliban or Friday, of recognizing Europeans as gods. At a later stage, however, Pigafetta introduced a new element into the drama of New World Encounter. Other giants appeared after Magellan had clapped two of them in leg irons. "When they saw later that they were tricked, they raged like bulls, calling for their god Cetebos to aid them."[126] It seems that they were not only monsters; their otherness was compounded by their calling on what sounds very much like Satan to aid them. The situation was extended and popularized in literature; in the *Tempest*, for instance, Caliban also invokes Cetebos. New World humans had begun the process of becoming demonized.

"Devilish arts" are always imposed on "other" people. Marco Polo observed that in an Indian city, "white Tartars began to mix with Indian women who were black." Later on, "they learned the magical and devilish arts."[127] Even though Greek observers of monstrous races were obviously non-Christians, at least the Greeks were "civilized." Europeans had little trouble with an easy equation of alien culture and savage religion. Mandeville had found giants, "folk of great stature," who possessed one eye; he had encountered "people without heads, with eyes on their shoulders." Both Marco Polo and Mandeville had thus confirmed the existence of monstrous races as non-Christians, and hinted at their total abandonment by God. The New World adventurers had to do as much, but they also had to save these creatures in the process.

Hence, Greek mythology, Latin speculation, and Alexandrine wonder became intertwined in early travel literature. As noted, when something was not found, it could still be situated and named. Therefore, Cibola, Brazil, the Antilles, and the Caribbean all now exist, along with the Amazon, Patagonia, and El Dorado (in southern Arkansas and Kansas).

What became important in New World encounters, at least for Europeans, was that a dream, a vision of a better life, was made possible. Nowhere did this manifest itself more distinctly than in the concept of the Fountain of Youth. Some of the ancient writers described people who lived for a long time, but no recipe for longevity was given until Prester John described it: "Which wood is situate[d] at the foot of Mt. Olympus when springs a clear fountain which has within itself every kind of taste. . . . Anyone who tastes of this fountain thrice, fasting, will suffer no infirmity thereafter, but remain as if of the age of 32 years as long as he lives."[128] In the version of the legend associated with Alexander the Great, fifty-six of his companions recovered their youth.

Prester John's letter appeared in 1165, although people had heard of him at least twenty years before. Written in Latin and widely translated, the letter was sent to specific European heads, particularly Manuel I Comnenus, the Byzantine Emperor, and Frederick I Barbarossa, the Holy Roman Emperor. Prester John's land, the letter stated, was rich, and Prester John intended to utilize his forces to put down the Muslims and retake Jerusalem. Many searched for him, but he was most elusive; his kingdom, it was thought, could be in Asia or even Ethiopia.

Marco Polo believed that he had identified Prester John's descendants in local Mongolian legends earlier on, Giovanni de Montecorvino and Giovanni da Pian del Carpini had sought out his kingdom. Finally, Prester John's territory, since he was Emperor of the "Three Indies," was thought to be located in Columbus' "Indies." For their Catholic Majesties, the plan was quite pragmatic; they wished to secure the aid of Prester John in order to attack the Turks from the East. One of Columbus' early biographers has Columbus, on his second voyage, citing Mandeville:

There he [the reader] will see that the city of Catayo is very noble and rich, and that its district has the name of the city. This province and city lie in the parts of Asia, now the lands of Prester John of the Indies in the district which dominates and looks towards the north, and in that direction in which the admiral sought it.[129]

Prester John, like other European images that had reached the New World, was imposed on it. But the difference between Prester John and the monstrous races from the medieval bestiaries is that Prester John was still a vision of possibility when the world seemed chaotic. True, he represented the imposition of a European order on that chaos, but his humility, as opposed to the arrogance of the conquerors, is truly touching. Even though he was "lord of lords" he preferred to be called simply "Prester" or "Priest."

Prester John's "Fountain of Youth" was likewise to be sought and found. Mandeville declared that he had drunk from it. Peter Martyr gave the account to the Pope, warning him, "Let not our holiness believe this to be a hasty or foolish opinion," for to the north was "an island called by us Boinca, and by others Aganeo; it is celebrated for a spring whose waters restore youth to old men."[130] When, like Prester John, it began to be sighted in the New World, we must note the process. The New World, partly nightmarish, was also becoming the repository of European idealization. We shall examine this more in a later chapter.

By special approval of Spain, Juan Ponce de León gained the opportunity to seek the Fountain of Youth. In his *Sumario* (1526) and *Historía General y Natural de las Indias* (1535), Gonzalo Fernández de Oviedo y Valdés, the official chronicler of New Spain, related this search for a distant dream. Peter Martyr in *De Orbe Novo* (1516) located it in Bimini where the water "makes old men young again." Antonio de Herrera also located the Fountain of Youth in his *Historía General* (1601), adding that an old man was known to have become completely rejuvenated.[131]

Finally, the goal of New World European exploration was to find Paradise. Once the monsters were overcome, once God's message was spread through conversion and conquest, then the physical search for Paradise would surely bring (as would the quest for Prester John and the Fountain of Youth) some semblance of peace and tranquility.

Just before the New World encounter, maps had placed Paradise across the Ocean Sea, surrounded it "with walls of flame and/or impenetrable rock" or with the "Vale Perilous," or had positioned it on an "unscalable height to which even the waters of the Flood had not reached."[132] Thus, the New World became the final place to discover Paradise, and, through language, writers tried to indicate its presence and point definitely to it. Amerigo Vespucci was exultant in a 1504 letter about what "we may rightly call a new world." The letter paints a picture of Edenic bliss. Vespucci then added that "this is new, indeed because our ancestors had no knowledge of them, and it will be a matter wholly new to all those who hear about them."[133] He decided that all arguments made by the Greeks must now be discarded, since his voyage showed that: "in these Southern parts I have found a continent more densely peopled and abounding in animals than our Europe or Asia or Africa and, in addition, a climate milder and more delightful than in any other region known to us."[134]

Paradise lay outside the known world, and what it symbolized was super-abundance, the cornucopia to which we alluded. But it was not possible to enter Paradise. Mandeville placed it "three days' journey from that sea," near "great mountains" but "Paradise terrestral . . . is the highest land of the world . . . closed all about with a wall . . . fire ever burning . . . for no man should enter."[135] Isidore of Seville placed Paradise to the east with many fruit trees and the tree of life. It was always eternal springtime there, and a spring ran from the center and watered the entire garden. Marco Polo described it as the province of "The Old Man" and his devotees.

Paradise came to the New World, quite physically and with jarring reality. Columbus mused on it, and, during his fourth voyage, finally concluded what the effects of the journey had been for him: "Gold is most excellent," he wrote a trifle wistfully. "Gold constitutes treasure, and he who possesses it may do what he will in this world, and may so attain as to bring souls to Paradise."[136]

The final vision is of paradise itself, not disguised in the fiction of El Dorado or as the gold and spices of worldly endeavor. During the third voyage, Columbus reasoned hard, citing Bede, Strabo and others. In a way, he discarded some of the ancient writing on which he had previously relied to reach his new conclusion: "I do not find and I have never found any writing of the Romans or of the Greeks which gives definitely the position in the world of the earthly paradise."[137] But, then came his revelation, just off the coast of South America, near the Orinocco delta:

I believe that the earthly paradise is there and to it, save by the will of God, no man shall come. And I believe that this land which Your Highnesses have now sent [me] to discover is very extensive. . . . I do not hold that the earthly paradise is in the form of a rugged mountain as its description declares to us, but that it is at the summit, there where I have said that the shape of the stalk of the pear is, and that, going towards it from a distance, there is a gradual ascent to it. And I believe that no one could reach the summit as I have said, and I believe that this water may originate from there, though it be far away and may come to collect there where I came and may form this lake. These are great indications of the earthly paradise, for the situation agrees with the opinion of those holy and wise theologians, and also the signs are very much in accord with this idea, for I have never read or heard of so great a quantity of fresh water so coming into and near the salt. And the very mild climate also supports this view, and if it does not come from there, from Paradise, it seems to be a still greater marvel, for I do not believe that there is known in the world a river so great and so deep.[138]

Columbus could now admit at least to an "*otro mundo*" that had become the ultimate vision — the Terrestrial Paradise. Although his journey ended in disaster and he was sent back to Spain in chains, he had helped to redefine the New World for Europeans. He had not substituted another myth of Eden for the legend of the lair of the Wild Man, nor had he anticipated some of the absurdities of the myth of the Noble Savage. Instead, he partly sought to correct one false mythology by placing on the New World a different but equally unreal one, which was only more indicative of the idyllic aspirations of the European newcomer.

Paradise, in essence, negated the European world — although Columbus did not. This image of Paradise, existing just off the coast of South America, began to free Europe of its view of the New World as a distorted grimace of itself. The concept of Paradise assures us that, in the end, the adventurers "discovered" not new continents but themselves. But we are still left with the New World as an enormous fable. Indeed, even to call it "New World" compounds the problem, since the term "new" obviously implies that it is being seen from an "old" world standpoint. At the same time, we cannot be too fastidious or purist. "America" expresses the same problem of naming in two ways. First, the name was wrongly applied by a zealous German mapmaker, Martin Waldseemüller, and, second, even when the term was used, it signified only the southern portion of the continent.

We have already noted how the terms "Carib" and "Caribbean" foisted the Plinian Wild Man onto the entire area. Current research by Louis Allaire has shown that the people in the entire area where Columbus encountered his "cannibals" were of the Taíno culture.[139] Thus, even the utilization of the term "Carib" to refer to the islands is quite wrong. Further, the Taínos were probably trying to frighten Columbus off or, since he did not speak their language, he may have misunderstood what they tried to communicate. Did their sign language set off one of the monsters in Columbus' head?

The fantastic image of the New World could and would, in time, develop into one of exoticism. Since "India," "the Indies," and New World "Indians" were all confused in the European mind, artists ascribed to native Americans a regalia and posture that were not appropriate. Thus the Noble Savage was born, further distancing the New World from reality and continuing to lend it a degree of quaintness.

Albrecht Dürer admitted to his own excitement when he, like Bartolomé de las Casas, witnessed a traveling exhibition. In 1579, Cortés dispatched six Aztecs and a number of artifacts back to Spain. The "exhibition" toured Seville, Valladolid, and Brussels at the time of the coronation of Charles V. Dürer saw the exhibition as a major change in his own artistic life. He confessed in his diary to an ecstatic delight: "I saw the things which have been brought to the king from the new land of gold. . . . All the days of my life I have seen nothing that rejoiced my heart so much as these things."[140]

Jean Michael Massing has shown that the golden and silver discs from the New World excited the greatest curiosity and this was indeed part of the problem. His article goes on to say: "The identification of these two discs as sun and moon seems to stem from the traditional relationship between planets and metals found in Western astrological and alchemical writings; in short, the Aztec objects, were interpreted in European terms."[141] Massing has suggested that not understanding the two objects to be representations of Quetzalcoatl meant that las Casas, Dürer and others speculated wildly. They could, as Massing has noted, "only try to accommodate them to their own system of values."[142]

This was disastrous, for again, according to Massing, "Indians were prettified, even by reputable artists like Dürer." Massing's article reprints a page from the *Gebetbuch* of Emperor Maximilian, in which, with Psalm

24:1, Dürer placed an "Indian." He dressed him in Roman-type sandals and had him carry a primitive lance and shield. His hair was bushy and he wore a necklace and grass-skirt. Below him were fish, above birds, and he himself stood on a snail.[143] Native Americans were being conscripted in yet another direction; they were in the process of losing their monster status and gaining the nobility of the savage.

Europe did "discover" America, by inventing it, in that what Europe visualized, verbalized, viewed, and envisioned in the Americas was based on phantoms of the European past. Whatever type of fancy was inflicted — Amazon or El Dorado, Dürer-painted "Indians" or Patagonians, Carib cannibals or simplistic monsters — spoke more directly about the perceiver than it did about those who were perceived. In any event, the fantasy involves us in a manipulation of historical fact that we need to examine further if we are to come a little closer to objective truth.

European Myth
Exported

Four "proto-texts" document how Europe viewed the outside world, particularly Asia and Africa. First, Pliny's *Natural History* (c. 77 A.D.) established a kind of "scientific" background against which the others could be seen. Second, the "Alexander Romances" (dating from around the second or third century A.D.) placed much of this material in the personal context of Alexander's conquests in Egypt and India. Third, "The Wonders of the East," based on the "Letter of Farasmanes to Hadrian" (between the second and sixth centuries A.D.) attempted to itemize, almost encyclopedia style, the various "marvels" and "wonders" of the world beyond Europe. Finally, the "Letter of Prester John" (written in 1165) continued the idea of a fantastic world beyond Europe. All of these texts bring us to a consideration of Muslim, Jewish, and early Christian travel writing, through which we shall attempt to see how fictions evolved into facts and how the earlier "known" world of the "East" anticipated and prescribed the later "unknown" world of the "West."

These European accounts give us a clear understanding of popular beliefs about the world outside the fixed perimeter of Europe. But none of these originated as a "popular" accounting; they were all, in their different ways, nonfictional expressions of "informed fact," skewed it is true, but fact nonetheless that Europeans largely accepted. The ideas were illustrated and disseminated, sometimes via an original Latin or Greek text, into numerous European languages. Even if these accounts could not be read at the popular level, they were nevertheless told and retold until they formed part of a popular and agreed upon concept of the world.

PLINY

As already noted with regard to Pliny, there were no contending viewpoints. Pliny was the authority of ancient research whom few could dispute. Pliny was clear in Book VI that Ethiopia took its name from "Aethiops the son of Vulcan" and that "the outermost districts of this region produce animal and human monstrosities."[1] He continued that people there existed "without noses" and that some "have no upper lip and others no tongues." He likewise described people who "never wear any clothes."[2] In Book VII, Pliny wrote of "Three-span men and Pygmies," of races of men, including the "Long-lived Ethiopians," who lived to be one-hundred-forty.[3] Pliny also wrote that he "saw in Africa a person who had turned into a male on the day of marriage to a husband."[4] The world of wonder is constantly reiterated in his writings.

As far as Pliny was concerned, the Egyptian pyramids:

Rank as a superfluous and foolish display of wealth on the part of the kings, since it is generally recorded that their motive for building them was to avoid providing funds for their successors or for rivals who wished to plot against them, or else to keep the common folk occupied. Much vanity was shown by these kings.[5]

Regarding the Sphinx, Pliny believed it to be merely the symbol of some ridiculous superstition. It was, plainly put, ugly: "The face of the monstrous creature is painted."[6] Perhaps this opinion was not only an example of Roman jealousy, but also an early attempt to debunk Egypt as cultural archetype.

Beginning with Pliny, the achievements of the non-European world have been downgraded and mocked, and the people, animals, and landscapes beyond Europe have been constantly mentioned as oddities. Columbus cited Pliny's mistaken beliefs as authoritative, asserting that "Pliny writes that the sea and land together form a sphere, but that the ocean forms the greatest sphere," and that "this ocean sea is the greatest mass of water and that lies towards the sky, and that the land is beneath it and supports it."[7] Hence, as late as the third voyage, New World geographical configurations could still be seen as Plinian manifestations.

Pliny was considered all the more acceptable because of his research and methodology. In his dedicatory letter, he mentioned how he had utilized his sources and credited them — "I have set down the very names of those writers, whose help I have used in compiling them." The statements that Pliny made would be accepted at face value for almost two-thousand years, for, even though his sources had been lost, his account seemed to demonstrate an honest desire to achieve veracity.

HERODOTUS AND OTHER SOURCES

Early European ideas about the world were based largely on accounts put forward by Herodotus and Pliny. These would have remained as "learned" tomes, however, were they not revived by the "fictions" that followed them and that lent authority to works that were still to come, such as Marco Polo's *Il Milione* and Sir John Mandeville's *Travels*. Put differently, were it not for the "wonders" and "monsters" portrayed in the earlier works, there would have been neither the "legitimacy" nor the fictional "space" for Marco Polo, Mandeville, or the earlier literature of travel to the East.

Sources for such fantasy may be seen as early as the fifth century B.C. in Herodotus (c. 404–c. 420 B.C.). Herodotus was a personal researcher, actively involved in travel to Egypt, the Black Sea and Scythia, the Euphrates and Babylon, Cyrene and the North African coast, as well as to the Greek Mediterranean and Asia Minor. He readily accepted the marvelous and the miraculous, and passed this belief down to later writers.

Both Ctesias of Cnidos (c. 398 B.C.) and Megasthenes (c. 303 B.C.) probably undertook personal travel also. In their cases, they located the source of marvels in India, but the strange, the odd, and the macabre could have been found anywhere beyond the "known" areas of the European world. The further afield the account was placed, the more it manifested an antithetical relationship to Europe. Ctesias' *History of Persia* in twenty-three books was, for instance, used by Plutarch, while Megasthenes' *Indika* in four books, although at times highly inaccurate, was still utilized as source material by later Greek writers.

Even though writers of the Alexander romances, which followed Alexander the Great's invasion of Egypt in 332 B.C. and India in 326 B.C., might not have been familiar with some of these earlier works, the common alacrity for dealing with the fantastic defines all these previous endeavors as travel books of the mind. Strabo (64/63 B.C.–21 A.D.) dismissed the earlier writings as worthless and contributing nothing, as he put it, either to adorn or to improve life, but his views ran counter to prevailing opinion. Most writers saw in Pliny's *Natural History*, with its zest for the fantastic and the bizarre, a solid foundation on which to model their own peregrinations into the unknown.

For example, when Gaius Julius Solinus in the third century A.D. put together his *Collectanea rerum memorabilium*, he scanted the more factual elements of Pliny and instead extracted only the strange and marvelous. This tendency was bequeathed to the Middle Ages through writers like

Ambrosius Theodosius Macrobius (c. 400 A.D.) and Martianus Capella (c. 400 A.D.). Macrobius was a prefect of Africa, while Capella was born in Carthage, but whatever reality they had encountered abroad did not prevent them from passing on imaginings about European culture, particularly the monsters and marvels that were to be found in "other" places.

Encyclopedias and maps gave factual representation to the fantastic in the Middle Ages. Pierre d'Ailly's *Imago Mundi* (1410), which was most significant because of the influence it exerted on Columbus, showed the extent to which fantasy was sometimes the norm. D'Ailly followed Ptolemy in concluding that, in the "uninhabitable" parts of the world, people "have greater ability to perform wonders."[8] He agreed with St. Isidore that Ethiopia (using the supposedly Greek derivation of its name), "was named from the color of the people who are burned by the sun's proximity."[9] Again following St. Isidore, he identified the so-called Gorgodes Islands as being inhabited by "women of destructiveness, with coarse and hairy bodies."[10] In just these few words, he gave active approval to the condemnation of Blacks and females.

Such a concept of the world assumed normality at its European center. Only outside of this locus was the "abnormal" to be observed and even expected. Descriptions in these proto-fantasies occurred at the levels of landscape, people, and object. What was observed tended most often to be the opposite of European "normality" — hence, the landscape is large, ominous, at times evil. The objects within such an environment were either odd, like giant ants, or desirable, like gold, spices, and lascivious women. Non-European males were considered peculiar, in that they did not recognize the importance of objects desired by Europeans (gold, spices, women). Moreover, because such men existed in an odd environment, they tended to behave and act in a non-European and hence abnormal manner. This could explain their "otherness," their distance, their departure from a human norm, and their total separation from the ordinary.

ALEXANDER'S LETTER TO ARISTOTLE

Several works about Alexander exist as proto-texts but two will suffice for our consideration at this stage: *Alexander's Letter to Aristotle* and *Wonders of the East*. By our reckoning today, they are both delightful "fakes," stuff manufactured out of thin air. But Mary B. Campbell has pointed out the documentary nature of the work, since much of the content was received not as fantasy, but as material that had the weight of scrupulous observation, through what we would term today "research."

Having said this, we must add that the world of *Alexander's Letter* and *Wonders* was not simplistic. It was merely girded by different ideas of organization and representation, thereby degrading the significance of the other.

Alexander's impact on the ancient world was tremendous. There were reliable reports, such as that of Ptolemy Soter (c. 367–283 B.C.), a close friend and general. His account of Alexander's life was considered responsible and, indeed, was heavily relied on by Flavius Arrianus (Arrian) (c. second century A.D.) for his *Anabasis* in eight volumes. Arrian was seldom indiscriminate or sweeping; indeed, his *Indica*, an account of the people of India, was not based on wild speculation but depended on a Greek who had visited India. Aristobolus (c. 320 B.C.) was also reliable, a primary source on which Arrian depended as well. Because he was an officer in Alexander's armies, Aristobolus' accounts of the campaigns, of which Strabo approved, seemed all the more realistic, especially because he wrote *The Ephemerdes* in diary form.

Mere physical presence — being a "witness" — did not guarantee veracity, of course. Callisthenes (d. 328 B.C.) wrote about expeditions that he had actually made with Alexander, but he still tended to be inaccurate. Equally, Onesicritus (third century B.C.), who was made chief pilot by Alexander, later compiled a biography of Alexander, but the problem was the same. Like Callisthenes, Onesicritus tended to exaggerate. Similarly, Cleitarchus (c. 280 B.C.) has been accused of sensationalism.[11]

The problem in any biography of Alexander is inherent in reporting about a subject larger than life. In his own lifetime, Alexander was greeted by the Egyptian priest at Amun as the son of a god. Indeed, just a few years before he died, he had demanded that all his subjects prostrate themselves before him, imposing a new cult of Alexander the God on all cities in Greece.

Alexander may be forgiven — he was only thirty-two when he died in 323 B.C. But the stature of the man surrounded him with myth, for his conquests were the stuff of legends. In turn, these legends were told and retold, orally and in written versions, until they achieved a life of their own. It has been argued that the earliest written source can be traced to a Greek folk epic from Alexandria, written during the second century A.D. Many translations of this were made in Greek, Latin, Armenian, Syrian, Ethiopian, and Coptic. Alexander thus became world lore.

In the newer legends, Alexander was a kind of savior, his birth a type of miracle. He encountered the Amazons in India, and magic helped him to defeat his enemies. He is even present in the *Koran* 18:84 to 18:97 as Dhul-Qarnayn, a messianic and godlike figure:

We made him mighty in the land and gave him means to achieve all things. He journeyed on a certain road until he reached the West and saw the sun setting in a pool of black mud. Hard by he found a certain people.

"Dhul-Qarnayn," We said, "you must either punish them or show them kindness."

He replied: "The wicked we shall surely punish. Then shall they return to their Lord and be sternly punished by Him. As for those that have faith and do good works, we shall bestow on them a rich reward and deal indulgently with them."

He then journeyed along another road until he reached the East and saw the sun rising upon a people whom We had exposed to its flaming rays. So he did; and We had full knowledge of all the forces at his command.

Then he followed yet another route until he came between the Two Mountains and found a people who could barely understand a word. "Dhul-Qarnayn," they said, "Gog and Magog are ravaging this land. Build a rampart between us, and we will pay you tribute."

He replied: "The power my Lord has given me is better than any tribute. Lend me a force of men, and I will raise a rampart between you and them. Come, bring me blocks of iron."

He dammed up the valley between the Two Mountains, and said: "Ply your bellows." And when the iron blocks were red with heat, he said: "Bring me molden brass to pour on them."

Gog and Magog could not scale it, nor could they dig their way through it.[12]

By sealing off Gog and Magog, Alexander here personifies the task of locking away the "ultimate other," which, interestingly enough, is passed on even to the "other" world of Muslims as a strict theological credo. The two tribes had reached the West, by way of the Bible (Ezekiel 38:1–9 and Revelations 20:7–8), as the forces of the Antichrist which would be unleashed on the Day of Judgment. In the thirteenth-century Psalter map in the British Library, Alexander's wall is identified with the Great Wall of China.

Through European history, Alexander has evolved, therefore, as a legendary *Christian* hero, God-sanctioned and omnipotent. Interestingly, he made a transcultural leap from "West" to "East." Hence, in the Christian and Islamic eras, Alexander moved past the historical reality that Plutarch (c. 48–c. 127 A.D.), for instance, was still able to impose on him. By contrast, Quintus Curtius Rufus' *History of Alexander the Great*, initially in ten volumes (the first two are lost, as are parts of the remainder), belongs more to fiction than to historical literature. As Mary B. Campbell has added in *The Witness and the Other World*, "The farther one got from Home, the Temperate, reasonable mean, the more outlandish, *unheimlich*, became the bodies and manners of men."[13] The Alexander legends aided this process as they moved away from the historical representation of Alexander.

Although an account of Alexander is to be found in a ninth-century Old English translation, Europe inherited the corpus of legend and lore through translations made into Middle Irish in the eleventh century and a Middle High German version in the twelfth century. A Middle English romance entitled "King Alisaunder" and a Franco-Provençal version called "Roman d'Alexandre" also belong to the twelfth century. There are many accounts in Latin of Alexander's supposed "letters," of which one of the most important is "Alexander's Letter to Aristotle."

The entire corpus of writing about Alexander helps us to understand later travel writing and the context into which it fits. If we are to come to any conclusions about the manner in which "myth" and "legend" become intermingled with "history" and "fact," indeed become so intertwined that they are inseparable, then the Alexander romances and letters are good illustrations of how the process occurs. They are important to us not only because they distort Alexander but also because, in so doing, they disfigure the world with which Alexander came into contact. Recall that this "known" world had Europe at its center, and Asia (India) and Africa (Egypt) at its periphery. Alexander's name lent a credence to the accounts, implying that this was indeed what the rest of the world looked like, once one moved away from the European center.

At first, the voice of the "Letter to Aristotle" moderates the excesses of the romances.[14] The tone is personal, with the specific purpose of informing Alexander's teacher, Aristotle, about India. Indeed, because what Alexander is about to relate will be so fantastic, he reminds his tutor that he will "observe the boundary line of fairness and . . . understate all matters."[15]

Alexander relates that he is quite wealthy as a result of his successes; even his army bears gold-plated arms. This constant emphasis at the beginning of the letter stresses a consideration that goes beyond physical possessions. Against the background of an army at once almost crippled by its rich possessions and yet almost dying of thirst, the "magic" and "wonder" of the alien environment are presented, for his people's enormous wealth and lack of water set the macabre tone.

A vast landscape looms before them. Alexander and his party reach a river along which they observe canes sixty feet high, beyond a stream of bitter water. They encounter "semi-nude Indians who immediately took shelter."[16] Both the oppressive landscape and the meek "Indians" will

become part of the later narrative of conquest, as will the aggression on
the part of the invaders:

When no one appeared, I ordered that a few arrows be shot into the city so that they
might be moved to show themselves because of fear of war if they should be unwilling
to come out on their own free will. When they hid so much the more on account of
fear, and when no one appeared for a long time, I sent 200 Macedonian soldiers with
light arms to swim through the stream.[17]

Were it not for the "arrows" and "Macedonians," we might be reading a
sixteenth-century text about the Spanish conquest. The stage is set,
complete with meek "natives" and triumphant "overlord." This is the
scenario Columbus and all the conquistadors would later replicate.

Next, as in the European New World encounters, several important
incidents occur. First there is the sight of monsters — here they are
"hippopotami with bodies larger than elephants . . . monsters from the
water." In Columbus' case, the "monster" was the "Carib" or "cannibal"
(both words have the same root; in other words, Columbus "named" his
"monster"). Second, there is the loss of life, as the hostile environment
attacks the newcomers; there some of Alexander's men are inadvertently
eaten by the hippopotami. Third, as a result, the encountering party
moves on: "For what did it profit to stay in such a place when we were
lacking water?" Then, the loss of life is reversed — in the New World
encounter these new "Indians" died. Fourth, as with Alexander, the in-
vading group moves on to other places of "discovery," other islands,
another part of the Americas. Finally, much as Alexander was deified in
Egypt, so too were the conquistadors, at least according to their own
versions.

Alexander's *Letter* indicates several other concerns that we shall
observe in later travel writing. Fear of the unknown probably produces
the monstrosities, for, as the letter states, "Through the whole night we
kept resisting onrushing lions and bears as well as tigers, panthers, and
lynxes." In this first incident, they reach their goal, "the stream . . .
enclosed by a very old and thick forest."[18] In the case of the
conquistadors, the goal was not only water, but the wealth of the land
and the domination of its people. As the *Letter* goes on to relate, these
were also Alexander's goals.

In this way, "marvels" and "monsters" are revealed through
Alexander's *Letter*. First, there is the "journey," with its attendant problems of thirst, hunger, and monsters; second, there is the "battle," whereby Alexander and his men wage war against their surroundings their
enemies and themselves. Next, a "sacrifice" takes place, a blood-letting,

followed by a "tryst" through which a kind of temporary peace is won. Then the cyclic "journey" begins all over again.

Alexander's adventures are thus placed within the structural format of a neat fabrication. The important concern is not the manufactured elements that contain the whole, but rather the opportunity afforded to describe "reality" outside the domain of Europe. Donald Davidson and A. P. Campbell have contended that "historical material, famous battles and kings, accounts of travels and terrain are mentioned but not elaborated upon."[19] The fabulous itself becomes the sole motive for the account — fantastic golden ornaments, beasts of the sea and land, everything exaggerated to the nth power — so that Europeans may be even more conscious of the degree of distance between "us" and "them."

The concepts of "themness" and "otherness" cause macabre events to occur in such an alien setting, thereby rendering Alexander's savagery acceptable. At one point in the "sacrifice," the letter reports, "I ordered that 100 of these [Alexander's own men] be flung into the river."[20] At another point, his own guides are "punished by the breaking of their limbs,"[21] and, in response to the supposed hostility of the landscape, "I ordered that the grove be cut down."[22] As with New World adventures, internecine slaughter goes hand in hand with the slaughter of local people and the despoliation of landscape.

Throughout the account, the monstrousness of the environment is stressed. There are menacing scorpions, "Indian serpents with two or three heads," "crabs in great numbers covered with the skins of crocodiles," "boars of immense size," an animal that was a "beast of a new kind . . . larger than an elephant, armed with three horns," "pests of various colors," "trees [that] were 100 feet in height" and "reeds as thick and tall as 300 ordinary reeds."[23] Such a landscape is not only inherently grotesque but also helps the European observer to place the non-European observed in the same incredible perspective. The people whom Alexander encounters are like the three-headed serpents or the boars — plainly, what Alexander himself calls, "the barbarians and the Indians."[24] We shall find these terms over and over again in new World delineation. Even Porus, King of India, possesses qualities that Alexander condemns — "The arrogance and deep audacity of the barbarian."[25] Any conquistador might recall similar sentiments being expressed in the confrontations between Cortés and Montezuma and between Pizarro and Atahualpa.

These strange people possess treasure, also a goal of New World voyagers, which may be taken from them in battle. Only after Porus is defeated does he show Alexander his treasures, "of which [Alexander] was not aware. From these he enriched me and my companions and the whole army."[26] Therefore, even though both landscape and people conspire against them, there is still booty to be gained. The formula of the quest for treasure requires hostile actions against people who are "nine feet tall."

At this point, we note how the alien humans become one with the environment and the monsters. The letter goes on "[W]e saw men and women in the open field who had hair over their whole body like beasts."[27] This is the final point at which the non-European is made into the Ultimate Other, demonized and totally banished from human consideration. Thus, it becomes a moral duty to deprive the "barbarian" of his life and his property.

Women are specially singled out, Amazon fashion, for the same misogynistic treatment that New World explorers would later accord them. For instance, when Alexander is on his way back from India, he comes upon a combination of Greek sirens, mermaids, Amazons, and whores:

These women suffocated my men while they, ignorant of the area, were swimming. [They did this] either by holding them in the eddies or when they were caught in the thicket of reeds. Since the women were extraordinary in appearance, the men, who were completely overcome with their fond feeling [for them], the women [were] treated violently or killed during sexual pleasure. We captured only two of these. Their complexion was snow-white, [and] like nymphs their hair spread over their backs.[28]

These Amazonian women reappear in New World accounts, and show how misogynistic feelings continued to be reflected by male European adventurers. After all, later medieval inheritance even demonized women as witches.

Only to some extent can Pliny as observer be regarded as a "culture hero," for Pliny was supposedly writing an objective account of people in *other* places. The hero of the Alexander romances has no such problem. He represents the conqueror, and, in the *Letter*, he seeks ultimate immortality in the Sacred Grove, as Alexander himself sought in real life by declaring himself a god.

Because the "India" of the letter is indeed merely the antithesis to Europe as such, on his journey there, Alexander observes "next to the ocean, in Ethiopia, promontories reaching to the sky."[29] There ought to be no geographical confusion here, for "India" is only a metaphor for the darkness and horror of the unknown. Thus the people, "clothed in the skins of panthers and tigers"[30] are not merely Indians, but members of a race of nonhumans, distant and apart. As if to make this point with dramatic directness, the priest of the oracle (when Alexander seeks to know his destiny) is described as "10 foot in height, with a black body, and with the teeth of a dog."[31] He too is described as a "barbarian," and his blackness pinpoints his complete outsider status.

Within this setting, the magical may be invoked. Some normal laws of logic and discourse are reversed: For instance, trees speak, and Alexander is told "you will see the two trees of the sun and the moon which speak Indian and Greek. The male tree is the tree of the sun, and the other, the feminine tree, is the tree of the moon. From these you will be able to learn what good or evil impends for you."[32] The trees are over one-hundred feet high, although it never rains in the grove. At this point, the ever-impulsive conqueror must be restrained from his decision "to make a sacrifice and to slay sacrificial victims."[33] After this, the oracle foretells Alexander's death, at first unnerving him, before he realizes the opulence that surrounds him:

[T]he priest himself, covered with skins of wild animals, was sleeping, and there was a large piece of frankincense placed on the table in front of him which was left for him from yesterday's dinner. There was also an ivory knife there. In fact they lacked copper and iron and lead and silver [but] have plenty of gold.[34]

On his way back, Alexander and his men find serpents with large emeralds round their necks, and Alexander is able to erect two enormous gold pillars as testimony to his accomplishments. This persistent obsession with gold fueled the entire European New World enterprise.

Alexander is fact, not fiction. First and foremost, he was a real man. Second, his version of the world verified previous accounts, written and verbal, that had been given credibility over a long period of time. As a culture hero, Alexander showed that it was possible for the European to dominate alien lands and foreign peoples and, through a kind of crude individualism, to overcome any and all obstacles placed in his way. Thus, although we know that Alexander must die, we are less concerned with his mortality than with his ability to outwit, outfight, and outlive his enemies. We shall see, as we pass on to further investigations of the proto-text, how the Alexander myth in turn became an authoritative buttress for justifying yet more wonders and marvels, as well as the segregation of the "other."

WONDERS OF THE EAST

Wonders of the East exists in three manuscripts, the first in Old English, the second in Latin and Old English at the British Library, and the third in Latin alone at the Bodleian Library, Oxford. Paul Gibb has added that there are eight related texts, seven in Latin and one in Old French; he has termed these the "Continental relatives." I shall concern myself here mainly with Gibb's modern English version that makes use of the two Old English texts.[35]

Although *Wonders* is also in the form of a "letter," what emerges is not merely its epistolary flavor, but the itemizing of wonders and marvels in the world outside Europe. The author is very concerned with establishing geographical preciseness (mentioning that particular sights are near Babylon, in Egypt, near the Nile, etc.), and Greek measurements are stated for specific areas. Once he has done this for the sake of credibility, however, he moves on to describe the strange and alien environment of "non-Europe," as an inversion of the accepted way of visualizing the European world.

We are told that one place, termed the "colony," is one of merchants, and further proof of its authenticity is given by reference to Alexander: "The great wonders are there, the works Alexander, the great Macedonian, ordered built."[36] If we still have doubts, perhaps about the race of men who live for an extremely long time, then we are informed that "Alexander, when he came upon them, wondered about their humanity. He did not wish to kill them nor in any way to do harm to them."[37] Alexander is thus used to verify the existence of such monstrous people. Alexander is also cited, in a more recognizable context, in the description of women who, "[b]ecause of their uncleanliness . . . were killed by the great Macedonian, Alexander. When he could not take them alive, he killed them because their bodies are foul and contemptible."[38] In the middle of the text, Alexander's two trees of the sun and the moon become two lakes: "that which is of the sun is hot by day and cold by night. And that which is of the moon is hot by night and cold by day."[39] By carefully placing references to Alexander at the beginning, middle, and near the end of the text, the author of *Wonders* reminds us that we need to take this particular account of the non-European world seriously, since Alexander is presented as its authority.

Alexander has thus sanctioned the familiar misogyny that is most potently symbolized in the Greek Amazons.[40] Women "have boars' tusks and hair down to their heels and oxen's tails growing out of their loins"; furthermore, these women are thirteen feet tall and possess "camels' feet and donkeys' teeth."[41] Here the writer goes beyond the Amazon legend, justifying the murder of the women and siding with Alexander's brutality. Indeed, throughout the text, women are considered so monstrous that, in one case, they are described as "having beards down to their breasts and horses' hides for clothing,"[42] and, as above, being gigantic.[43] It is always stressed that their color is an odd and peculiar type of white, reinforcing, it seems, a way of showing a degree of non-European abnormality, even in European women. From the very beginning, women are seen as alien creatures who, whenever mentioned, are antithetical and often hostile to European males, indeed to progress itself, unless they are sexually compliant, as in one instance when a group of "generous men" insists on giving each European guest "a woman before they let him go away."[44]

Unlike women, males in the subhuman category tend to be non-European. *Wonders* describes men with "the mane of a horse, the tusks of a boar, and the heads of dogs,"[45] hairy men whose diet is raw fish, enormous men who live near "the prince of foul rivers" [the Nile], who are "fifteen feet long," with "two faces on one head, feet and knees very red, and a long nose and dark hair."[46] In another area, men exist "begotten of three colors . . . twenty feet tall and they have a great mouth like a winnowing fan." The writer pertinently adds that these are "thought to be men."[47] In still another place, men "have feet and legs which are twelve feet long, [and] sides with chest seven feet long."[48] At times, the human monstrosities exhibit both animal and human characteristics, like the "Double Ones," who have "a human shape down to the navel, and from there on they resemble a donkey."[49] Perhaps, in this instance, the merger of the brute and the monster offers a glimpse of strong homophobic tendencies; these continue in later travel literature and may account for the enslavement of early New World populations.[50]

Animal monstrosities are numerous.[51] There are rams "as big as oxen,"[52] red hens that are "unheard-of instances of sorcery,"[53] monstrous wild animals with eight feet that are also "unheard-of animals,"[54] serpents with two heads,[55] animals that have the "ears of a donkey, wool of a sheep, and feet of a bird,"[56] dragons "thick as stone columns,"[57] and so on. In another manuscript version appear birds with "four feet and the tail of a cow and the head of an eagle."[58] Animals and humans lie in a landscape totally at variance with the normality one might expect in Europe.

Both the humans and animals are "barbarous," because they subvert the European order. In one instance, we are informed that "the worst men and the most barbarous," possess a total inversion of the European concept of royalty: "they have kings under their power — one hundred ten of them it is said."[59] The monstrous humans are made completely alien by their indulgence in the ultimate act of barbarism — the eating of human flesh. In an island of the Red Sea, a group of monstrous men are reported to exist who speak all human languages and whose sole intent is first to beguile the unwary traveler; afterward, "they devour him all but the head, and then they sit and weep over the head."[60] Part of this lore was later foisted on Caribs and Africans, but it originates in the Alexander creations, the so-called monsters termed "Donestre."

Particularly intriguing are three elements of the text that demonstrate how the writer distances himself from the material he is recounting. First, there is the occasional reference to "us"; at times, this merely represents an attempt at "objective" distancing between the recorder and his subject. The narrator thus mentions that one race of monstrous men is "called by *us* Donestre."[61] At other times, the comparison is made to stress a contrast, as, for instance, with the mention of the monstrous red hens, first described as "hens like those among *us*."[62] Indeed, the whole of *Wonders* becomes a way of relating, in the starkest of terms, the differences between references to "they" (monsters outside the European pale) and allusions to "we" (people within the European framework). To put it this way is perhaps to make a judgment based on the knowledge of our own times. But St. Augustine of Hippo, the early fifth-century Church Father and an African, had no problem with such a polarity. Indeed, St. Augustine argued that to challenge the idea of monsters is to regard God's wisdom as the product of an imperfectly skilled maker. In *City of God*, Augustine concluded that "if such people exist, then either they are not human, or, if human, they are descended from Adam."[63]

Second, ultimate otherness is established by allusion to place. There are constant references to the Red Sea and Egypt, as well as "the southern part of Babylonia." The manner in which the writer uses "they" becomes even more intriguing, for its mere repetition is enough to establish an enormous gulf between the oddities being described and European normality. Most interestingly, the men with three colors have to go to India to propagate their species. We are told that "they travel in ships to India and there bring their kind into the world."[64] In this way, India, Africa, and the Middle East become one and are all identified within the text as sites for extreme abnormality.

Third, there are references to people "of a black color,"[65] to "another race of men .... of a black color in appearance,"[66] and to "another mountain where there are black men, and no other men may travel to those men because the mountain is all aflame." Blacks are therefore placed in a kind of nether zone, beyond even subhuman contact. True, there are also allusions to monstrous people who are White, but we know that the males are non-European because their skin color is "as white as milk,"[67] and that the females are European oddities because their skin possesses the "whiteness of marble,"[68] a kind of whiteness-beyond-whiteness. The writer does not obfuscate the fact that the ultimate monsters are Black; indeed, he is most specific that "One calls them Ethiopians."[69] These are the very last words in one of the versions and are meant to make a final impact.

It follows almost naturally that these are lands of great wealth. Snakes guard a pepper forest, which we shall later encounter in the travels of Marco Polo and Mandeville. The city of El Dorado is anticipated in the references to gold and wealth, as in these descriptions: "These lands are near the cities which are filled with all the worldly wealth that is the southern part of Egypt."[70] There is also a "golden vineyard" whose trees contain "pearls and gems."[71] Nearby, "in another kingdom in the land of Babylonia . . . precious gems are found."[72] The gold-digging ants, later mentioned by Marco Polo and Mandeville, are also present: "[T]he ants dig up gold from the earth before the night until the fifth hour of the day."[73] Another area possesses trees that yield "the most precious oil,"[74] and still another has the "kinds of trees upon which the most precious stones are found, and upon which they grow."[75] As Gibb's translation further shows, the other version of *Wonders* continues to stress abundant wealth, as in the reference to "a land in which vineyards grow most greatly, where there is a couch of ivory."[76] We must not forget, however, that all of this is still associated with the odd and the monstrous. Put differently, marvels and monsters are two sides to the same coin. Both wonder and wealth simply represent a way of visualizing another world totally at variance with Europe.

Additionally, references to Alexander indicate ways of showing how textual accretions occur. The text of *Wonders* itself not only *actively* utilizes these references to establish its authority, but also *passively* incorporates strains from earlier oral and written accounts to carry on tradition. We therefore see, even in the so-called proto-text, the extent to which the creation of a literary palimpsest becomes increasingly evident. Particularly intriguing, especially in the midst of such a recital of the grotesque, is the reference to "a noble and gentle priest" who "governs the halls and keeps watch over them."[77] He sounds very much like Prester John, whom we shall next consider.

LETTER OF PRESTER JOHN

According to Vsevolod Slessarev, Alberic de Trois Fontaines confirmed the arrival of Prester John's letter in 1165. Slessarev has noted that it is probable that the Byzantine Emperor Manuel I Comnenus (1143–1180) forwarded the letter to Frederick I Barbarossa (1152–1190). In any event, such a letter was in circulation, for on September 27, 1177, Pope Alexander III (1159–1181) sent a reply to Prester John. Although the letter was supposedly composed in Greek, no Greek original has been found; still, over a hundred manuscripts exist in various European languages.[78]

The *Letter of Prester John* continued the same type of "fiction" we have been describing. This document is a little more blatant, in that it was created for a specific political purpose. Additionally, unlike the other texts that we have looked at, this had both a spiritual and a psychological function. What the writer did was to incorporate, quite intentionally, several elements of mythology that were already accepted by Europeans and to place these side by side with the facts of recent history, particularly the fall of Jerusalem, the rise of Muslim power, and fears about the collapse of Christendom. By the mid-fifteenth century, Fra Mauro's map had been illustrated with a picture of an Emperor of Ethiopia, who was closely associated in all minds with Prester John. The myth had now been validated.[79]

In the letter, Prester John first sends greetings to Manuel, with the pert remark that Manuel is only "governor of the Romans." He, Prester John, is a mere human being, whereas Manuel (the letter scoffs) is considered to be a god by his subjects. Prester John goes on to state that he is extremely wealthy and that seventy-two vassal kings are under his control. He intends to go to Jerusalem with a mighty army and fight the enemies of the Christian world.

Having established this political ploy, the *Letter of Prester John* returns to the familiar world of monsters and marvels. Prester John's kingdom is the "Three Indias," full of exotic animals, monsters, and the familiar monstrous races, Gog and Magog. To counterbalance these, as in the other works considered, the idyllic is also presented — kindly creatures, a river of clear water that flows through the kingdom on its way from the Earthly Paradise (later, recall, to be "discovered" by Columbus on his third journey), the usual precious stones, the familiar pepper forest infested by snakes, and numerous miraculous medical cures, including the suggestion of an elixir that is reminiscent of Ponce de León's Fountain of Youth.

The *Letter of Prester John* connects the mythological world of Pliny, Alexander, and other nonreligious authoritative sources to the "divinely inspired" viewpoint of the Bible. The word "prester" itself means priest, and, in one of the addenda to the original letter, Prester John describes himself as a descendant of one of the Magi. His ideal state anticipates Sir Thomas More's later Utopian vision of the New World. What we observe imbedded in Prester John's letter are layers of mythical belief previously discussed, but quite intentionally used here in the context of Christian faith.

Prester John describes (in accordance with biblical injunction) how he feeds and shelters all pilgrims and strangers. As a result of his conscientious outlook and Christian rule, no destitute people, thieves, robbers, or adulterers exist in his country; indeed, everyone is quite wealthy, curiously lacking only horses. Prester John himself exudes the qualities of splendor. When he goes to war, he is preceded by thirteen crosses made of gold and jewels; during peacetime, a wooden cross, a vessel full of gold, and another of earth are carried before him, the last to signify his humility.

Prester John's palace is similar to the one built for a king of India by Saint Thomas who allegedly carried Nestorian Christianity to the East. The building is constructed of precious woods and stones and, at night, only balsam is burned. Because of the materials used, the furniture and palace have a wholesome effect on the people who live there. Prester John has several beautiful wives who approach him only four times a year for the purposes of procreation.

The letter continues to describe the opulence of Prester John's court: the emerald table at which they eat rests on columns of amethyst which, in turn, prevents over-inebriation. In front of the palace is a tower with a magical mirror in which the enemies of Prester John may clearly be seen. The fact that seven kings, seventy-two dukes, and 365 counts attend him further testifies to his physical grandeur. Masses are said for Prester John around the clock, emphasizing his spiritual magnificence.

After a detailed description of a second royal palace, the *Letter* ends with another direct address to Emperor Manuel, in which Prester John explains why he wishes to be termed simply "priest." His explanation is so completely contrary to his intent that it is difficult to see Prester John in any context other than that of a god-king:

We have in fact at our court many subordinates who are endowed with more important titles and positions in the church hierarchy and whose divine duties are greater than ours. Thus our steward is a patriarch and king, our butler is an archbishop and king, our chamberlain is a bishop and king, our marshal is a king and an abbot, and the first cook is a king and a prior. Therefore our Highness does not suffer to be called by these names or to be designated by such titles of which our court abounds.[80]

If Prester John could be "verbalized," he also needed to be "visualized." A 1558 atlas by the Portuguese, Diogo Homem, shows Prester John secure in Africa. By then, Europeans had been searching for him in all the wrong places for four-hundred years. On Homem's map, Prester John's image straddles North-East Africa. Behind him are the turrets of three glistening palaces, as he gazes toward the Indian Ocean. He is clad in blue with red sandals and a golden cloak, wearing a golden crown, bearing a cross-like scepter, and seated on an enormous golden high-backed throne. With the Homem map, Prester John had finally moved from the misty area of myth to the specific region of a cartographer's reality.[81]

At the same time, Prester John's kingdom reflects the promise of splendor that undergirds biblical belief. People should not lay up treasures on earth, since, ultimately, the reward of heaven provides the supreme boon. Prester John, in his life and by his rule, shows that it is possible to have kings who are divine but who do not become the divinity, even though Prester John, as stated before, is decidedly a demi-god.

Additionally, the letter offers the original writer and subsequent scribes with an opportunity to gloss the text, which allows us to learn some of the important preoccupations of the twelfth and thirteenth centuries. Friederich Zarncke, in his exhaustive study *Der Priester Johannes*, has identified a number of interpolations. Zarncke has argued that there are over a hundred Latin versions, but that there is an original letter that precedes the others. He has pinpointed five major types of interpolations in the later versions, termed A, B, C, D, and E.[82] I shall briefly discuss these.

The first or "A" interpolation significantly enlarges on the story of the pepper forest. This is extremely important for our consideration, since it demonstrates how the desire and need for oriental spices become of more and more interest to Europeans. By the fifteenth century, this was one of the major motivating factors that dispatched Portuguese caravels around the southern tip of Africa and indeed, a significant reason that Columbus himself set sail in 1492. At the very basic level of European gastronomy lay a desire for spices that would help preserve food and add taste to an otherwise bland diet.[83]

The second or "B" interpolation shows the extent to which the "editors" of the letter utilized accretions that were part of the general belief of the time. In this instance, they were most concerned with establishing wealth as a prerequisite for both physical and spiritual well-being and, even more importantly, as a very desirable and practical reason for Europeans to be interested in Prester John's kingdom. Indeed, as late as 1600, the English editor of Leo Africanus' *A Geographical Historie of Africa* "updated" this African/Arab text to include specific descriptions of Prester John's kingdom, regarding how it was governed and how it obtained and retained its wealth.[84]

According to Zarncke, the "C" interpolations had become an official part of the letter by 1221. Here we receive a fairly long account of the nations of Gog and Magog. This places the letter within the "fictions" of the Alexander romances, or, as Arthur Newton concluded in *Travel and Travellers of the Middle Ages*, "the popular legends of Alexander the Great lay at the root of all the amazing statements of the forgery."[85] Indeed, in one version, translated from French, Alexander is specifically mentioned as the person who locks up the tribes. The *Letter of Prester John* therefore established the background for the ongoing creation of a document of the mind, which learned Europeans composed about the outer reaches of the world beyond their own.

The final interpolations, "D" and "E," continue to stress the glory and magnificence of Prester John. To some extent, the writers of these addenda had to be extremely careful to balance the humility of Prester John with his worldly possessions and accomplishments. It was equally important that Prester John should provide hope, especially within the historical context of an apparently shrinking Christendom. Columbus himself realized that his greatest appeal to King Ferdinand's sponsorship of further explorations lay in this — that New World adventurism would provide the funding to retain Jerusalem and restore it to Christendom.

In Slessarev's translation of one of the French manuscripts, most of the familiar elements are present. Prester John's land is full of "gold, silver, [and] precious stones." His empire, the Three Indias, is enormous, encompassing a "Greater India," another "India" near Babylon, and "another province toward the North," where "there is a great abundance of bread, wine, meat, and everything necessary for the human body."[86] This kind of abundance is stressed to contrast it with the grim realities of Europe in the Middle Ages. Prester John's land (like the New World later on) becomes a desired haven, a cornucopia, filled with everything that could be desired. It was sought for over four centuries in Asia, Africa, and the New World as a panacea for European ills, in part for its restorative power and for its symbolic ideals.

As part of this upside-down version of Europe, Prester John's kingdom has its fill of Plinian and Alexandrian monstrosities such as "wild asses with two little horns, wild hares as big as sheep, and swift horses with two little horns who gallop faster than any other animal."[87] Note that in the expanded version, horses, albeit monstrous ones, are now present, since, in reality, a powerful kingdom lacking horses could hardly be conceived. Horses, for Cortés and Pizarro, and indeed for Columbus after his first voyage, represented extra advantage over Native Americans, allowing Europeans to assume control over indigenous peoples. Of particular interest to us is the contention of the conquistadors that the Native Americans perceived the Spaniards as fearful "monsters" — half-man and half-horse. One must wonder to what extent this was a product of European fancy. After all, descendants of indigenous New World peoples were the first to domesticate the horse in Asia.

Other monsters are listed — birds that feed horses or oxen to their young and, as in *Wonders of the East*, birds "of fiery color,"[88] that, phoenix-like, easily regenerate their young after a sixty-year life span. Other "birds called tigers . . . lift and kill with ease an armored man together with his horse," this version of the letter relates.[89]

Monstrous people also exist in Prester John's kingdom. Again, there are the familiar Homerian "horned men who have but one eye," except that they now have an additional three or four eyes behind it. Once more, brutish men and women are described, like the horned men who have "women who look similar." Cannibals are likewise there, except here they are identified as belonging to Gog and Magog. Humans with "hoofed legs like horses" exist as well.

We obtain the familiar dose of misogynistic attitudes. Once more, non-European women are singled out as Amazons, existing in a separate and distinct area:

In another region of the wilderness we have a country that extends for forty-two days' journey and it is called the Great Feminie. Do not think that it is in the land of the Saracens, for the one we are talking about is in our country. In that land there are three queens and many other ladies who hold their lands from them. And when these three queens wish to wage war, each of them leads with her one hundred thousand armed women, not counting those who drive the carts, horses, and elephants with the supplies and food. And know that they fight bravely like men: No male can stay with them over nine days, during which he can carouse and amuse himself and make them conceive. But he should not overstay, for in such a case he will die. This land is encircled by a river called Cyson that flows from the terrestrial paradise and is so wide that nobody can cross it except in big boats or ships.[90]

Like Blacks in *Wonders of the East*, women are physically removed from any type of everyday human intercourse, literally existing in a no-man's-territory surrounded by a river flowing from the Earthly Paradise, through which none may venture. On his third voyage, as Columbus also encountered the Earthly Paradise off South America, he too mused that it was impossible to journey there. And, when Orellana finally arrived there, he also encountered an extreme — women who engaged in fighting so fiercely that their actions were "foreign," for what they did was "independent of and without association with male beings."[91]

Humans exist in Prester John's kingdom who are "as small as seven year old children," who "from the waist up are men but whose lower part is that of a horse." These are the people Pliny referred to as Hippopodes, centaur-like creatures with horses' hooves for feet. It is interesting to note in passing that Cortés claimed that this was how native Americans viewed Spanish horsemen, and it is reasonable to wonder whether the myth was not really Western, having been transplanted to the New World and simply inflicted on its unfortunate indigenous inhabitants. This version of the *Letter* goes on to describe unicorns that kill lions, men who were once giants, the phoenix itself, and other oddities.

These strange creatures are balanced by the land's bounty. There is, in addition to the abundance of food, the riches that would drive Europeans to seek El Dorado:

Between us and the Saracens there flows a river called Ydonis which comes from the terrestrial paradise and is full of precious stones. It flows through our land mostly in small and big arms and many precious stones are found there, such as emeralds, sapphires, jasper, calcedoines, rubies, carbuncles, "scabasses," and many other precious stones which I have not mentioned; and of each we know its name and its magic power.[92]

Additionally, there exist many herbs to ward off spiritual and physical ailments and special "birds of a more hot-blooded nature than elsewhere"[93] that can also cure ailments.

Specifically, there are five features in this amazing place, some of which we have previously observed and all of which we shall see in the worlds of Marco Polo and Sir John Mandeville. First is pepper, which grows wild in the kingdom. As in *Wonders of the East*, the pepper turns black because it is burnt. This explanation is a little like the Plinian explanations for the color of the Ethiopians who have "burnt faces." In *Letter of Prester John*, however, there is no mention of serpents guarding the Pepper Forest.

Second, a Fountain of Youth exists, and Prester John asserts that he has benefited from its waters by living 562 years. The tone of the letter is almost poetic at this point:

Near this region is a fountain and whoever drinks of its water three times on an empty stomach will have no sickness for thirty years; and when he has drunk of it, he will feel as if he has eaten the best meat and spices, for it is full of God's grace. A person who can bathe in this fountain, be he of a hundred or a thousand years, will regain the age of thirty-two. Know that we were born and blessed in the womb of our mother five hundred and sixty-two years ago and since then we have bathed in the fountain six times.[94]

Observe the important addition to the document, which suggests that God is responsible for the "wonders" — the cures and longevity — if not for the "monsters," the malformations, and the disorder.

Third, there is what is termed here the "Sandy Sea" (in later texts the "Gravelly Sea,") which actually is the initial European observation of a desert landscape. The letter describes its "swift surf" and "frightful waves." Earlier texts describe large fish that can be obtained from its banks, which may be a reference to the Nile. Near the sea, "there flows a river in which one finds many precious stones and herbs that are good for many medicines."[95]

Fourth, Prester John symbolizes most potently the incipient figure of the Emperor of El Dorado. Near "a river full of precious stones," he has established "forty-two castles which are the strangest and most beautiful in the world." Indeed, "no Christian king has as many treasures as we do," Prester John declares, later adding that his palace walls "are of crystal, the ceiling above is of precious stones and it is adorned with stones similar to those of the sky."[96]

Fifth, in Prester John's kingdom there exists "the tree of life from which the holy oil is coming," guarded by a serpent. The tree is "only a day's journey from the earthly paradise."[97] In sixteenth-century exploration, this tree is merged with the Fountain of Youth and Paradise itself.

As news spread about Prester John, he was seen not only as a great ally to counteract Muslim power, but also as a desirable symbol of the civilized European world versus the "other." Merchants, missionaries, and Pope Alexander III's own physician, Master Philip, all attempted to find him, and, in the process, revealed other aspects of mythologies about the regions where they sought him, particularly in western Asia.

With the advent of Portuguese exploration of the African coast, the myth was once more revived. By then, Prester John would have been over 800 years old, but no matter. Prince Henry specifically gave instructions that explorers should seek him out, and King João II of Portugal dispatched an overland expedition to the Middle East in search of him as well. When the Portuguese finally reached Ethiopia, they attempted, however lamely, to equate the Ethiopian emperor with Prester John. The search had continued, not merely for the verification of a legend, but for the establishment of religious and political associations to contain Muslim power.

These elemental attributes of Prester John's kingdom would reappear, redefined or simply copied, in the literature of actual travel. Later writers did not even have to read Prester John's letter, since its ideas and images expressed an agreed-upon assembly of images constituting the European way of visualizing non-Europe.

The *Letter of Prester John* utilized the monsters and marvels not merely to be informative, as did Pliny, or simply to titillate, as in the Alexander romances or *Wonders of the East*. Instead, the *Letter* situated its major concern with the macabre within the context of established belief in order to be persuasive. Thus, by using certain cultural appendages, the *Letter of Prester John* succeeded in making itself into a kind of super-text, from which still other texts would emerge, among them the accounts of Marco Polo (who actually traveled), Mandeville (who probably did not), and actual travelers journeying to the Holy Land in the thirteenth century and before.

Additionally, the *Letter of Prester John*, especially after its relatively wide dispersal, moved from existing as mere "text" toward becoming an important cultural landmark, shared by Europeans at all societal levels. Thus, the gold and diamonds, the pepper forest, the Fountain of Youth, the Amazon women, and indeed Prester John himself became fact within this new, agreed-upon European outlook. They became not symbols of a mythical journey but motivating reasons for European exploration in the sixteenth century, in order to "discover" what had only been imagined, to "name" what had never existed, and to "invent" a New World from their original mental fiction. Certainly, in this way, there can be little dispute that Europe exported its mythology first to Asia and Africa, and later to the New World.

From Pliny and Alexander, we obtain a view of just how distant this "other" world is. Not only are the people taller and/or shorter, not only does their appearance verge on the monstrous, but "we" clearly cannot identify with "them." Because "they" are so different, they possess worthwhile things that they count as worthless, (particularly gold and spices). The reasoning behind acquisition thus becomes the entire justification for European exploitation, which begins with exploration, continues through colonization and neo-colonization, and extends itself into the "New Europe" of post-1992, with its trade pacts, alliances, and sanctions.

Pliny's *Natural History* and the Alexander romances and letters may be termed "fiction," as Mary B. Campbell has done in her important study, but they were interpreted as "fact," especially in the long line of correspondence that continued to describe a world other than Europe. In a way, therefore, *Wonders* and *Alexander's Letter to Aristotle* were the forerunners of "fictions" that differed only slightly in their approach from later missives, such as the *Letter of Prester John*, Columbus' supposed "Letter to Luis de Santangel," or even Cortés' five letters to Charles V.

Note that all the letters, in whatever terms we choose to regard them today, were expressions of "truth." First, they were personal, written from one individual to another of either revered or peer status. Thus, one would expect that "truth" would be foremost, either to gain favors or to represent the writer as an honest purveyor of fact, although this was seldom the case.

Moreover, the letters not only showed the personal state of mind of a writer, but described the state of belief of the society from which the writer came. They therefore became public accounts that incorporated wonders, magic, and monsters into projected or actual historical conquests. In this way, the *Letter of Prester John* fit in with the formula of myth and magic while still conveying a tough political promise of dominance over the heathens.

All the letters reveal how the world "beyond" appeared to the world "immediate." The latter was the province of the letter's recipient, who would seem fairly certain of her/his own reality. But, since a recipient was constricted by his time to a specific place, he or she could not seek alternative explanations. The process of "remembering" for Alexander or the author of *Wonders* was thus much the same as for Columbus. In the absence of "instant dictation," memory tended to fuse the immediate past with the mythical or, put differently, to associate remembered facts with what had already been spoken about or written down. Only when writers are able to break away from accepted versions of history do they become free to liberate their own recollections. It is a problem that is still with us today.

MUSLIM INTERPRETATIONS

The Thousand and One Nights, known by various names in the West and dating as far back as the ninth century, is as good a point as any to show the interest in travel that Arabs possessed. Sinbad the Sailor was most likely a composite figure, who related the adventures of Arab seamen along the Red Sea, down the coast of Africa as far as Zanzibar, to India, Malaysia, and even China, and up along the eastern Mediterranean. In all, according to the legend, Sinbad embarked on seven voyages, all ending in shipwreck. Constantly he would vow never to return to sea, but the promise of wealth ever beckoned him to go back again and again. Despite the monsters and cannibals he encountered, as well as the adverse weather conditions, he, like many unnamed Arab seamen of old, plied these ancient trade routes.[98]

Marco Polo noted that Arab ships had no iron and were assembled with wood, ropes, and coconut shells. Traveling southwest between April and December, during the monsoon period, the dhows went along the African coast as far as Zanzibar. A second route took them eastward to India, the Malay Peninsula, and as far as China. One of their types of vessels, the *ganja*, was used as a model by Portuguese explorers. Were it not for their skill, Vasco da Gama could not have completed his voyage to India, for he had to make use of an Arab navigator.

Today, Arab dhows still have the same lateen sail and stern post rudder, the latter added in the twelfth century according to Chinese specifications. Arab interest in traveling introduced the compass to the West. Equipped with lateen sail and compass, the Portuguese could forge ahead on their New World and Far Eastern quest. Arab technology coupled with Muslim conquest helped Arabs to maintain their solid control of the spice trade. Without this state of affairs, it is unlikely that mere curiosity alone would have encouraged the Portuguese and Spaniards to venture out.[99]

From the classical to the medieval periods, from, say, Isidore of Seville's seventh-century world picture to the medieval *mappae mundi*, concerned European mapmakers of an earlier period had drawn versions of the world. All were adjusted by Arab cartographers such as al-Idrisi (Abu 'Abd Allah Muhammad [1100–1165]). By the time we come to early fourteenth-century mapmakers, such as Fra Paolino Minorita and Petrus Visconte, and early fifteenth-century ones, like Andrea Blanco (1436), a specific version of the world, particularly of the African continent, had become an accepted norm. Blanco's version placed an "indentation, named *nidus ahimalion* [nest of winged dragons] and decorated by two heraldic dragons "in Africa."[100] These creatures were not especially relevant to Africa, but quite significant in terms of the dragons of legendary lore who guarded the Fruits of the Hesperides.

Fanciful ideas about Africa were fed from the European continent to the Arabian peninsula and back again. A Muslim writer has stated, that between the twelfth and fifteenth centuries, "Muslim and Christian cultures were brought most closely together. The result was the creation of the core of new Europe."[101] He has further noted that, in these early European maps — the Psalter Map (1200), Hereford Map (1280), Marino Sanuto's world map (1321), the Borgia world map (1450), the Este world map (1450), Fra Mauro's "Africa" (1459), and the diagrams of *Imago du Mundi* (1480) — "acquaintance with Arab cartography and geographic information is revealed."[102]

When Arab mapmakers relied less on purely European sources, they could draw truly original maps. A case in point is the Hadji Ahmed world map of 1559, about which Michael Bradley has commented:

It shows lands and coastlines not "discovered" by Europeans for another two centuries. Although this map was drawn some sixty years after the first voyage of Columbus there is little doubt that maps of similar accuracy could have been made by Arabs a couple of centuries earlier. Hadji Ahmed did not rely upon European sources; his map shows the outline of the American continents more accurately than the European discoverers were able to draw it.[103]

Furthermore, R. A. Skelton has admitted, in *Explorers' Maps*, that Fra Mauro's 1459 map of Africa showing a Southern horn, was "derived no doubt from reports of Arab navigation along the east coast,"[104] for that feature to the south certainly does not appear on Martin Behaim's globe of 1492, which still shows Africa with a long landmass extending eastward toward Asia. Even after the voyages of Vasco da Gama (1497–1499) and Pedro Álvares Cabral (1500–1501), the general shape of Africa on maps remained malformed, even though it is now known that Arab and African pilots and sailors were very familiar with the African coast. It would seem that Arabs and Europeans could sometimes agree, especially when a mutually accepted "mythology" was in place.

We should not find it surprising that the Muslim world inherited several of the peculiar concepts of Western Christendom. After all, as T. W. Arnold has argued, they were "in many respects heirs of the same vivifying cultural influences."[105] Muslims, to some extent, both invented and shared in European culture. Additionally, they were motivated by reasons of profit and religious pilgrimage to explore the world. These geographers include Abu Al-Hasan 'Ali Ibn Al-Husayn al-Mas'udi in the tenth century, al-Bakri ('Abdul 'Aziz) in the eleventh, and al-Idrisi in the twelfth. Nafis Ahmad has listed several important geographers, among them Yaqut Hamawi (1179–1229), Ibn Jubayr (b. 1145), and the great Abu 'Abdullah Muhammad Ibn Battuta of the fourteenth century.[106] Ahmad argues that their work influenced both cartographers and writers in the West.

Ibn Battuta (1304–c. 1377) traveled for some thirty years, crossing "two continents, logging some 75,000 miles (tripling Marco Polo's travels) through 44 countries in today's atlas," as Thomas Abercrombie has noted in a recent *National Geographic* essay.[107] A Berber from Morocco, he first set out for Mecca, later journeying from Constantinople to China, India, the Maldive Islands, and afterward to Spain and in Africa as far as Mali. His book, the famous *Rehla* (c. 1356), which he dictated to a pupil on his return to Fez, seems to show a great deal of realism, until he comes to Africa. Although he quite naturally admired Mali emperors like Mansa Musa (fl. 1312–1337) and his brother Mansa Sulayman (fl. 1341–1360) for their devotion to Islam, what struck him most was the odd and the macabre. When, for instance, the *mansa* sends him a gift of food, he reports "When I saw it I laughed, and was long astonished at their feeble intellect and their respect for mean things." Sulayman, he complains, "is a miserly king."[108] One of Battuta's biographers, Ross E. Dunn, has concluded that "Ibn Battuta seems indeed to be harsher on the Malians than he does on other societies."[109]

As such, the familiar stereotypes of the alien crop up in Mali. Ibn Battuta recounts the story of a visit of cannibals from a nearby area:

The sultan received them without honour, and gave them as his hospitality-gift a servant, a negress. They killed and ate her, and having smeared their faces and hands with her blood came to the sultan to thank him. I was informed that this was their regular custom whenever they visit his court.[110]

He did find a few good qualities, but listed on the negative side that:

The woman servants, slave-girls, and young girls go about in front of every one naked, without a stitch of clothing on them. Women go in to the sultan's presence naked and without coverings and his daughters also go about naked. . . . Another reprehensible practice among many of them is the eating of carrion, dogs, and asses.[111]

In other parts of Ibn Battuta's world travels, he hardly ever condemns in this absolute way. For our purposes, we cannot help noting the way in which Mali, at the height of its power, is demonized, with familiar images of nudity and cannibalism. Indeed, the very same Wangara, whom Ibn Battuta has presented in this way, have been described by UNESCO historians, J. Devisse and S. Labib, as possessing "a large number of literate people among them who had clear knowledge of their environment."[112] This included contacts with Arabs and Berbers, as well as with Africans from the south. Indeed, to their east and west, Wangara merchants traded on foot, horse, and donkeys. The quick impression offered by Ibn Battuta is of a savage and barbaric race, more in keeping with European mythology than with Arab and African fact.

The general attitude of early Arab travelers toward Africans was a mixture of condescension and distaste. For instance, Ibn Khaldun (1352–1406), born in Andalusia and educated in Tunis, wrote *The Book of Examples* concentrating on North Africa. Since his main source was Ptolemy, his book states that "the equatorial regions and those further south were uninhabited," and even though he doubted this from "observation and continuing tradition," he could only tentatively conclude that "there may be a civilization in the equatorial regions and further south, as people say, but it cannot amount to much."[113]

Ibn Khaldun went on to suggest that "The waters receded from certain parts of the world in which God wished to create living beings and which he wished to populate with the human race."[114] Therefore, the idea of monstrousness is derived by a different method: according to Ibn Khaldun, much like St. Augustine, monstrosities must be the will of God. Ibn Khaldun thus concluded that once out of the northern area of Africa known to Muslims, one would encounter "Lamlam" slaves to the south "with scarred faces . . . men who are nearer to animals than to reasonable beings. They cannot possibly be counted as human beings [since] . . . living so far away from the temperate zone . . . their nature becomes closer to that of the brute beasts."[115]

Of course, we have heard all this before, but we are nonetheless surprised to hear it from an Arab source. Still, since none of the Arab geographers or travelers could live outside their own time, they too were very much captives of current European intellectual thought. Perhaps they were only too anxious to point out that they themselves were not part of the demonized non-European world of Pliny; hence, their need to identify the non-Arab (and non-European) world with barbarism.

The country of the "Lamlam" was therefore much like that of the "Barbarians." Devisse's chart in the *General History of Africa* places this country on the equator, at the very edge of the world — in fact, at the outermost point of the known world, with the land of Gog at the northeastern end. Indeed, both countries, Gog and Lamlam, are positioned at the farthest reaches, near the Sea of Darkness encircling the world.[116] The layout of these maps, with the south at the top and west to the right, was taken from the cosmographical school at Alexandria (founded there by Alexander, where he was supposedly buried) and later adapted by Muslim geographers. Muslim travelers identified the "monsters" as Africans and the "marvels" as located in Africa. In this way, they effectively tried to exclude themselves from becoming the European "other."

In *The Muqaddimah* (1377), subtitled an "Introduction to History," Ibn Khaldun definitely shows that he was a product of a pan-European/pan-Arabic world view of the period and reflected certain mutually agreed-upon assumptions. As a result, he never questioned the meaning of "civilization" nor the mandates of the "geographers" concerning the various zones of the world. As a result, people could easily be "scientifically" condemned because they lived away from the center and were thus "farther removed from being temperate in all their conditions."[117] His description of the inhabitants prepares us for Columbus' Caribs: they are like "dumb-animals," "live in savage isolation," and "eat each other."[118] True, his book describes Blacks as "characterized by levity, excitability, and great emotionalism," "eager to dance," and "everywhere described as stupid."[119] But recall that with the advent of exploration and conquest, these will become the way in which Africans and Native Americans will be known. Ibn Khaldun did not set the stage for this. He merely reminds us of the large degree of acceptability, regarding the "norm" and the "standard." This is only a hair's breadth removed from Ibn Khaldun's conclusion that "the Negro nations are, as a rule, submissive to slavery," possessing "little that is (essentially) human."[120] This is a point with which the conquistadors and colonialists could easily empathize.

One can argue that Arab writers should have known better and, indeed, did know better. But there were two major reasons why Arabs bought into the mythology of Europe. First, as stated, they wanted to establish a clear demarcation between themselves and the "monstrous" races. Second, and perhaps more importantly, they were drawing from a common source which Arabs themselves had helped create. After all, Islam had been an important life line between classical learning and the European Renaissance, and it had become heir to the cultural heritage of Europe. Nafis Ahmad in *Muslim Contribution to Geography* has contended that:

Whenever the West felt the need of deeper and fresh knowledge it invariably turned to the Arabic sources. Therefore, the main intellectual task of the twelfth and thirteenth centuries was one of translation. A vast amount of Scientific literature including geographical material was translated from the Arabic into Latin and the translators belonged to many parts of Europe.[121]

After the Middle Ages, scholars from England, Italy, Spain, France, and other areas came to seek out Arab scholarship. They translated material from Arabic into Latin, into Greek and then Latin, and into Hebrew. In the latter case, Jewish scholars played an important role in passing on knowledge and information. Even when translation proper did not take place, material was simply lifted and copied into other works. The Arab and European worlds touched and interacted with each other in Asia, Sicily, and, of course, Spain. With the fall of Toledo in 1085, much Arab knowledge was passed on to stimulate the European Renaissance.[122]

Therefore, we should not find it surprising that European and Arab intellectual outlooks coincided, for they were taken from a common storehouse. The problem was that a "victim" had to be identified and, judging from the work of Ibn Battuta, we can see that such a demonization pointed inexorably to Africa. Perhaps this is why, in the sixteenth century, Bartolomé de las Casas, while severely denouncing the enslavement of Native Americans, had no initial compunction about the introduction of African peoples as slaves. As the famous 1550 debate between las Casas and Juan Ginés de Sepúlveda illustrated, the entire justification for enslavement rested on a premise about what constituted humanity. Once Africans were dehumanized, they could hardly claim to be representative of God's creatures.

T. W. Arnold has given an overall view of Arab travelers between 1000 and 1500. From the eighth century on, Islam spread out of present-day Saudi Arabia, and "the journey of the Muslim traveler was facilitated by that brotherhood of Islam which . . . enables [a] community of faith to wipe out all differences of race and origins."[123] This was the historical motivating force behind Ibn Battuta's global peregrinations. Arab travelers set out from Egypt, Syria, Mesopotamia, and Persia, and from India and China as well. They journeyed to gain knowledge and to understand the variety of the empire. They also traveled for commerce, since the role of merchant is blessed in the *Koran*. Above all, they set out on pilgrimage to Mecca and, in the process, made side trips to other places. Because the *hadj* was incumbent on all Muslims, large numbers of Muslims had a greater impetus to journey than did their European counterparts. Like the Europeans, Muslims were also interested in trading precious stones, pearls, diamonds, scents, spices, silk, wool, furs, and various kinds of metal and food.[124]

Leo Africanus (c. 1485–1554) established a type of Arab proto-text, in that his *A Geographical Historie of Africa*, published in English in 1600, described areas with which most Westerners were unfamiliar. Africanus, who was persuaded to convert to Christianity by Pope Leo X, took on the Pope's name and acquired the Latin and Italian languages. Earlier on, he had visited the important city of Timbuktu, the valley of the Niger and, between 1516 and 1517, Aswan, the city of the Black Nubians. Captured by pirates, he was enslaved and presented as a "gift" to Pope Leo X who encouraged his writing. A note at the end of the ninth and final book of his *Historie* states that it was finished in Rome on the tenth of March, 1526.[125]

Africanus described himself as "born in Grenada and brought up in Barbary." He was a Moor with strong roots among the Berber, but if we expect his account to be relatively free from the mythologies of his period, we would be asking too much. Africanus epitomized in his own life the type of synthesis between the Arab and European worlds that was so typical of his period. Even though born in Muslim Spain before the fall of Grenada, he was still a pragmatic creature of his time. He converted to Catholicism because it was expedient and looked toward Africa, as we shall see, with very European eyes. Indeed, from the very beginning of his own work, he himself was not even conscious of how hard he attacked Africa, and so he offered this caveat: "Neither am I ignorant how my own credit is impeached when I myself write so homely of Africa, into which country [sic] I stand indebted both for my birth, and also for the best part of my education."

This statement occurs quite early in the first book, after he has listed what he termed the "vices" of Africans. These include the following (I have modernized Africanus' text). Africans are covetous, possess an unforgiving nature, are "void of good manners," "believe impossible matters which are told them," are "ignorant of natural philosophy," and observe no "certain [definite] order of living nor of laws." He continued that Africans are always angry, aggressive, and:

By nature they are a vile and base people, being no better considered by their rulers than if they were dogs. They have neither judges nor lawyers, through whose wisdom and counsel they ought to be directed. They are utterly unskillful in trades or merchandise ... they are a rude people and (as a person might say) born and bred to theft, deceit, and brutish manners.[126]

The victim has now been named and located, interestingly enough, by a "victim" himself, who probably used this racist denunciation to claim some individual difference and distinction for himself. Note that, although the book is describing the land of his ancestors, Africanus' use of "they" effectively distances him from the object of his contempt.

Africanus was really expressing a "loyalist" point of view, in keeping with the Euro-centric and Arab-centric views of his time. Put differently, this was the "learned" opinion about Africa, from the viewpoint of the civilized Arab world. Africanus conceded only that Pliny "erred a little in some matters concerning Africa." On the whole, he continued, Pliny's work could be said to possess "a little blemish [which] ought not quite to disgrace all the beauty of a fair and amiable body."[127]

Much of Leo Africanus' book, therefore, continues to place Africa within the world of European mythology. Even though he himself claimed to have traveled on both the Nile and the Niger, he nevertheless still asserted "that the said river of Niger is derived out of Nilus," because this was received opinion. Likewise, he excluded Ethiopia from active consideration in his work for this very interesting reason: "These people have an Emperor, which they call Prester John, the greater part of that land being inhabited by Christians."[128] Africanus was thus suggesting that the mythology associated with Prester John — his royal court, his subject kings, and his Christianity — did not fit in with the barbaric Africa that Africanus sought to portray. In a way, therefore, Africanus was even more vindictive than Arab and European writers of the period.

Whenever Africanus encountered African countries that had been "redeemed" by Christianity or Islam, he tended to be generous with his praise. Otherwise, he was quick to invoke the spectacle of the "barbarian." He even explained this word in the context of Africa:

The tawny people of the said region were called by the name *Barbar*, being derived from the verb *Barbara* which in their tongue signifies to murmur, because the African tongue sounds to the ears of the Arabs, no different than the voice of beasts, which utter their sounds without any accent.[129]

Not only did Africanus' view of Africans incorporate and accept the otherness of the non-European world found in Pliny and Alexander, but Africanus was also prepared to reinterpret and justify his own demonization. Recall that he described himself as coming from the Barbary coast of North Africa.

Throughout the work, the familiar categorizations occur. In Libya, a people thus live "without all law and civility," wearing a small piece of cloth "wherewith scarce half their body is covered."[130] Africans are a people who possess no religion and who, when the Arabs first encountered them, had no form of writing, according to Africanus. Nevertheless, a page further on, we read that the enemies of the Caliph of Baghdad "burnt all the African books," "[f]or they were of the opinion that the Africans, as long as they had any knowledge of natural philosophy or of any other good arts and sciences, would every day more and more arrogantly condemn the law of Mohammed."[131] Furthermore, even though Africanus had himself visited Timbuktu, admired it, and must have known about its famous library, he was content to dwell only on the material wealth he found there, much as any European visitor would have done.

Abnormal longevity is also singled out, as we have noted in the previous European descriptions. The people of Barbary live to sixty-five or seventy years, but, "in the aforesaid mountains, I saw some who had lived a hundred years, and others who affirmed themselves to be older,"[132] Africanus stated, reminding us of the Fountain of Youth and of Prester John's longevity.

According to Africanus, Africans live outside the realm of "civilization" and possess no religion or social organization. Africanus, himself an African and the main authority on Africa for 200 years, firmly identified the Plinian savages of Africa as:

Great numbers of people who live a brutish and savage life, without any king, governor, commonwealth, or knowledge of husbandry. They were clad in skins of beasts, and had no specific wives. In the day time they kept their cattle, and when night came they resorted ten or twelve, both men and women, into one cottage together, using hairy skins instead of beds, and each man choosing the companion he most fancied.[133]

Africanus' African thus merged with the mythical man of Pliny and the Alexander romances, but now, in the Christian era, what Africanus stressed was their clear lack of moral guidance. This kind of argument could very easily justify the slave trade, first from Africa to Europe and later to the New World, for all could agree that such action was being undertaken for the good of the Africans.

Africanus' English editor, John Pory, a Cambridge University don, wrote a lengthy appendix that detailed the land of Prester John. Africanus himself took Prester John for granted, often mentioning him in passing as he told about various places in Africa. In addition, Africanus' fascination with the gold of Timbuktu and the wealth of its emperor derived partly from visual representations in atlases and verbal recountings of Prester

John that Africanus must have heard at the palace of Pope Leo X. In part, Africanus described the Emperor thus: "The rich king of Timbuctoo has many plates and scepters of gold, some of which weight 1300 pounds. When he travels anywhere, he goes on a camel, which is led by some of his noblemen. He rides like this also when he goes to war, when all his soldiers ride on horses."[134] Recall that Prester John went forth in much the same manner and that, according to the later interpolations in the letter, Prester John's kingdom possessed an abundant supply of horses. Also, in keeping with the *Letter of Prester John*, Africanus' account makes a distinction between how the Emperor of Timbuktu rides in time of war and peace. Much time is devoted to describing his wealth and his devotion to religion. The description of the Emperor of Timbuktu is almost a word-for-word copy of that of Prester John.

Buried, therefore, in Africanus' work, are the same major mythologies of the non-European world. Indeed, it may be argued that this similarity made it more palatable to Italian, Latin, and later English readers. Africa thus became the ultimate place where non-Europe existed. There the people lived in a barbaric state, removed from the world of European man and God. Obviously, Africanus was a confused man who, in attempting to please his benefactor, was quite willing to sacrifice his own known truth to the European legend. At the same time, one cannot be sure that he had much of an alternative. In Vatican circles, he was received as a prodigy, even as visible proof that the Church could and should penetrate the remotest corners of the earth. Leo X was the pope who excommunicated Martin Luther. What might he have done to a mere African ward who had no appeal beyond that of seeming to be a supreme compromiser? And, had Africanus not made some kind of concession, especially during the period of the Counter-Reformation, it is more than likely that we would never have heard of the travels of Leo Africanus or Al-Hasan ibn Muhammad Al-Wazzan Al-Zaiyati, as he was known in the Arabic world. Leo Africanus represented an early African-European who walked between cultural extremes, a Muslim-Christian who balanced on a religious tightrope. For our purposes, his work shows us more than ever that "Euro-centric" perceptions of the "other" were actually the "learned" views of the combined "East" and "West" concerning the "rest" of the world, at first Africa, and later the New World.

JEWISH TRAVELERS

We should also make a cursory examination of the works of Jewish travelers, in an attempt to note any differences from Muslim and

Christian sojourners of the period. Particularly relevant in this context are Jewish travelers between the ninth and fifteenth centuries.[135] Jews journeyed mainly as traders, but their accounts give us interesting glimpses of Jewish life in ghettoes and palaces. Always, the travelers defined "home" as a place that is a mixture of a real and an unreal Jerusalem. This is the most startling difference from Christian writers in that for Jews, Utopia is both known and found, neither "discovered" nor elusive.

Jewish travelers helped to spread learning from North Africa and Spain to Baghdad and, like Isaac the Jew in 801 A.D., served as the bearers of exotic gifts: Isaac brought an elephant from Africa to Pisa in the company of an African envoy.[136] Still, these early Jewish travelers imposed their own version of history on others and, as with Eldad the Danite in 1480, also absorbed the mistaken notions of the very European states that had rebuffed them. For example, Eldad described "black Ethiopians, tall, without garment or clothing upon them, cannibals, like unto the beasts of the field."[137] Although the rhythms are unmistakably Hebraic, even down to the familiar phrase "beasts of the field," the sentiments adhere to European belief.

Conquest is part of what is understood, assumed, taken for granted, and accepted, except that here the reference is Jewish conquest. Eldad, using an Alexander-type boast, commented that "there was none like us men of war."[138] As a result, the conquest of Egypt was inevitable: "[T]hey [the Egyptians] had to pay tribute to Israel, and we dwelt with them many years, and increased and multiplied greatly and held great riches."[139] Again we observe the heroic stance and the national trumpeting, but here in a new ethnic format.

With Jewish travelers (as with European and Muslim sojourners), indigenous culture became a force that gave a sense of purpose. Thus, Judah Halevi (traveled 1085–1140) composed a paean to the God of Israel, as a type of arch-protector, even "when the Christians sail in Moslem main" or "when the ship by monsters of the deep / Is chased."[140] All adventurers seem to operate from their own cultural reference points, secure in their own beliefs. The exception here, which is so obvious that it need hardly be stated, is that Jews were not engaged in conquest, although this does not suggest that Jewish travelers were not also in search of material wonders. Rabbi Benjamin ben Jonah of Tudela is perhaps the best known of the Jewish travelers. He was fascinated by the ornate "pillars of gold and silver and lamps of silver and gold more than a man can count"[141] that he observed at Saint Sophia in Constantinople.

Rabbi Benjamin has also given us a taste of just how Jews were forced to survive. In his writings, he was frantic about oppression and Jew-baiting by zealots who "throw out their dirty water in the streets before the doors of Jewish houses."[142] At the same time, Jews, Christians, and Muslims in Baghdad all agreed that Daniel, the son of Hisdai, was a man to whom considerable respect was due. As he went forth to meet the Caliph, "He is mounted on a horse, and is attired in robes of silk and embroidery with a large turban on his head, and from the turban is suspended a long white cloth adorned with a chain upon which the cipher of Mohammud is engraved."[143] Rabbi Benjamin showed both the poverty and the power of Jews, but, in so doing, he always wrote from a celebratory Judeo-centric viewpoint. In many respects, however, he was a pioneer, in that he was one of the earliest travelers from Europe to visit the East.

Rabbi Benjamin seems almost realistic when contrasted with Rabbi Petachia of Ratisbon (traveled between 1170 and 1187) or Rabbi Jacob Ben R Nathaniel Ha Cohen (traveled c. twelfth century). Rabbi Petachia related strange customs, such as that of a people who became eternally bonded by drinking out of a special vessel.[144] Rabbi Jacob Ha Cohen recalled Egypt in this way: "There Alexander used to learn of his teacher Aristotle" and went on to describe a magical fire, so bright that it could be "seen in Acre, in Africa, and in Provence."[145] Jewish writers thus seemed to incorporate European mythology into their own, as with Elijah of Ferrara's "miracles and marvels,"[146] or Rabbi Jacob (termed "the Messenger of Rabbi Jechiel of Paris") who traveled 1238–1244 and his reference to a healing spring in Jerusalem.[147]

Quite naturally, Jewish travelers were interested first and foremost in the impact of distant societies on Jewish culture. As a result, Jewish beliefs bled into the itinerary. Rabbi Jacob (the Messenger of Rabbi Jechiel) encountered "a tree under which it was said that the angels partook of food,"[148] and Isaac Chelo in 1334 remarked on a society of people who existed in "happiness and tranquility, each according to his condition and fortune."[149] These writers can be forgiven, for, in both these instances, the ideal and real were blended; moreover, this was not an experience that non-Jewish writers could ever hope to replicate. Jerusalem has become for them both mystical fancy and domestic fact. Although some Jewish authors, like Rabbi Meshullam ben R. Menahem (traveled 1481), did mention Pliny as an authority,[150] the sight of the city of Jerusalem evoked real passion and wonder. He noted, "when I saw its ruins I rent my garments a hand breadth, and in the bitterness of my heart recited the appropriate prayer.[151] Whereas European travelers had only fuzzy notions of the idyllic in their minds, for most Jewish travelers, Jerusalem, when found, became both ideal and real. To arrive there was not to accomplish another stage in an eternal journey but instead to encounter heavenly perfection and bliss, which European explorers sought and never found, first in Asia and then in the New World. European travelers knew that a terrestrial paradise existed; Jewish travelers found it in Jerusalem.

Paradoxically, Jerusalem as state of mind and attainable perfection might even be achieved through Islam. David Reubeni (traveled 1523–1527) continued his travels in the sixteenth century, learning this much in Portugal from the Muslim Moors:

From the day that I saw the king drink water and his brother also drinking water, . . . I vowed in my heart to drink no wine but only water, and the reason is that I have come from the east to the west for the love of God and for the love of his people, and the love of the land of Israel, and I am in Galuth (captivity) and from the day I began to drink water I have eaten at my table at a meal more than I eat [sic] before, and water is better than wine.[152]

Perfection becomes possible, not through rejecting the world or discarding its people, but through an acceptance of life in all its wonderful diversity. Perhaps in no small way, the long-term, historical intolerance and prejudice against Jews did help them to develop a more sympathetic understanding of the possibilities of all human life. Since Jews were engaged in neither crusades nor conversion, they could take a more balanced view of the real world as they encountered it, without the constant European obsession to alter what they found into their own image. Also, the Spanish Inquisition must have left in later Jewish writers a total disdain for the self-righteousness of would-be converters.

GUIDES TO HOLY LANDS

Even when "guides" were factual, fantasy tended to be an important element. Why? Because the fantastic is very much a part of an acknowledged, even credible, belief system. We note that Jewish writers downplayed the incredible in favor of the ecstatic. Although the unusual was acknowledged nevertheless Jerusalem, as both a physical place and a spiritual idea, constantly served as a guiding purpose and direction.

I shall briefly examine three non-Jewish authors of guidebooks, to show how the imaginary could creep into apparently authentic accounts.

Take Benedict, a canon of St. Peter's, who in 1143 authored *The Marvels of Rome*. The volume is important because it provides an account of the contrast between the old Rome of the Caesars and the new Rome of the Church Fathers.

Benedict was most intent on displaying the presence of ancient glories, especially the profusion and wealth. His stated purpose, as he revealed at the end, was "to bring back to the human memory how great was their [what he terms "the heathen"] beauty in gold, silver, brass, ivory and precious stones."[153] Therefore, the "marvels" of Rome include both its pagan and Christian glories — the Alexandrine Baths, the Four Pillars of Gilded Brass, the numerous palaces, churches, bridges, and statues. These were important to him because they significantly pointed away from a well-defined Christian world toward the protean possibilities of a pagan past.

In the second part of Benedict's little guide subtitled "The Legends Behind Rome's Monuments," ancient accounts vie with Christian beliefs. For instance, Octavian sees a vision of "a virgin exceedingly fair standing on an altar holding a man-child in her arms."[154] Here then exists a world in which, for no historical reason, ancient Romans are given constant intimations of the possibilities of perfection in Christ.

This is also a world of dazzling barbarian splendor. The Colosseum, we are informed, is the "temple of the sun . . . of marvelous beauty and greatness . . . all covered with a heaven of gilded brass."[155] Cleopatra is "wealthy in gold and silver, precious stones and people"[156] (the verbal arrangement almost seems hierarchical in her case). Indeed, everything in Rome is "splendid." Castel Sant' Angelo is noted as "'a temple built of marvelous greatness and beauty,'"[157] while the Capitol is "completely adorned with marvelous works in gold, silver, brass, and costly stones."[158] Note again how pagan and Christian elements blend.

We begin to see, therefore, that even pilgrims who seek an "other" worldliness have to be wooed in these travel guides in terms of the splendor of El Dorado, and by "marvels" such as magic fountains and baths. Ronald G. Musto has commented on the German monk Theoderich's *Guide to the Holy Land* (c. 1172)[159] that Jerusalem is both "center of the world" and a marvelous site with "rivers that run underground, the Dead Sea that once a year, on the anniversary of the destruction of Sodom and Gomorra, throws up their stone and wood, and the pillar of salt that was once Lot's wife."[160] This approach is different from the Jewish accounts for, in this instance, the natural phenomena are logically explained in cited Bible accounts, thereby making wonder dependent on religious faith.

Theoderich's *Guide* sets a tone that we can later identify in the accounts of the conquistadors namely that the world is a mixture of observed fact and speculated fictions. Note that here there is little attempt to visualize the Holy Land in terms of a historical-religious symbiosis, which is different from the approach of Jewish writers. Instead, Christian writers exalted holy sites as places where the miraculous, the "marvel," is still possible. Not unnaturally, familiar images are present — "water bubbles out of the earth like a fountain and . . . after filling the pool and running down to another pool close by, it disappears."[161] At another place, "a great fountain bubbles forth, which supplies the Garden of Abraham and the whole plain around it with water."[162] Obviously, here is the Christian association of water with restoration, baptism, and renewed spiritual life, but in a new form in both Prester John's fountain and Ponce de León's spring. Seemingly, the conquistadors opted for a more immediate gratification and for instant physical, not merely spiritual, longevity.

Like many other writers of guidebooks, Theoderich betrayed the prejudices of his age, especially a contempt for both Jews and Muslims. But, as the French scholar Pierre Gilles showed in *The Antiquities of Constantinople* (c. 1544), the eastern enemy of his time, the Seljuk Turks, possessed much that could be admired. Gilles experienced more of a scientific approval, in that his interest in marine life helped to objectify his account. Nonetheless, his xenophobia emerged in the final sections of Book IV:

I was a stranger in the country, had very little assistance from any inscriptions, none from coins, none from the people of the place. Having a natural aversion for anything that is valuable in antiquity, they rather prevented me in my inquiries so that I scarcely dared tackle the dimensions of anything; and I was menaced and cursed by the Greeks themselves if I did.[163]

In his accounts, Gilles repeats that he had to bribe would-be acquaintances with large quantities of wine. Their conversation, he adds, was "frothy and insipid."[164].

Thus, although Gilles was able to express his delight in the gardens and parks of Constantinople much as Cortés and Pizarro did in Mexico, there existed in all of them a basic contempt for the alien, the outsider, and the infidel. As we have seen time and time again, travelers assume that their habitat is the norm; the slightest deviation by foreign peoples from certain expected modes of behavior may suggest either eccentric oddness or calculated savagery. Constantinople, Mexico, and Peru did not resemble "home," and, in many respects, accounts of conquest arose from disillusionment. Whatever is distant or remote can never resound with the pleasing familiarities of what is near or accessible. The essential differ-ence between "here" and "there" initiates the process of disillusionment and finally leads to the wholesale condemnation of otherness. These early guidebooks continued to validate this process.

CARPINI, RUBRUCK, AND ODORIC: LOOKING EAST

The first European to travel to the empire later established by Kublai Khan and to record his adventures was an Italian friar, Giovanni di Plano Carpini, who journeyed between 1245 and 1247. His fellow Franciscan, Gillaume de Rubruck (William of Rubruck) traveled there between 1253 and 1255 under the auspices of the French king, Louis IX, shortly after Carpini returned. In 1260, Marco Polo's father and uncle went to the land of Kublai Khan. Before the Polos even began their journey back to Venice, another Franciscan, John of Monte Corvino, traveled east as a representative of Pope Nicholas IV. He would later be visited by Odoric of Pordenone, who departed for Asia around 1316 with the noble intention of converting the entire area. Also journeying after Marco Polo, Niccolo de Conti traveled throughout southern Asia, returning to Venice in 1444.[165]

With the possible exception of the Polos, these travelers set out, under the aegis of popes or kings, on what were considered "civilizing" missions of Christianization. In the process, however, they reported about the new cultures they found: Carpini, for instance, witnessed a coronation at the royal court of Syra Orda in the northern portion of the Gobi Desert. William of Rubruck reached the capital of the Mongol Empire and was amazed at its grandeur. Quite different were the Polos, who had set out as merchants from Venice seeking trade in jewels and gems. They encountered Kublai Khan's cousin, Barka, and, when war broke out, met the Khan of Turkestan, a descendant of Genghis Khan. Later, they met and impressed Kublai Khan himself, as Marco later recounted. The young Marco returned to Asia with his relatives, at first in the company of two emissaries sent by the new pope, Gregory, finally reaching Kublai Khan in 1275. Kublai Khan appointed Marco a type of emissary, and he traveled extensively throughout the area, up to Tibet and by sea along the eastern and southern coasts of Asia. Marco Polo did mention other foreign traders, but his importance for us at this point is to lend validity to the travelers being discussed. We shall look at Marco Polo later as the initiator of a certain type of fiction.

Here we shall first examine these early travelers, noting the mental images they offered.

John of Monte Corvino went across Persia, to India, and along the China Sea, reaching his destination in 1294. He built a church opposite the khan's palace and was appointed Archbishop of Beijing by the Pope in 1307. This encouraged a number of other Western bishops to visit, such as Odoric of Pordenone who left a record of his travels, for Odoric did not return to the West until 1320, taking a difficult route over the Himalayas.

In the writings of both Carpini (1246) and William of Rubruck (1253–55) the familiar attitudes are present.[166] In Richard Hakluyt's version of Carpini's text, some of the people encountered are quickly found to be the inverse of Europeans. They speak "filthy and immodest words," "are angry and of a disdainful nature towards other people, and beyond all measure deceitful," and "full of falsehood."[167] Carpini added that they were vindictive and unhygienic in their eating and drinking. He contended that "drunkenness is honorable among them, and when any of them has drunk more than his stomach can bear, he vomits it and begins drinking again."[168]

Having established that some of the people encountered exhibited tendencies that placed them outside the European realm of humanity, Carpini was then free to go into the question of monsters:

Returning through the desert, they came to a certain country where we were told in the emperor's court by certain clergymen from Russia [that] they [the clergymen] found certain monsters resembling women, who being asked by many interpreters where the men of the land were, answered that whatever women were born there were imbued with the shape of males, but the males were like dogs. And delaying their time in that country they met with the said dogs.[169]

Pliny had mentioned this before, relating an account of a people who had a dog for their king. Here the twist blends the misogynistic Amazonian legend with Pliny's version, incorporating what seems an earlier Egyptian version in which the first Amazons were actually men. Of course, the usual distancing is supplied here, between Carpini and the narrative, by interposing the clergymen of Russia as the source of the news. In macabre New World tales, the omnipresent "Indian" became the agent of verification and transferral.

Other Plinian accounts crop up in the writings of Carpini. For instance, Pliny gave an account of people who eat their parents — the Anthropophagi. In his "Christian" version, Carpini was careful to point

out that he was referring to pagans, before adding, "These people have a
strange or rather a miserable custom. For when any man's father dies, he
assembles all his family, and they all eat him."[170] Later, he and his
companions traveled to a country near the fabled Ocean Sea, "where they
found certain monsters, who in all things resembled the shape of men,
except that their feet were like those of an ox, and they had indeed men's
heads but dog's faces,"[171] a reference to the Alexandrian Cynocephali.
Thus, we encounter again the familiar horrors that these travelers located
in the non-European world. Quite naturally, when Europeans traveled to
the New World, their monsters accompanied them. For instance, Raleigh
reported on monsters in Guiana with heads between their shoulders,
resembling the Plinian Blemmyae.

Carpini's horror tale is balanced with the magnificence of the court.
When he and his party were finally admitted to the Emperor's court, they
were fascinated by his great wealth and even more by the albeit strange
report that "[c]ertain Christians of his family earnestly and strongly
affirmed to us that he himself was about to become a Christian."[172] Of
course, we must remember that Carpini's account was intended for papal
consumption. It should be noted, however, that a Christian baptism was
also Montezuma's supposed last wish before he was killed, as Charles V
was duly informed.

In *Marco Polo's Asia*, Leonardo Olschki has noted how, as early as
1236, the Hungarian Dominican, Friar Julian, shifted the border of the
unreal even closer to "home." Being particularly concerned about the
advance of the "Tartars," his brief report was "symptomatic of all
subsequent reports of travel to Asia . . . [contained] the same mixture of
fable and truth."[173] In a way, the old mythology lent credence to the new
travel accounts — fiction fed on even more fiction.

Finally, Carpini's journey home is the classic stuff of the legendary
hero. They traveled all winter, through deep snow, for instance, marking
their progress back, during spring and summer, as a clear indication of
their mission itself, with reference to the Christian calendar of holy
days, from the Feast of the Ascension, through Pentecost, until near the
time of the Feast of St. John the Baptist. When they arrived back in
the West, there the people, "having intelligence of our approach, came
forth all of them to meet us with great joy." The language here assumes
the rhythms of the Bible, the "tidings of great joy" that herald the birth of
Christ. And, lest we be in any doubt about the spiritual consequences of
the journey, Carpini added that "they rejoiced over us, as over men that
had been risen from death to life."[174] The language, therefore, clearly
conveys and emphasizes the religious equivalent of the birth and death

of Christ Himself, without actually daring to state so by direct comparison.

Likewise, William of Rubruck's journey was also spiritual. Both Carpini and Rubruck were "messengers"; Carpini had been dispatched by the Pope and William was sent by King Louis IX of France. Rubruck left Constantinople on May 7, 1253, crossed the steppes, and encountered Batu Khan. Afterward, he and his party were ordered to set out for the court of the Great Khan Mongke. Around May 26, 1254, after staying at the khan's encampment, they were ordered back home. They journeyed in a more northerly direction, again marking their progress with the Christian calendar of holy days.

Rubruck's composition is in the form of a letter, but it differs from many other medieval travel accounts in that it aimed more at realism and less at fantasy. Mary B. Campbell has written that it recorded "the things William [Rubruck] saw, when and as he saw them, in an order integral to the shape and purpose of the whole."[175] But, despite Rubruck's humor, the negatives persisted: people ate "all kinds of mice with short tails"; some subject people insisted on washing their clothes only when being soundly beaten; one man's wife had probably cut off her nose in order to appear flat-nosed — Rubruck added that she "looked hideous." Moreover, the people he encountered were totally unfamiliar with Western good manners: "If they were seized with a desire of relieving nature they did not go away from us . . . indeed they performed their filthiness by the side of us, chatting to each other."[176] Rubruck sought refuge in the comical, but the fun was always directed at the "strange" people he encountered. Those who joined with him, like his interpreter, aptly named "Homo Dei," were exempt from condemnation. Likewise, those from whom Rubruck and his party sought some favor, such as the khan himself, were accorded qualities of perspicacity in line with Euro-philic piety: "The monk told me that the Khan only believes in the Christians."

All the familiar mythology is present in his account, so one cannot totally exonerate Rubruck. For instance, he wrote of Gog and Magog, although he did not name them:

The next day we crossed a valley where the base was visible of walls running from one mountain to another, and there was no path along the crests. These used to be Alexander's barriers, which held in check the barbarian peoples — namely, the herdsmen from the wilderness — so they might be unable to overrun the cultivated regions and cities.[177]

Rubruck added that "[t]here are other barriers that shut out Jews," reflecting a type of legend that fit well with the terrible love/hate relationship of the period. These Jews, apparently also locked away like the vicious tribes, were eagerly sought by Dominican friars. According to one account, supposedly by a writer termed "Pseudo Methodius" around the third and fourth centuries, the Jews had also been imprisoned with the tribes.[178]

There are hints of the travelers' proximity to Paradise. "Below this city," Rubruck wrote to his king (much as Columbus would later say to his royal benefactor), "the country used to resemble Paradise." Also very much like Columbus, more than two centuries later, however, Rubruck merely hinted at the possibility. Furthermore, there was also the merest suggestion of a Fountain of Youth. Rubruck wrote that "beyond Cataia there lies a country, and that whatever age at which a man enters it he remains at that age."[179] Still, he prefaced this with the statement that "I was further told for a fact, though I do not believe it." Therefore, far from being a kind of objective realist, as Campbell has suggested, Rubruck carried on the imaginative tradition of the myth-mongers — merely distancing himself from giving full credence to the stuff of legends, as others would later do.

According to Rubruck, Prester John is located geographically "on a plateau among these highlands" and historically as a person who "[o]n the death of Coir Chan [Khan] . . . set himself up as king."[180] But Rubruck took care to appear objective, for he added that "only a tenth" of what his people said of the Khan was true. Rubruck's very ambivalence itself lent credence to the wonder of Prester John: "When I myself crossed his pasturelands, nobody knew anything about him." This may sound sceptical enough, except that it is followed by this statement: "It was in his grazing grounds that Ken Chan [Khan] used to live," once more rendering Prester John in huge, nonhuman terms. By giving Prester John a brother, the very real Ong Khan (d. 1203), Rubruck restored apparent historical validity to Prester John.

Although Rubruck's mythical city of gold and plenty is not named El Dorado, a comparable city is located:

Where they are mining gold and manufacturing weapons; and consequently I was unable to visit them on my way there or back. On my outward journey, however, I did pass fairly near the town, possibly at three days' distance, though I was unaware of the fact, and could not have made a detour from the route even had I known.[181]

Rubruck was careful, never expansive. Nonetheless, in his description of Tibet he noted: "Anyone in need of gold digs until he finds some, takes so much as he requires and puts the rest back in the ground." The land of abundance, but, even more, the existence of a country where the inhabitants do not understand or care for the value of gold, is thus validated. Such a place would not only be fictionalized in Sir Thomas More's *Utopia*, but would be "discovered" time and time again in the New World of the conquistadors.

In the final analysis, Rubruck's world was little different from earlier European models of what lay beyond Europe. The environment itself is described as gargantuan, with large animals and donkeys the size of mules. Similarly, in Tibet, there existed "a race whose practice was to eat their dead relatives,"[182] an idea obviously originating in the Plinian Anthropophagi.

Columbus would later claim that, on his first voyage, he had "so far found no human monstrosities." Nonetheless, he quickly added, as if to confirm his own close reading of d'Ailly's *Imago Mundi*, "except in an island 'Quaris,' the second [island] at the coming into the Indies, which is inhabited by a people who are regarded as very fierce and who eat human flesh."[183] Columbus' description of the inhabitants of Quaris confirmed the ancient mythology of Europe and thereby imposed an enormous burden on the indigenous people of the entire region.

Several years after Rubruck, between 1316 and 1332, Odoric of Pordenone undertook a journey to the east. Odoric was a Franciscan friar, and his mission was very clear. As he journeyed to Turkey, Persia, India, Indonesia, and China, before returning to Europe via Central Asia, his duty was to convert and baptize. Later on, Mandeville would "adapt" much of the second part of his book from Odoric, and, through Mandeville, Odoric was passed on to Columbus and Raleigh. Therefore, in every direct way, Odoric's world was inherited by those living a century and a half later, before Columbus and Raleigh left their native shores.

Most of what Odoric encountered was strange and undesirable. He lacked both Rubruck's humor and his subterfuge, since he reported *directly* on monstrous beasts, the legendary pepper forest, the bounty of trees that yielded food, and the miracle of fishes that threw themselves ashore. Odoric marked his narrative progression with biblical reference points, like Mt. Ararat, the supposed resting place of Noah's Ark. At this point, he utilized a neat device, which later writers copied, of citing the difficulties of the journey itself as reasons for his failure to observe particular phenomena. This was useful, since the forward movement of the "plot" became a means for explaining away a "marvel." Another useful device was to invoke God; in the case of Noah's Ark, "the people of the country report that no man could ever ascend the said mountain because (say they) it pleaseth not the highest God."[184] Both the reference to God and the offhand allusion to "say they" took the burden of credibility away from the writer.

Odoric, therefore, did not explain his world, for he assumes that his readers would take it for granted. When he made references to miraculous phenomena, such as manna (which allegedly fell from Heaven to feed the hungry Israelites), he mentioned it almost cryptically and moved on to the next section: the sentence, "Here also Manna is found in great abundance," is succinct and bare in style, posing little to challenge its cryptic rendition.

When Odoric hinted at gender alteration, his language was more descriptive, and his very excessiveness, especially when contrasted with his previous austerity, emphasized his amazement even more:

The men of the same country [Chaldea] used to have their hair kempt, and trimmed like unto our women; and they wear golden turbans upon their heads, richly set with pearl and precious stones. The women are clad in a coarse smock only reaching to their knees and having long sleeves hanging down to the ground.[185]

The women's lack of refinement and the men's exaggerated finery suggest a gender disparity, perhaps even a sexual confusion. This was a new element added to the constant criticism and defamation of women, who act "contrary to the nature of their sex," suggesting the hermaphroditic qualities of the Plinian Androgini as well as medieval sexual problems.

Because the realms that Odoric described were beyond Europe, the animals were once again large, monstrous, and omnipresent: "There are divers kind of beasts, as namely black lions in great abundance, and apes also, and monkeys, and bats as big as our doves. And there are mice as big as our country dogs, because cats are not able to encounter them."[186] The use of "our," as in *Wonders*, helped the reader to feel a sense of security, in that the monstrosities were not part of his immediate world. They belonged elsewhere, outside the area of rational discourse, in a land of contrasting opposites.

Naturally, the people of such a place could not possibly value human life. Pliny had told of people who worshipped a dog; in Odoric's account, a group worships an ox, washing themselves with its urine and annointing themselves with its dung. The entire ceremony is performed with gold and silver basins, once more demonstrating the total disregard of non-Europeans for what Europeans held most dear.[187]

The city of gold was itself located in Malabar, according to Odoric. An idol there was manufactured of "most pure and glittering gold." It resembled a man and indeed looked very much like St. Christopher. Around its neck was a silk ribbon, full of precious stones. The house of the idol was made "all of beaten gold, namely the roof, the pavement, and the sealing of the wall within and without."[188] Later, this became the standard description of El Dorado when the indigenous "Indians" of America played European myths back to the Spaniards.

In Columbus' mind, there was a link between God and gold from the very start of the "discovery." In his letter to his sovereigns regarding his fourth voyage, Columbus stated, albeit a trifle nostalgically: "When I discovered the Indies, I said that they were the richest dominion that there is in the world. . . . Gold is most excellent. Gold constituted treasure, and he who possesses it may do what he will in the world, and may so attain as to bring souls to paradise."[189] Following the accounts that southwest Native Americans replayed to the Spaniards, Francisco Coronado, for instance, sought "Cibola" and "the Seven Cities." Pedro Castañeda was a contemporary reporter entranced by the elusive nature of the quest and the phantom-like quality of his own mythology that spurred him on. He wrote of Coronado's expedition as if Coronado were motivated by a wish to reach what "the Indian said was to be crossed toward the North Sea."[190] But Coronado himself wrote to his king about barbarous people, cannibals, the hostile environment, and his abject disappointment: "All that I am sure of is that there is not gold nor any other metal in all that country."[191] Castañeda's wishful thinking contrasts with Coronado's cryptic conclusions.

Odoric anticipated this in that he passed on the inherited myth of abundant wealth, and his account was popularized, verbatim in some parts, by Mandeville. Particularly interesting was the version, in the accounts of both Odoric and Mandeville, of a holy city to which "the Indians go on pilgrimage." The setting is India proper, but it evokes the same schema of a god-king, a lake, the casting of precious objects into the water, a golden chariot, and the total local disregard for the precious metals.[192] Although Odoric was writing almost 200 years before Castañeda, his descriptions are pertinent since they evoke a later New World manifestation. Odoric wrote of how the faithful "cast gold, silver and precious stones. . . . And therefore when anything is to be adorned or mended, they go unto this lake taking up the treasure which was cast in."[193] As in accounts of Prester John, the idol in this instance is borne along with pomp and ceremony.

The misogyny continued unabated, only now directed by Odoric toward some alien and distant "other." This obsession is also concerned with the male obsession of woman as property, as yet another mark of male wealth and power. Again Mandeville lifted this word for word: "In this country all women are common, so that no man can say this is my wife."[194] Odoric was here resurrecting the Wife-Givers in the *Wonders* text. The exaggerations of the *Wonders* tradition also pervaded Odoric's account, thus, there were canes "as big as trees,"[195] tortoises "as big as oxen," an island with "all kinds of ravening and wild beasts," "fowls as big as our country's geese, having two heads," and so on.[196] The misogyny and the marvels not only continued the tradition of travel fantasies discussed before but also added new legitimacy to them.

Item by item, Odoric's preoccupations were an attempt to justify the Plinian and Alexandrian monsters. He found Pygmies (later to be located in Africa in the Ituri forest) "three spans" high; cannibals who specialized in "fat men"; "men and women [who] have dog faces,"[197] and most of the other basics for an extra-European encounter.

In a way, this was all preparation for the "boon" of reaching the Great Khan's court. There were some hints of splendors to come, such as the palace in Java, described as "brave and sumptuous," with a roof of "pure gold."[198] Thus, despite the privations of the journey, the reader instinctively awaits the "climax" at some distant place, where the means exist for the enlargement of possibility and the depiction of ideals. This search for perfection — material and spiritual — may be seen as a direct contrast to the background from which the seeker has evolved. For Odoric as well as for the post-Columbian journeyers, the synthesis of perfection lay in just this — the manner in which the Emperor of Cathay "says every day 300 prayers unto his god," while "wearing upon his finger also a stone of a span long, which seemed to be a flame of fire."[199] Cortés would view Montezuma in much the same manner as the embodiment of God and gold.

For Odoric, therefore, the "monsters" were the necessary travails that the good Christian must face to reap any reward. There was no doubt in his mind that a kind of perfection existed out there somewhere, and such glimpses of the ideal increased as he neared the palace of the Great Khan. In Ceylon, the image of near-perfection is depicted in terms of the king of the island being close to the spiritual and material apex. Odoric accomplished this nicely by suggesting that the island contained a lake that some said "proceded from the tears of Adam." Odoric was quick to deny this, but the mere suggestion hinted at the image of a non-Europe,

of Paradise in another place. Along with heavenly abundance, there was
earthly amplitude:

From this lake the water runs even to the sea, and at a low ebb, the inhabitants dig
rubies, diamonds, and pearls, and other precious stones out of the shore. Where upon it
is thought that the king of this island has greater abundance of precious stones, than
any other monarch in the whole world besides.[200]

This was Odoric's true achievement. He both showed the bleak
medieval landscape of his predecessors and hinted at new alternatives. He
was not afraid to be positive, even when alluding to non-Europeans; for
instance, he found that in India "the men of the province are of a fair and
comely persuasion [and] the women are the most beautiful under the
sun."[201] So, side by side with monsters, abominable customs, and all the
expected paraphernalia of the journey, Odoric was able, through contrast,
to suggest an alternative vision.

This was summed up most succinctly in a visionary rapture, in which,
on a journey over a mountain, the language of the Bible, particularly of
the Old Testament prophets, revealed Odoric's view of life. He wrote of
his journey "*over* a certain great mountain" [emphasis added]. Note his
choice of preposition and the symbolism of the nameless mountain. Here,
through a unique balance, Odoric discarded the notions of good and evil
associated with white and black, thereby challenging Pliny, Alexander,
and certainly the crude equations of *Wonders*:

I went over a certain great mountain, upon the one side whereof I beheld all living
creatures to be as black as coal, and the men and women on that side differed in manner
of living from others. Howbeit, on the other side of the said hill every living thing
was snow-white, and the inhabitants in their manner of living, were altogether unlike
unto others.[202]

This was the province of real rapture, but Odoric's contention was one
that later "discoverers" never took up. Odoric presented the world here in
an elegant allegory, making no judgments; his plea was simply for the
recognition of differences in disparity.

Odoric dictated his account to a fellow friar before he died on January
14, 1331, and before he could accomplish a proposed visit to Pope John
XXII. He never did know to what extent his own "letter" was understood, nor whether his description of the Great Khan and his mighty
power, influence, and wealth had been seen, or could be seen, in the
context of the human search for God, Paradise, and a new "other" world.

For the khan was the perfect embodiment of the ideal medieval ruler, holy man, and merchant prince. Odoric surpassed his previous descriptions as he discarded artistic demarcations in order to exalt the khan. At one point, the lake of an earlier mentioned king (later, El Dorado's river) and the bounty of an earlier place (later, the New World itself) came together:

Within the precincts of the said palace imperial, there is a most beautiful mount, set and replenished with trees ... having a most royal and sumptuous palace standing thereupon, in which, for the most part, the Great Khan is resident. Upon the one side of said mount there is a great lake ... [with] a great abundance of geese, ducks, and all kinds of water fowl.[203]

The superlatives conjure up more than Prester John's land. Odoric was hinting quite positively at the Kingdom of Heaven. In any event, this is still a reversal of the medieval world, proffering a differing concept of the "other," but, it is still, unfortunately, equally farfetched as the earlier, more negative, versions.

Toward the end of his account, Odoric let us understand more graphically the nature of his testament. When he left China, he returned by way of Prester John's kingdom. There Odoric emphasized "great plenty of all victuals," reminding us that Prester John was one of the vassal kings of the Great Khan. Nearby, probably in Tibet, another kingdom "is in subjection to the great Khan." There too food for the body was stressed: "I think there is more plenty of bread and wine than in any other part of the world besides."[204]

There is reason enough for this emphasis. Despite a jarring reminder of a Plinian race of people who eat their fathers, the journey continued more or less positively until, toward the end of the narrative, Odoric revealed his final hand. He described an old man, wealthy and famous, who lived in a palace and was fed by singing virgins. Odoric implied, almost autobiographically, that the man represented the rewards of a good life. His health was a result of his piety: "Near unto the wall of the said palace there is a mount artificially wrought with gold and silver, whereupon stand turrets and steeples, and other delectable things for the solace and recreation of the aforesaid great man."[205] As Odoric traveled on, what the man represented became complete. This man was allied with another, an Alexander-type icon, "who round about two mountains had built a wall." But, unlike Alexander, his wall did not seal off chaos; instead it contained heavenly perfection, reminding us of the Fountain of Youth, "the fairest and most crystal fountains in the whole world. And about the said fountains there were the most beautiful virgins in great numbers."[206] The "virgins" (perhaps a trifle sexist by latter-day standards) did not exist to merely satisfy the lust of either of the old men. Their presence instead conjures up images of the Virgin Mary herself. Perfection and purity, along with power and possession, thus constitute the appropriate rewards of the good life. Recall that for a disappointed Columbus in 1504, gold was the means by which humans could achieve Paradise. Odoric anticipated Columbus in that Odoric concluded the narrative with an actual identification of this place, which, because it possessed "everything that could be devised for bodily solace and delight . . . therefore the inhabitants of the country call the same place Paradise." Naturally, more than a little of the *Koran* had rubbed off here as well.[207]

Odoric's journey revealed the variations of Paradise (and indeed Hell) that humans had to encounter before perfection could be achieved. Indeed, the personification of the two old men and their representational qualities suggested that Odoric well understood that this was no mere journey from one external point to another but, instead, an internal search for spiritual perfection. Later writers did not follow his model. Perhaps they either failed to understand his intent or were more concerned with the superficialities of exploration and plunder. If Odoric has a descendant, then it must surely be Cabeza de Vaca, whose cyclical journey was concerned not with the conquest of the "other" but with the surrender of the "one." In this connection, Odoric combined elements of the entire mythology — the Fountain of Youth, the City of Gold and its Emperor, the Amazons, and the monstrous races — to suggest the possibility of human perfectability, even among those outside the European frame of reference. Indeed, with Odoric, we have come full circle past the horror and the monstrosities to the perfection of Paradise, the obverse of non-Europe, which would soon be explored by Francis Bacon, Thomas More, Tomasso Campanella, and others in their literary evocations of the utopian state.

Finally, it bears emphasizing that these early travelers to the East were, in a way, trying to move away from a totally negative image of the Mongol as Tartar," or what Matthew Paris had condemned as "devils from Tartarus," "inhuman and beastly, rather monsters than men."[208] Rubruck and Carpini visited the Mongol courts of Kuyuk Khan and Mangu Khan; Odoric traveled east some two decades after Marco Polo. What they all found were not merely versions of the mirror images they carried, but extensions of new terms of differing human dimensions. After all, they had been dispatched as emissaries when the European world was in the balance, torn, it seemed, between Muslim and Mongol. What they all craved was respite and reassurance that no ultimate doom awaited the West at the hands of the victorious Mongols. In attempting to give some solace to the West, they had to avoid overdoing images of the dark savage so embedded in medieval belief. Instead, they had to offer a new hope of the possibility of survival for both Christian civilization and God's Church on earth. This subtext of their accounts redeemed their message and helped maintain, if not a balance, then at least an avoidance of extremes. Being so imprisoned by their own fancies, they could not set the record straight, but they could at least suggest that beyond "home" lay more homes, with new people and fascinating life-styles. Popular opinion, however, preferred their concept of the "alien," so it was still difficult two centuries later to convince even rational men that Native Americans had souls. These early writers had begun a search to validate the humanity of the "other"; today we still seek to find an easy acceptance of this notion.

Chapter 3

Discovering West and East in Literature

There are degrees to the elements of "fiction" found in the accounts of St. Brendan, the Vikings, Marco Polo, and Sir John Mandeville, yet they all claimed an authenticity that, within a twentieth-century frame of reference, we find difficult to accept. Within the orbit of their own concerns, however, these four accounts mirrored their times and existed as metaphors for larger spiritual concerns — the search for the ideal.

All four dealt with the world from a European, Christian, male standpoint. At one extreme, St. Brendan, an Irish monk, was concerned not so much with "discovery" as with affirming his own Christian beliefs in his travels. At the other extreme, Mandeville was interested in incorporating the body of current belief into his text and then displaying its manifestation within the context of supposed travel. Somewhere in the middle lay the Viking sagas and Marco Polo's work. The sagas looked west and Marco Polo east, but both sought to reinforce patterns of belief taken from the societies within which they were manufactured.

In varying degrees, all "borrowed" from a shared European past and imposed this world view on areas outside of Europe. Thus, St. Brendan's voyages owed much to the Bible, manifesting an almost literal belief in the physical embodiment of angels and biblical personages. By contrast, the Viking sagas, belonging to a northern European tradition, stressed Scandinavian will and persistence, rather than Christian virtue. But just as St. Brendan recognized the creatures of his faith on his voyage, so too did the Vikings as they moved away from "home" to encounter geographical similarities in distant North America.

Of course, outright "fantasy" has its place in all these accounts, as does the demonization of the non-European world. We have already noted that this tendency was initiated quite early in European travel literature. One must be wary, indeed, in categorizing fantasy, since neither the world of St. Brendan nor that of the Vikings owes anything to the "monsters" and "wonders" of the Plinian or Alexandrian frame of reference. It is almost as if, in setting out for the "West" rather than the "East," they freed themselves from the cultural baggage related in *Alexander's Letter to Aristotle* and *Wonders of the East*. This was, of course, not the case with Columbus.

By contrast, both Marco Polo and Mandeville sought to justify the world of the marvelous within the context of the journey. As they traveled, familiar signposts indicated and supported previous encounters with the non-European unknown, including obsessions with Prester John, the Fountain of Youth, distorted and perverted images of women and, of course, gold.

Since all these narratives are male-centered, the women in them fare badly, in that they are either ignored or exploited. True, each account tries to retell history, but the attitude toward women, particularly in the medieval work of Polo and Mandeville presages that contempt shown by the all-male conquistadors. Arguing about the link between misogyny and courtly love, R. Howard Bloch has posited that "the denial of history to women entails an abstraction that also denies the being of any individual woman."[1] Thus, we find a two-sided approach that seeks always to find the "ideal" in women, but balks at the representation of the "real." Because the "ideal" is never found, the "real" becomes demonized as the whore/witch. Except for St. Brendan's higher calling, we should note how this results in women being reviled, castigated, and misused.

From all these works, but particularly from the widely disseminated texts of Polo and Mandeville, Europeans confirmed, through apparently authentic travel texts, a vision of the world that they themselves had nurtured. Moreover, because in this period, little attempt was made to distinguish between "fact" and "fiction," we have to see in these works efforts at displaying a kind of mirrored reality. As the writers journeyed outward, they also traveled inward toward European belief and an inversion of the non-European world constructed in Europe's image. This is why the chief commonality among all these works is a striving to attain a glimpse of idyllic perfection beyond the barriers of evil.

ST. BRENDAN: SEEKING PARADISE

St. Brendan's (c. 484–c. 578) "discovery" of the New World (c. 539–551) was only partly outside the tradition of European travel literature, in that St. Brendan's account did not owe anything to what may be termed a strict European formula of travel. More definitely an account of an "inner" voyage in search of the self, the legendary voyage of the Irish monk shared with later voyagers, however, an evangelizing fervor.

In effect, the Christianized version of the Irish *imram* spread throughout Europe. Latin versions date from the late ninth century, and the *Navigatio Sancti Brandani* survives in several European versions that show little or no reference to Ireland. In addition to over a hundred Latin manuscripts, both prose and verse variations exist in Norman French, English, Dutch, German, and other European languages. The journey may therefore be described as "European" in that many language groups identified with it.

Most probably, St. Brendan's epic narrative was based on authentic seamen's accounts of trans-Atlantic voyages. In a voyage to Ireland before 1492, Columbus himself seemed to suggest that the Irish were familiar with the possibility of trans-Atlantic human life. On a visit to Galway Bay, he reported that two bodies with "strange features" had been washed ashore in two boats.[2] Columbus also sincerely believed that St. Brendan's Island existed, and he looked for it on his first voyage. According to his son, Ferdinand, Columbus not only believed in the existence of the island but also in the "many marvels" told about it.[3]

This island appeared on most maps and globes, including Martin Behaim's 1492 globe, the Piri Reis Map of 1513, and, as late as 1621, an illustration in Caspar Plautius' *Nova typis transacta navigatio*.[4] In these visual accounts, St. Brendan and his party were depicted astride a sea monster, climbing up or sitting on its back. Most illustrations prominently featured the cross.

Like Columbus, Cortés, De Soto, and other conquistadors, St. Brendan's motivation for the journey was, first, to take the cross to pagan lands, and, second, to seek his own New World, here called "the Promised Land of the Saints." In the manner of any epic hero, he and his party would have to undergo the challenge of an alien environment in order to be worthy of the "boon." As St. Brendan and his monks journeyed, the challenges were a mixture of Bible lore and fantasy, all marked by the strict timekeeping of the Christian calendar. On Christmas night, for instance, they found Judas cooling himself on a rock. Jonah's whale from the Bible was the sea monster on which they landed.

In order to demonstrate St. Brendan's appeal as a European "discoverer," I shall make use of Latin, Anglo-Norman, Italian, and German versions,[5] although I will not overconcern myself with stylistic differences or variations. Instead, I will show the manner in which, despite its Christian thrust, the account conveys both a European view of

the non-European world and a definite insistence on maintaining this as
the sole constant of spiritual authority.

In all the versions, the narrative development is relatively straight-
forward. We learn that St. Brendan, after hearing a story told by one of
his kinsman about the Island of Delights that the monk had visited,
resolves to set out in accordance with God's wishes. After a forty-day
fast, St. Brendan and his monks set out in a westward direction. They
encounter unusual creatures, observe Judas, land on a whale's back, visit
the outskirts of Paradise, and return home to the center.

Most editors of the various versions have inferred an oral basis in the
narrative. In addition to this, each account was linguistically confined
within a specific culture. Thus, although the broad outline of the plot is
maintained, St. Brendan and his fellow monks speak the specific dialect
of each particular audience, thereby identifying themselves with that
group. Geographical place names offer no distraction, since the narrative
is told against a neutral background that suggests both a recognizable
plausibility and a degree of allegory; the latter allows the story to have
ramifications that are easily comprehended within the common context of
Christendom. Rolf Fay, a German editor of one version of "Sankt
Brandan," has confirmed that this version not only differs from the
Navigatio,[6] but that its direct sources may be found in Low German
dialects that led to the printing of a High German version, accompanied
by woodcuts, as early as 1476 in Augsburg.[7]

Scholars have noted that Italian versions show Brendan as more
Catholic than Irish. Even though a specific place name might be
mentioned, the language of the possible Brendan model, "Brenainn," was
very often that of the Church; there are thus references to "divine graces
of the Holy Spirit," "words of devotion," "sacred ecclesiastical rule," and
so on.[8] These suggest a rigid conformity to the rituals of the Roman
Catholic church and clergy, a type of behavior much stricter than that
required of an Irish monk. Especially since Italian scholars have seen this
as a source for St. Brendan, an argument can be made that the story of
St. Brendan was "nationalized" (indeed, even with reference to sources)
as the text moved from country to country.

In editing the Anglo-Norman version of St. Brendan, E.G.R. Waters
has shown that there are five Anglo-Norman texts, three in England at the
British Library, the Bodleian Library, and the Dean and Chapter Library
in York, and two in France, at the Bibliothèque Nationale and the
Bibliothèque de l'Arsenal. The editor has designated the manuscript at the
Bibliothèque Nationale as the oldest but noted that only this one is a Latin
translation. Not only has he concluded that it was probably composed in

England, but he has also shown the very Anglo-Norman context (Old English and Norman French) in which the poem is situated. The creator of the Anglo-Saxon poem utilized a prologue, expanded and summarized the Latin account, and reorganized the story. As a result this version makes for a better imaginative work.[9]

Nearly all the various European versions emphasize the "Christian" nature of the Brendan voyage. St. Brendan's desire to visit the Other World is rendered in the *Navigatio* as mere curiosity, whereas the German, Italian, and Anglo-Norman versions stress his piety. In the *Navigatio*, after Barinthus has recounted the tale of an island he visited, St. Brendan merely announces this to his fourteen chosen monks: "My most beloved co-warriors in spiritual conflict, I beg you to help me with your advice, for I am consumed with a desire so ardent that it casts every other thought and desire out of my heart."[10] In the localized European versions, Brendan prays, beseeching God that he might visit Paradise and Hell before he died.

St. Brendan's bearing is not merely religious; he is equally conscious of what the later conquistadors also clearly understood — the need to find both God and gold. So, in the German version, quite early in the narrative, St. Brendan and his brothers come to an island where "it became very dark and they could not see earth or heaven," but "the ground was full of gold and precious stones."[11] This passage dramatizes the dual nature of the quest for the material and the spiritual, for there, in the darkness, in the midst of spiritual ambivalence, the stones shine through, bringing hope.

Paradise, thus defined, is the hoped-for reward. Throughout the Middle Ages, Paradise was first sought in the East, and only later in the West. St. Isidore had said as much: Paradise lay to the east, and it contained many fruit trees and the tree of life. Springtime lasted the year round and, as the Bible had said, from the center of Paradise, a spring watered the entire area. But Paradise was surrounded by a fire that reached up to Heaven, and this made it difficult to enter. Pierre d'Ailly confirmed that the origin of the Euphrates existed in Paradise, and Columbus noted, in one of his annotations in d'Ailly's book, that this Paradise of d'Ailly could be equated with the riches of the world.[12] Because Paradise was seen as attainable in very earthly terms, many medieval writers stressed not only the walls of flame but added impenetrable rock. Cosmas Indicopleustes, as Mary B. Campbell had shown, "places the Earthly Paradise in the circle of land he postulates as surrounding the impassable Ocean Stream."[13]

All of this tells us that "St. Brendan" is a very *medieval* creation. The entire journey is directed toward reaching Paradise. Early on, St. Brendan reaches the Paradise of Birds, "where white birds perch," and a bird instructs St. Brendan on the fall of Satan. In the *Navigatio*, Brendan wishes to drink from a nearby spring but is warned against this by a messenger from God. When St. Brendan reaches the Earthly Paradise (a little too early in the *Navigatio*, but dramatically reserved for a climax in the Anglo-Norman texts), the picture painted is one of great beauty. Not only are biblical and medieval notions utilized, but, in addition, in the non-Latin accounts, there is great imaginative force.

In the *Navigatio*, Paradise is a land of abundance. The voyagers wander through the land for the religiously significant forty days, eating apples and drinking spring water, preserving what one writer has called "the Celtic pagan conception of the promised land."[14] Put differently, this is the country of the "Betha Brenainn," "a land secret, secure, delightful, separated from men."[15]

St. Brendan's voyage therefore retains much of the common matter found both in "legendary" travel (including legendary accounts based on real people like Alexander) and, more importantly for our purpose, the archetypal mythology of the literature of "discovery" and conquest. Against the overall background of a journey, a man and his companions travel westward, battle natural and unnatural elements, attain Paradise, and return with the spoils of their quest. St. Brendan, the Vikings, and Columbus all have a basic common denominator. They all share an adversarial relationship with their environment. They battle storms at sea and fight against the internal and external "monsters" that they bring with them.

Part of the cultural baggage includes demonizing any people beyond the "discoverers'" own frame of reference. This occurs less in St. Brendan's accounts, since, apart from him and his men, there are few real humans present. Most of the figures that emerge are "monsters," some frightening, like the enormous whale, and others soothing, like the talking bird. When humans are mentioned, they are usually either other monks, who are godly and helpful, or biblical figures, like Paul the Hermit.

Nonetheless, one exception is the persistent "other," which seemed to haunt medieval tales. At the very center of *Navigatio* is the "infantem ethyopem" (Ethiopian boy). He symbolizes the devil and associates easily with a monk who stole a silver bridle or, in other accounts, a golden goblet. The Ethiopian boy flies away from the monk's bosom once the monk repents. The horror is captured well in this translation of a Latin version:

The rest of the monks cast themselves to the ground and begged the Lord to save their brother's soul. Brendan lifted the culprit to his feet and the rest of the monks stood up — to see a little Ethiopian boy pop out of the culprit's breast and cry out: "Man of God, why are you expelling me from the home I have lived in these past seven years? You are casting me off from my inheritance."

"In the name of Our Lord Jesus Christ," Brendan replied, "I forbid you to harm any man from now till the Day of Judgment." Then, turning to the monk, "You must receive the Body and Blood of the Lord, for your body and soul are soon to part company. You will be buried here, but that brother of yours who accompanied you out of the monastery will rest only in hell."[16]

This dark "other" is the same as Grendel, Caliban, and Friday, just as we observed in *Wonders*, except that here he speaks with a Christian tongue and is thus all the more dangerous. Like Native Americans and Africans, he recognizes the superiority of St. Brendan as a "man of God," with the power to disrupt his life. The conquistadors and colonists could and did "expel" their conquered and colonial peoples, and "cast" them off from their "inheritance" of social cohesiveness, language, custom, and sense of place. As if to make the point abundantly clear, the symbol of the Ethiopian boy is rendered in other non-Latin accounts (for instance, the Anglo-Norman text) as "a devil."[17]

The image of the Ethiopian boy takes us back,to what has been said of Paradise. In the midst of Paradise, the serpent exists, constantly seeking to bring down chaos on an idyllic life. It becomes the duty of monk and master to prevent disorder in the form of Eve's seduction. In a vision on the previous night, St. Brendan had "witnessed the machinations of the evil one. He saw a little Ethiopian boy holding out a silver necklace and juggling with it in front of the monk."[18] Because St. Brendan has been forewarned, he is able to take decisive action.

As las Casas was to write about the Yucatan in 1552, four centuries after the Brendan accounts were first committed to writing:

It was a kingdom where great Spanish cities could have been built, where people could have lived in an earthly Paradise, had the Spaniards been worthy. But the cities were not built, because of the greed, the sinfulness, the insensitivity of the Spaniards. . . . [They] assembled all the Indians they had allowed to survive and sent them away on the many ships that came, attracted by the smell of slaves.[19]

As with the Brendan allegory, New World conquerors recognized Paradise but associated its inhabitants with the antithesis of virtue. As with the Ethiopian boy in Brendan lore, Native Americans were demonized, derided, and driven far from Paradise. And when las Casas finally won his own crusade, another victim was located in another place, only to be subjected to the same fate.

As a final corollary to St. Brendan's Island, perhaps another nearby and equally mythical place, Antilla, can help us to understand the drive West, which forced Europe to seek a non-Europe. Embedded in the word "Antilla" are "anti" and "ilja," suggesting that the mythology that Europe sought beyond its own west was in direct contrast to itself. We shall explore how these mythologies of perfection and imperfection continued to affect peoples in lands beyond Europe, beyond the western coastline, far from the locus of assurance, in a literature of imagined contact.

THE VIKING SAGAS: TOWARD VINLAND

Two narratives are most relevant in the present context: the "Greenland Saga" and "Eirik's Saga," both of which, with slight variations, give an account of and Viking travels and explorations in the New World. The "Greenland Saga" tells of Bjarni Herjolfsson's (c. 970) accidental glimpse of North America when he is blown off course while sailing from Iceland to Greenland. Leif Eiriksson's expedition (c. 1000) is considered different, in that he plans it and arrives at places he calls "Helluland" (Slab-Land), "Markland" (Forest Land), and, finally, "Vinland" (Wineland). Thorvald Eiriksson's (c. 1000) Vinland expedition is mentioned in the "Greenland Saga." In it, he fights the indigenous people and is killed. Thorstein Eiriksson, in both the "Greenland Saga" and "Eirik's Saga," makes an unsuccessful attempt at his own version of "discovery." In both sagas, accounts are given of Thorfinn Karlsefni's (c. 1002–1007) expeditions, which had several women and extensive provisions including cattle on board. In the "Greenland Saga," Karlsefni trades and fights with the locals and leaves after two years. In "Eirik's Saga," Karlsefni specifically goes to Helluland, Markland, and Vinland, which had previously been visited by Leif Eiriksson. Finally, in the "Greenland Sage," Freydis, Leif's sister, leads an expedition on which she takes both men and women; internal bickering and internecine strife occur, during which she kills five women. After remaining in Vinland for one year, she returns.[20] We shall attempt to see what significance lies in these Viking sagas that purport to relate their New World contacts around 1000 A.D.[21]

On the "visual" side, a map exists that confirms the Viking journey. In *The Vinland Map and the Tartar Relation*, a number of scholars have discussed the authenticity of the map.[22] They date it to around 1440, almost 500 years after the actual voyages. But, even before we relate the journeys of the Vikings, the map (genuine or not) affords us an opportunity to examine further the exportation of mythology.[23]

West of Europe, in the northern half of the "Mare Oceanum," in the northwest corner of the map, Vinland, Greenland, and Iceland are represented as islands. Vinland, with two large Scandinavian-type fjords running from west to east on the map, is positioned at the west, southwest of Greenland. At the very top of the map, a Latin text declares that Bjarni and Leif Eiriksson "*discovered* a new land, extremely fertile and having vines" [emphasis added]. It further adds that the island was "named Vinland" and that Eirik (or Henricus) later came to "this truly vast and very rich land, in the name of Almighty God."[24]

Even before looking at the "verbal" representations in the various sagas, we may note three elements that link Viking enterprises with later European conquest: The lands are "discovered," "named," and Christianized. In addition, the pictorial representation of the map further attempts to place them within a familiar European context. Greenland and Vinland, in particular, are covered with fjords that reproduce Scandinavia, although at least one anthropologist who has found Viking remains in the area has argued that "the narrow and most northerly indentation which terminates in a lake makes one think of Hamilton Inlet in Labrador" and "the somewhat broader fjord to the south may be the Straite of Belle Isle."[25]

J.R.L. Anderson has contended in *Vinland Voyage* that Leif Eiriksson probably crossed the latter day Davis Strait, making his first landfall somewhere on:

The northern coast of Labrador or perhaps even as far north as Baffin Island. . . . [He] gave it a name — he called it "Helluland," which means literally "Land of Flat Stones." . . . He sailed on southwards and came to . . . a coast densely wooded but with not much else in favor of settlement. Leif called this "Markland," which means "Land of Forests." It was not worthless to the Greenlanders, for they needed timber almost as much as food — timber for building ships and houses. Greenland and Iceland had no timber.[26]

As early as the eleventh century, an economic reason for "conquest" was already apparent. This becomes even more interesting because the expedition carefully avoided what the map depicted further south, off the coast of Spain — the "*magnae insulae*" (*large islands*) of St. Brendan, as well as the "Fortunate Islands" off the coast of West Africa. As the Norsemen well knew, such travels would bring them into a collision course with other European powers, a contest they could ill afford at a time when "push" factors were driving them out of Scandinavia.

In a 1590 map, originally drawn by Sigurdur Stefansson, and redrawn in 1670, the "named" areas are clearly marked. Some scholars have argued that the map was drawn in accordance with the "heard" versions of the sagas. Here, this map reveals an interesting detail that appears over and over again in the sagas — the presence of a place termed "Skraelinge Land." In Stefansson's Latin appendix to his map, he related this land to the people (later termed "Indians") who "obtain their name from the aridity; they are dried up just as much by the heat as the cold." South of this area lies a promontory jutting out northward. This is identified as "Vinland" and described by Stefansson as a place "which is called the Good because of the fertility of the land and the abundant produce of useful things."[27]

Even though the earlier Vikings had lived apart from the more Southern European conventions associated with Plinian and Alexandrian monsters and marvels, note how carefully they went about concocting their own representation of the unfamiliar. "Otherness" was conferred on the indigenous people by the scurrilous term "Skraeling," translated by one scholar as "wretches." Stefansson's Latin description suggests a monstrous race of people, ill-adapted to natural climatic change. Furthermore, since *"ab ariditate nomen habent"* (they obtain their name from the aridity), the Latin suggests not merely an environmental desert but a cultural one as well. Thus the Skraelings, as they came to be known in the sagas, represent victims who lack the ability to alter their environment and to produce a culture. These are opprobriums that will later be identified with the negative mythologies of Europe and applied to people in Africa and the New World.

Side by side with the dismissal of indigenous peoples are the laudatory effusions about the land and landscape, as well as the vision of a perfect other world, in the manner of St. Brendan and Columbus. The Norse concept of Valhalla was thus transferred, in the perverse pattern whereby a relationship with a new territory and its people becomes established and more easily understood. At the "visual" level, Stefansson appended the description of the "Promontorium Winlandiae"; at the "verbal" level, in both the "Greenland Sage" and "Eirik's Saga," the occasional ascent to near rhapsody is proof enough of how the new land was equated with the promise of bliss in the great halls of Odin himself. For instance, in the saga, when Bjarni and his crew first sight land, after grim days of fog and no wind, they see "that the country was not mountainous, but was well wooded and with low hills."[28] As the crew reveals afterward, the

land is the material representation of what they believe they want most —
firewood and water. Similarly, when Leif and his men first reach the area
of Vinland, they are rapturous: "They went ashore and looked about
them. The weather was fine. There was dew on the grass, and the first
thing they did was to get some of it on their hands and put it to their lips,
and to them it seemed the sweetest thing they had ever tasted."[29] The
superlatives speak to the wonder and the awesome majesty of what they
had located.

Vikings were not known for their benevolence. No less an admirer of
power than Winston Churchill credited them with what he termed the
"discovery of America," but castigated them for the "plunder of the
civilized world."[30] Not surprisingly, therefore, the sagas reveal a sorry
record of their contacts with the Skraelings. The "Greenland Saga" relates
that Thorvald Eiriksson's instant instinct, on seeing nine indigenous men,
was to capture and kill eight of them. His action, quite naturally,
provokes retaliation; he is killed, and soon after the party returns to
Greenland.

Like the conquistadors, the Vikings arrive as Christian propagandists.
Thorvald instructs his men with his last dying words to place crosses at
his head and feet after he is buried.[31] The discord that they have
introduced contrasts directly with a land in which "[t]here was no lack of
salmon in the river or the lake, bigger salmon than they had ever seen,"[32]
and where they could gather grapes and vines during the winter for the
voyage back to Greenland.[33]

According to the sagas, when Thorfinn Karlsefni later makes his own
visit, he goes with a group of sixty men and five women. Before he
departs, he makes an agreement with his crew that "everyone should
share equally in whatever profits the expedition might yield."[34] They may
even have been thinking in terms of a "permanent settlement," but this
early trading venture proved as one-sided as those that followed centuries
later. According to the saga, "They made use of all the natural resources
of the country that were available, grapes and game of all kinds and other
produce." When they first meet the Skraelings, they see them as
simplistic and child like, fleeing at the sound of a roaring bull and
attempting to make for Karlsefni's domicile.[35]

Thus, they are easy to handle. The Vikings satisfy the Skraelings'
eager appetite for milk in exchange for furs, sables, and pelts. As the
chronicler records with some satisfaction: "And so the outcome of their
trading expedition was that the Skraelings carried their purchases away in
their bellies, and left their packs and furs with Karlsefni and his men."[36]
But by next winter, the Skraelings refuse to be exploited. Soon the two

sides are fighting again, but the Skraelings are naive to the point of alarming stupidity. One of them, apparently unfamiliar with the use of an axe, kills a man standing near him.[37] Another, "tall and handsome" and identified as their leader by Karlsefni, has the good sense to throw it into the water before they all flee into the forest.

The concept of indigenous people as simple "children of nature" belongs to a later epoch, but it is intriguing to see the first glimmerings of savagery and nobility in the sagas. Recall that the Vikings are relating how they see their "perceived." Particularly interesting is Karlsefni's instant ability to identify a "leader," based on his own notions of beauty. Such mythologies will persist throughout the encounter between the Old World and New World. Newcomers in the later period likewise claimed that they could identify "leaders"; they dealt with them and then inevitably betrayed them, as the nefarious instances of Cortés with the Aztecs and Pizarro with the Incas easily demonstrate. Furthermore, within the perception of the Skraelings as the ugly and bestial, the callous and cruel, are foreshadowings of literary concoctions such as Aphra Behn's *Oroonoko*, William Shakespeare's *Othello*, Jean-Jacques Rousseau's *Émile*, and Daniel Defoe's *Friday*, among others. Out of this curious European dualistic view of the "other," the Noble Savage emerges as the supreme ethnocentric measure of cultural abnormality.

A major problem of European/New World contact has been the inability of the participants to communicate with one another, or, put differently, in the assumption that "language" is somehow the province of the European. Later on, the Spaniards, Portuguese, Dutch, and English would all fall prey to the belief that their own linguistic province was somehow "global," that their signs, symbols, and words would be understood by all people throughout the world. The failure of words began with the Vikings and continued even more dramatically when Columbus took an Arab translator with him on his first voyage. At least the Vikings, despite their crudeness, could admit that "[n]either side could understand the other's language."[38]

In another instance cited in "Eirik's Saga," Karlsefni and his party discover that the Skraelings now have a yearning for red cloth, which they trade for gray pelts. When the cloth is in short supply, Karlsefni merely cuts it up into smaller pieces. The saga gleefully reports that "the Skraelings paid just as much or even more for it."[39] Skraelings are condemned as brutal and vicious, lacking chivalrous ritual in their battles. When they come to battle, they are presented as an insane lot, waving sticks in a counterclockwise direction and "howling loudly."[40] Earlier, on, they are described as "small and evil-looking, and their hair was coarse; they had large eyes and broad cheekbones."[41] In appearance and behavior, the Skraelings fit the pattern of medieval monstrosities, incapable of the ordinary attributes of human appearance.

As in the lore of more southerly portions of Europe, Viking women are subject to the same disgust as indigenous people. One account is given of how Freydis, Thorvald's wife, conspires to set one Viking clan against the other. After Thorvald has slaughtered the men of the opposing group, she is still not satisfied, for the opposing women are still alive: "Freydis said, 'Give me an axe.' This was done, and she herself killed the women, all five of them."[42] Leif denounces her and warns that her children will never prosper.

In another example, Gudrid, Karlsefni's wife, has a supernatural encounter. She meets a "shadow" who is "wearing a black, close-fitting tunic [with] a band round her chestnut colored hair." She tells Gudrid that her name is also Gudrid, but her appearance merely presages the slaughter of a Skraeling, "for trying to steal some weapons."[43] Of course, the Vikings, much like later European adventurers and settlers, are not troubled by such niceties as cultural differences in ideas of ownership. But the point here is that Gudrid is the sole witness to the presence of imminent evil. In a way, she stands for Gudrid's other self, who is non-human, supernatural, and, above all, Black, as seen in the color of her apparel. The important fact is that she is described as a "shadow," reminding us of the priest's "shadow," the Ethiopian boy in St. Brendan's account, and other references in *Wonders*.

Yet another instance occurs in Greenland, when Gudrid is visited by a mysterious, abnormal woman, who "wore a black lambskin hood lined with white cat's fur."[44] She is the epitome of the medieval witch and prophesies for the company, having been "supplied with the preparations she required for performing the witchcraft." Gudrid herself confesses to her own knowledge of the spells and songs associated with witchcraft. Women, as in other narratives of the period, find themselves equally as damned as the new indigenous people encountered in alien lands. Apparently, both gender and race remove people from proximity to the European cultural center. Neither indigenous inhabitant as "barbarian" nor woman as "witch" can be situated within any accepted concept of "normality."

Thus, Viking women and Skraelings both contribute to a sense of the monstrous, which we also observe in later journeys. In "Eirik's Saga," one place of landing is called "Furanstrands" or "Marvel Strands."[45] The sagas readily admit, as does later travel literature, that the outer world is strange and exotic. On one expedition, Thorhall the Hunter goes along

for the simple reason that "he had considerable experience of *wild*
regions,"[46] and, when Leif arrives on the land, he sees "fields of *wild*
wheat growing"[47] [emphasis added]. As with land and agriculture, so too
the inhabitants: In "Eirik's Saga," Karlsefni and his party see "five
Skraelings clad in skins, asleep; beside them were containers full of deer-
marrow mixed with blood." Karlsefni sums up the situation instantly,
deciding that the men are "outlaws" and dispatching them quickly.[48]

Especially because all these journeys are "symbolic" (even those made
by the conquistadors) and not really rooted in hard fact, the true purpose
is not exploration but seeking home, the center. One part of "Eirik's
Saga" neatly sums up reasons and motives, and establishes in a few
words why, despite their early victories over the Skraelings, Scandi-
navians pulled back: "Karlsefni and his men had realized by now that
although the land was excellent they could never live there in safety or
freedom from fear, because of the native inhabitants. So they made ready
to leave the place and return home."[49]

At the center, far from the Skraelings, the Vikings could concentrate on
European lands to their south. As Normans, occupying Normandy in the
tenth century, they would demonstrate a much greater tolerance for the
foreigners among whom they found themselves, blending and merging
the culture of disparate European peoples into a new pattern. By 1066,
with the Norman Conquest of Britain, they were making ready for yet
another journey that would indirectly lead their English descendants back
to the land of the Skraelings. It is a great pity that, by then, the earlier les-
sons of the Vikings' contact had faded away in the lost pages of another
people's history, never Anglo-Norman or British. Karlsefni's return
anticipated the collapse of British imperialism by almost a millennium.

MARCO POLO: PARADISE IN THE EAST

When the young Marco Polo traveled to Asia with his father and uncle
in 1271, he was about seventeen years old. Given semi-official status and
letters for the Mongol emperor by the newly elected Pope Gregory X, the
family journeyed through southeastern Turkey, eastern Turkey, and
northern Iran, crossing the desert of Lop, and reaching Hormuz on the
Persian Gulf. Deciding against a sea voyage to India, they continued
overland, crossed another desert, until they reached Khorasan in eastern
Iran. They then turned toward Afghanistan, remaining there for probably
a year, during which time the young Marco probably visited other nearby
territories, probably as far as Kashmir. Continuing east, they went across
the main Silk Road, until they came to the borders of China.

There the Polos lived for several years, journeying to northern and southern China. They returned to Venice in 1295, having been granted permission by Kublai Khan to accompany a young princess to Persia. They sailed south, stopping at present-day Vietnam and on islands off the coast of present-day Malaysia. After visiting present-day Sri Lanka, they rounded the west coast of India to Hormuz. From there, the Polos finally departed for Europe, after spending in all some twenty-five years in Asia. Marco was imprisoned in Genoa and dictated his *Il Milione* to a fellow inmate in a Franco-Italian language that was rendered into English by John Frampton in 1579.

Marco Polo's adventures were real, in that he was a historical person who made very specific journeys to places unknown to Europeans. What interests us more is the manner in which Marco Polo, in his forties, "recollects" the events of two decades before. In his account, there is the stuff of "fiction," in that Marco Polo, as a European, could not possibly have recollected the exotic East without a heavy reliance on the fantasies propagated by the world from which he came.

In a way, therefore, his work establishes another development of a kind of proto-text, in that, for several generations, it would be regarded as an authority. It was blatantly plagiarized and copied, most notably by Sir John Mandeville, who was himself most likely an armchair traveler. Nonetheless, even as proto-text, Marco Polo's version of the world beyond Europe, while establishing its own authority, borrowed heavily from other versions.

This is surprising, if only because Polo's realism in his *Travels* cannot be ignored. He was careful to note the geographical peculiarities of regions and the customs of people, and also to point out distinctions between, for instance, Muslims and Buddhists. In addition, he had access to Kublai Khan, presenting him with sacred oil that they had painstakingly carried from Jerusalem and giving him the letters from Pope Gregory. Indeed, he probably was able to practice his skill at "remembering" in Kublai Khan's court, where he became a favorite and often recounted his adventures to the Mongol emperor.

Not only are Marco Polo's "recollections" colored by European imaginings, but the popular reception of the book also caused it to be further sensationalized in many adaptations that seriously distorted what Polo had originally rendered. And, since Marco Polo dictated his account before the invention of the printing press, some 140 manuscripts exist, presenting the modern commentator with a most beguiling problem. What did Marco Polo actually say? The answer is complex, since in the intervening centuries, some editors have seen fit to tone down what they regarded as improprieties. It is best to consider the work therefore as a kind of culmination of medieval speculation on the extra-European world, with all its fabulous distortions and wild speculations.

Editors A. C. Moule and Paul Pelliot have pointed out that three Paris copies are the best possible source of a lost copy that was based on an original manuscript. They have added that a later Latin text could also be used to complete and correct these earlier ones. In addition, if one were to attempt to reconstruct what they have termed "the original words of Marco Polo," they have suggested a Franco-Italian text in the Bibliothèque Nationale, an Italian version, and a third Latin text in the Chapter Library at Toledo.[50] Early printed editions date from the fourteenth century.[51] Because of its wide dissemination, Polo's work became the main source through which both "verbal" accounts like Mandeville's and "visual" accounts like the Catalan Atlas version of China in 1375 established themselves as authorities. On Fra Mauro's map of 1459, the island of "Zimpangu" (Japan) was lifted from Marco Polo's "Chimpangu," and Polo's descriptions of the imperial city of "Chambalech" and the summer palace of "Sandu" were all rendered with profuse illustration, ornamentation, and lavish description.[52] Even as late as the sixteenth century, both Gerardus Mercator's (1569) and Abraham Ortelius' (1570) maps were rife with what R. A. Skelton has called "misinterpretations" of Marco Polo.[53] Even though these representations were:

Often curiously reconciled with new dates, [they] continued to be drawn from Marco Polo, whose topography of the mainland of China was not superseded until the Jesuit surveys in the 17th and 18th centuries. . . . Mercator himself was responsible for a striking perversion of Marco's geography of south-east Asia which was to mislead geographers until the 18th century.[54]

As a result of this heavy over-reliance on Polo's text, mapmakers created a southern continent, an idea not dispelled until the voyages of James Cook in the eighteenth century. What should most concern us is not the accepted "authenticity" of the account, but the manner in which Polo's book became "representational," permitting the views of a mythical Europe to become an eyewitness account and merely substituting these at times with alterations, accretions, emendations, and even distortions, as if they were confirmed facts.

Polo's work, despite its earlier title "The Description of The World," seems to develop toward the climactic point where the khan, his court and feasting, his palace and wealth, and indeed even his spirituality, are all exalted as ends in themselves. As Leonardo Olschki has admitted, Polo saw the larger part of the world as "barbaric or exotic," from the viewpoint of "a true Venetian, a European."[55] Hence, as the "plot" develops, the cities of Asia are "noble," in direct contrast to his fascination with the Mongolian emperor who, after all, was a nomad. In large measure, however, Polo remained a foreigner, dependent on interpreters for his contacts with the Chinese. As a linguistic and cultural outsider, and also as a man torn between admiration and disdain, he was very much like the conquistadors who followed him in a different direction nearly 300 years later.

As a medieval man, Polo was subject to the fears and prejudices of his time. Going through the Desert of Lop, he recalled "deluding spirits . . . talking in a way that they seem to be their companions, for they call them sometimes by their names."[56] These were nothing other than the Alexandrian Donestre who, as Friedman has pointed out, "pretend to speak the language of any traveler they meet."[57]

Marvels abound in Polo's work, related with the usual excessive superlatives that we have noted before. There are "sheep large as asses" with tails weighing thirty pounds. In this part of the world, Polo learned of the "Caraunas," who remind us of the monsters who must go to India to mate. The Caraunas have Indian mothers and Tartar fathers. They represent the medieval fear of an ultimate and gruesome act of "otherness" in sexual merging, which would seemingly bring out the most horrible qualities. In this instance, the fear of blackness, of the extreme alien noted in *Wonders*, is once more apparent in Polo's words: "And the white Tartars began to mix with the Indian women who were black, and begat sons of them who were called Caraunas, that is in their language, mixed."[58] As a result of this mongrelization, they "are a most cruel and wicked race and robbers who go scouring the land and doing great harm." To them belongs the ultimate power of darkness, which they conjure up at will so that "they make the whole day become dark like a dark night by their enchantments and by devilish work."[59]

As with other travelers discussed, Polo's landscape often threatened and seldom reassured. Equally, until he arrived at the court of the khan, much of his homophobia was reserved for people who looked different and toward whom a great deal of the negative mythology of the European world was directed. In Zanzibar, people resemble giants (whom Alexander had defeated in India and Antonio Pigafetta had seen in Patagonia in 1526):

And they are all black and go quite naked except that they are covered in their natural parts. And they do so wisely to cover them for they have them very large & horrible to see — And they have so great a mouth also and the great and red nose so flat and turned upwards the forehead like an ape. . . . They have the ears large, and the lips thick, turned outwards . . . [and] whoever should see them in another country would say of them rightly that they were infernal devils.[60]

Polo was not simply describing his shock at meeting Blacks; he was reiterating certain stock opinions that had been orally transmitted, including those about their nudity, unusual gender appendages, and resemblance to apes. Many of these characteristics were imposed on the peoples of Africa and the New World, continuing a tradition that Polo himself, despite his own firsthand contacts with objective reality, helped to distort and perpetuate. The Plinian "Amyctyrae," for instance, were visually depicted in medieval bestiaries with a lower lip resembling two protruding horns, so large that it must be held up for support.

Polo thus lent additional credibility to this amazing view of the world by defining himself as a viable witness: "For I the said Master Marc Polo who saw all this tell you that we ourselves tried them sufficiently," confirming that trees that grow flour exist. Likewise, he used the language of confession, sincere and emotional in its appeal, as he related his account of the Cynocephali or dog-headed men:

Now you may know quite truly that all the men of this island have the crown of the head like the head of a dog and teeth and mouth and eyes and nose like dogs; nor must you doubt of this for I tell you in short that they are just like the heads of great dogs which we commonly call mastiff dogs.[61]

The method used here is intriguing. Polo was appealing directly to the listener or reader, giving his own personal assurance and relating what he has seen in terms of familiar European images. By linking the "normal" and the "absurd" and by grounding them in modern observation and ancient reference, Polo was ensuring that the mythology would be received as reinforced truth. Sometimes, under the guise of restating older wisdom, Polo used a device of mock attack to propose a new mythology. Such was the case with people in Java who only *resembled* monkeys. Therefore, by putting the lie to certain beliefs, Marco Polo established a new authenticity for himself.

Man-eating monsters were derived from the Plinian "Anthropophagi." Even the relatively low-key, sympathetic account of Cabeza de Vaca's eight-year sojourn (published as the *Relación* in 1542), mentions man eaters, but, in Cabeza de Vaca's unique method of reversing the stereotype, the descrip-tion is of the shock of *Indians* as they see "five Christians quartered on the coast . . . eating each other."[62] Olschki has remarked that Polo's obsession with the crass was intentionally meant both to titillate and to point to ethnographic differences. We could add that the "differences" were ways of assuring medieval European readers of the normality of their own world, a feature that obviously contributed to his book's immense popularity. Polo's Asia confirmed a European view, not of Asia alone but of Africa as well. This is why the work is of such immense value, for it brings together an oral legendary past, a written view, and a more contemporary account of a non-European journey in a phantasmagoria. Olschki has concurred that Polo's heed to this tradition influenced his interpretation of the "medieval teratological zoology of legendary and literary tradition." This tendency *"makes him discover"* the unicorn in Sumatra [emphasis added]. But, because Polo sought veracity, even within the province of legend, he had to add that this particular unicorn was "quite different" from the ones that Europeans imagine. Olschki has rightly added that this was "an indication of his Western culture under stress of personal experience."[63]

Nevertheless, given our assumption that *Il Milione* is a compendium of medieval belief, one would be quite surprised if the usual staples did not occur. Prester John is naturally mentioned, but a "revisionist" view naturally modifies his power. Since the entire thrust of the book points toward the glorification of Genghis Khan, Prester John appears as his opponent in a battle that Prester John must surely lose. Here, Polo is not positioned as a "witness" but merely as a recorder. The narrator hides behind the narrative with the words "Now the story says." There is no personal accountability here, only an attempt at setting straight the "historical" record of Prester John, whose letter of 1165 preceded these events by over a hundred years.

Polo, in effect, updated the account. Some scholars have argued that the major purpose for the *Letter* had been to help resolve the bitter church/state dispute personified in Pope Alexander III and Holy Roman Emperor Frederick Barbarossa. Prester John became the representative of the exemplary ruler, combining in his office and person the kindred qualities of priest and king. By 1219, the situation had changed, as Genghis Khan, supposedly a descendant of Prester John, became the new force against the Muslims. But when Genghis Khan established himself in Russia, that dream had to be discarded, for he was much too near the homefront. Olschki has commented that:

Whereas the original phase of the legend had made of Prester John the mythical Christian ruler of a large part of the Asian continent and the allegorical figure of a political utopia, the new trend that began toward the middle of the XIIIth century limited his dominion to a tribe in Mongolia, which was governed by a Christian dynasty. His power and prestige were thereby reduced, and his exploits associated with the history and legend of the recently formed Chinghizide empire.[64]

In Polo's thirteenth-century restoration, Genghis Khan battles Prester John with "many Nestorian Christians & also many Saracens." The astrologers' prophecies bode well for Genghis Khan and "at the last Ginghis Kan won the battle and Uncan, that is Prester Johan was killed in that battle."[65] Prester John is thereby relegated to the dustbin of history, because the legend is no longer as important as before. From Genghis Khan, power eventually passed to Kublai Khan, and Polo identified and shared in the glory of this all-powerful ruler. Here Polo again became quite subjective, with lyrical language exalting the new emperor:

And again I tell you a greater thing than I am telling you: that all the conquerors of the world and all the kings both of Christians and Saracens also, if they were all together, would not have so much power nor could they do so much as this Cublai great Kaan could do, who is lord of all the Tartars of the world, both of those of the sunrising and those of the sunsetting, for all are his men and subject to him.[66]

In effect, Polo substituted Kublai Khan for Prester John. When Kublai Khan died, Polo reported, everyone in the way of his cortege was slain with the worlds, "Go serve your lord in the other world."[67] This was certainly omnipotence, on a scale unmatched in Europe.

Polo's intention was therefore not merely to resuscitate the older legend, but also to refurbish it in the historical context of his time. His treatment of women offers a case in point here; the familiar misogynistic attitudes are subsumed within apparently explanatory contexts. In a way, placing the usual castigations within particular geographical contexts weakens the generalization. Specifically, then, on one of the small islands near Java, men and women "cover themselves with nothing whatever in the world [and lie] carnally together as dogs in the road wherever they may be without any shame, not having any respect, the father to the daughter nor the son to the mother, for each one does as he wishes and as he can."[68] Polo attempted to explain to us why this un-European behavior apparently occurred: "This people is without any law." This last sentence both provides an explanation and helps to distance such people further from European concepts of normality. Among another people, Polo found the women to be only apparently immodest, for, in this instance, "immorality" was circumscribed by strict conventions. Thus, "if a woman invites them in love they can lie with her without sin, but if they first invite the woman then they reckon it for sin."[69]

More and more as *Il Milione* develops, there is a craving for the ideal, the utopian world of non-European fancy. Polo was quite conservative in his views, constantly extolling virtue and praising one group because "for nothing in the world would the one touch the wife of the other." Particularly, he admired the women in one polygynous society for their devotion, adding that, in his view (and here he was referring to Christian infidelity), "there ought to be a most singular faith and chastity" in relationships, if "confusion of so great a sacrament of marriage" were to be avoided.[70]

Despite these doctrinaire aims in his writing, Polo still fell prey to revealing instances, as already noted, derived from medieval lore. The Wife-Givers were notorious, particularly in the *Wonders* tradition, for their generosity in providing "wives to any traveler who stops among them."[71] True enough, Polo did not generalize, but, in his own "description" of the world, such people too must be identified. He found them in "Camul" in the "great province of Tangu" where the men attend to "all that their guests need (none the less with payment from them); nor do they ever return home while the stranger stays there. And the stranger stays with his wife in the house and does as he likes and lies with her in a bed just as if she were his wife, and *they continue in great enjoyment*"[72] [emphasis added]. In reality, the disparagement of women was actually part of the medieval, male, European quest for his own unfettered license.

Such a view of a world without restraint would be one that the Spaniards in the Americas also sought for themselves. Hernán de Soto, when going through the American South, was supposedly given "a fine young girl" by one chief, while another leader allegedly presented him with his two sisters. Las Casas would complain in 1552 that "the Spaniards were allowed to choose, among one hundred and fifty Indian maidens the ones they liked best, paying for each one an arroba of wine or oil or vinegar or pigs, and the same for a comely boy."[73] Sexual promiscuity, according to Polo, was not only gender based. Its "victims" were instead identified with the defeated of the non-European world.

In Polo's account, the Mongolian emperor represents a corrective influence in the midst of sexual excess. Even though, in the context of Asia, he holds the position of "conqueror," his own humane and godly attitude is shown when he forbids his subjects, the "Camul," from forcing "their wives to comit adultery with strangers." Tradition triumphs, though; when the effects of this new policy are associated with crop failure, the people send a delegation to Mongke Khan, who reluctantly concludes:

"For my part I have done my duty, but since you wish your shame and contempt so much, then you may have it. Go and live according to your customs, and make your wife a charitable gift to travellers." And thus he revoked the order which he had made about this and consents that they do their will with their evil usage.[74]

Polo reported that "they went home with the greatest joy," thereby suggesting that the legend of the Wife-Givers had no "victims," since the "whole people," as he put it, rejoiced. Polo does not tell us how the women felt.

All of this helps reinforce the "character" of the khan, who, though human, yet possessed the metonymic equivalent of godly virtue. This point needs to be stressed, since for Polo the khan embodies perfection, in contrast to the wicked "Saracens," who believe steadfastly in the "abominable law of Mahomet," or the idol-worshippers of "Tangut," who sacrifice sheep and humans in their death rituals.[75] In a way, Polo was correcting some of the wild and diabolical beliefs attributed by Europeans to the Mongols themselves.

A major problem in elevating Kublai Khan to the level of a deity lay in the fact that he was not Christian. Polo rendered him, therefore, as a sensitive soul, always curious and interested in the Christian faith. "How do you wish me to make myself a Christian?" queries Kublai Khan at one point, arguing that "if I am converted to this faith of Christ and am made a Christian, then my barons and other people who are not attached to the faith of Christ would say to me, 'What reason has moved you to baptism, and to hold the faith of Christ? What virtues or what miracles have you seen of him?'"[76] He is presented as a sensitive man in a quandary, seeking the new faith but fearful lest it put him out of touch with his subjects. He requests of Polo that he ask the Pope to send him a hundred wise men who can demonstrate their power before the idol-worshippers. When this is done, the very pragmatic emperor says, "I shall be baptized, and when I shall be baptized, all my barons and great men will be baptized, and then their subjects will receive baptism."[77] Whether this occurred or not, it was certainly a familiar formula that the Catholic Church could easily recognize, as the example of Constantine the Great had shown in the fourth century. Incidentally, this was the same arrangement that Kublai's grandfather, Genghis Khan, had refused when Carpini had urged him to convert.

The European values are never forsaken, as Polo's account reaches its climax. The khan embodies the perfection of a virtuous man; he gives "great charity and provision and alms to the poor people." His generosity is confirmed in the personal accounting of Polo himself: "I believe I tell no lie, I believe that the poor men and women, more than thirty thousand of them, go there [to the palace] every day for bread."[78]

These descriptions offer as close an approximation of the Earthly Paradise as is possible. Within the confines of the khan's peregrinations, "six months in his city, and three months in the chase, and three months in his place of canes, . . . he leads his life in very great enjoyment." Because he is the epitome of the wished-for, medieval, European god/king, he rules over a land of perfection, "more valuable and healthy" with "no evil deed done in the city."[79]

Kublai Khan is generous to his own people and to foreigners alike. He is egalitarian, as Polo himself averred: "I tell you that there are as beautiful houses and as beautiful palaces in the suburbs as in the town." The khan banishes immorality, such as prostitution, outside the town's confines, but he does not outlaw its practice. The women are organized under the direction of a "captain," and, when ambassadors visit the khan's court, "this captain is obliged to give to the said ambassadors and to each one of this retinue one harlot each night."[80]

Naturally, the khan is wealthy, not only in gold and precious stones, but also in the much desired cloves. Again, Polo offered his own assurances: "I have told you more dear things and of greater value come to this town and greater quantities than into any town in the world, and more goods are sold and bought than in any other city, *so that so much of everything comes there that is without end*"[81] [emphasis added]. Here is the cornucopia that the Portuguese sought in the east and the Spaniards in the west.

The khan is also the very essence of moderation. This was particularly important for Polo's readers, since their own rulers (like Polo himself at times) were prone to divide the world into wicked infidels and good Catholics. Polo recounted that at the beginning of the year: "all people of whatever faith they are, all the idolaters and all the Christians or the Jews and all the Saracens and all the other races of the Tartar people who are subject to the rule of the great Kaan must make great petitions and great assemblies and great prayers, each to the idols and to their God."[82] On his birthday, the khan resembles the later image of the emperor of El Dorado, clad "in the most noble cloth of the purest beaten gold," with his attendants decked out in "cloth of silk and of gold."[83] Several times a year, the khan generously rewards his barons and knights with "robes adorned with gold, pearls, and precious stones . . . so that when they are dressed and thus richly adorned they all seem to be kings."[84] Polo confirmed, with particular reference to his European readers, that "there is no other lord in all the world who could do this nor continually keep it up, but he alone."[85]

Polo had visited other places of abundant wealth. In "Cail," the king is "very rich & abounding in treasure and wears on him many precious stones,"[86] and, in "Coilum," "brazil grows . . . in great quantity," as well as ginger and pepper.[87] But the khan's world is richer, since he is the moral equivalent of a perfect European king. The search for spices and precious metals inspired both Columbus and later conquistadors, but, despite their supposed adherence to the cross, they lacked the moral values of Kublai Khan. Therefore, even though Marco Polo ascribed to the khan the precious stones "traditionally associated with the legendary literary and geographical vision of Asia," as Olschki has affirmed, Polo utilized the symbols of wealth to project the khan as priest-king, in the tradition of Prester John.

Eulogizing the Great Khan seems to have been the main point of Polo's work, in which he celebrated the khan's power, wealth, and virtue. The khan is presented as a kind of ideal sovereign, who, in contrast with European kings, holds out the hope that unity can be achieved in places like Italy and Germany. Polo adopted the posture of a medieval knight errant, declaring that he was the servant and subject of this all-powerful emperor. Thus, this portrait is not that of a real khan, but rather an idealized depiction, not of an aging emperor but of a young man, neither short nor tall, with a fair and ruddy complexion, dark eyes, and a well-shaped nose. The description is certainly generic.

In this regard, Polo must not be faulted too harshly, since the descriptions of the European kings and emperors of the times were also very conventional. It is often difficult to find much individuality in either written or drawn portraits of them, since the current stylistic device was to render an ideal pattern. Within this convention, Polo succeeded in portraying the faraway Mongol emperor not as some exotic person but as an authority figure within the comprehension of his Western readers.

All these "great wonders," as Polo himself referred to his descriptions, would influence the European world for hundreds of years. With its lavish illustrations, the volume seemed most credible, and, because Polo himself assured his readers in the prologue of the work's authenticity, they believed even more in the world he related. It was not difficult for a medieval reader to accept an account of Christian prayer that moved a mountain in Tauris; after all, Christian teaching enjoined as much.

Polo's narrative is shot through with the deepest contradictions at the heart of religious faith. Particularly important is the allusion to the Old Man of the Mountain, "a follower of the law of Mahomet," with the power of evil over his followers, making them into "assassins" who do his bidding. This was probably Polo's attempt to explain the Shiah and their supposed use of "hashshashin" (hashish), after which the entire group was labeled with the derogatory derivative "assassin." The Old Man nonetheless dwells in Paradise, albeit of his own making, and Polo still wished us to accept the existence of this Earthly Paradise, reserving some of his best prose for this section. Hence, Polo described the land of the Old Man of the Mountain in this way:

He dwelled in a most noble valley shut in between two high mountains where he had made them [his followers] the largest garden and the most beautiful that ever was seen in this world. There are abundance and delight of all the good plants, flowers, and fruits of the world, and trees which he had been able to find.[88]

He has "The most beautiful palaces that ever were seen, of a wonderful variety, for they were all gilded and adorned in azure." To complete the sight of the "known" European Paradise:

He had made them make in that garden many beautiful fountains, which corresponded on different sides of these palaces, all these had little conduits there, for each one, through which ran that which they threw up; through some of which it was seen ran wine & through some milk & through some honey & through some the clearest water.[89]

Nearby, the most beautiful women play instruments and sing, and there are ladies who "were trained in making all the dalliance and allurements to men that can be imagined." Paradise is a land of abundance with "plenty of garments, couches, food, & all things which can be desired."[90] Indeed, the description here is not unlike the one in the *Koran*, suggesting that Polo may have asked the right questions of some of the "Saracens."

Despite an attempt to demonstrate that this is an "illusion" of Paradise, Polo as poet/visionary became quite carried away in his effort to do justice to this false Paradise. Indeed, this description of perfection is repeated twice. This is never-never land, the non-Europe that was as legendary as the monsters. Since this passage occurs quite early in the text, it prepares us for the real Paradise of the khan's court. Other versions of the Old Man's paradise, notably one found in the *Imago Mundi* of Iaccopo d'Acqui of the fourteenth century (in addition to Polo's account), put forward what Polo perhaps dared not do — the "ultimate" evil, the sexual "other," the presence of homosexuality and pedophilia in Paradise. In this later account, the Old Man is said to purchase "fine boys and fine and well formed girls," from as young as one year. They are "all brought up together . . . in one place where they have whatever in the world they wish for pleasures, and they mix together as they please when they are grown up." Exotica is also part of the medieval wish, with the text fulfilling an otherwise empty hope.

Paradise is a vision of unbridled delight and one with which the medieval mind was intrigued. Polo also proffered a vision of Paradise where a dualism exists, between ultimate delights and the attendant sin and evil that accompany indulgence. As already noted, Columbus, weakened and unhappy during his third voyage, found Paradise off the South American coast, where he noted "a quantity of fresh water," "mild climate," and "a river so great and deep"[91] — yet it remained a place he could not enter. Polo's quest for Paradise in the court of Kublai Khan equaled the conquistadors' search for El Dorado and the Fountain of Youth in the New World. Vasco de Balboa found it in the Pacific, Cortés among the Aztecs at Tenochtitlán in Mexico, and Pizarro among the Incas in Peru. But their very presence in Paradise sowed attendant ills, as Polo recognized, through which they initiated the wholesale genocide of the indigenous population and the destruction of the flora and fauna of the environment. Perhaps, as the medievalists knew so well, the Earthly Paradise could not really be entered by humans. When the conquistadors did, they irreversibly damaged its former pristine beauty. With the coming of European mythology, Paradise was transformed into an earthly extension of inter-European conflict. It was the *Reconquista* replayed once more, complete with a new Inquisition, revived for the indigenous peoples of the New World.

MANDEVILLE AS SYNTHESIST

If Polo's *Il Milione* is an example of what I have termed a "proto-text," the *Mandeville's Travels* (1351) must be classified as a "subtext." *Mandeville's Travels* "borrows" heavily from a number of other works, especially various travel accounts to the Holy Land, to the East (as in the cases of Carpini and Odoric), and Vincent de Beauvais' encyclopedia, published about 1250. In addition, Mandeville drew on "proto-texts" such as those of Pliny, Herodotus, the Alexandrian romances, and, above all, Polo.

So complete is the narrative "disguise" that not only are we unsure as to whether "Mandeville" traveled or not, but we cannot even be certain as to who he actually was. Suggestions have been advanced that he was probably one Jean d'Outremeuse, a Liège historian, or Jean de Bourgogne, author of *De Pestilentia*.[92] His real identity need not concern us too much, since we are examining the document for its significance in demonstrating European attitudes toward the non-European world.

Its claim to "European" status partly lies in its wide dissemination. Though the work was originally composed in Anglo-Norman, C.W.R.D. Moseley has contended that, by 1400, some version existed in most European languages, with some 300 surviving manuscripts.[93] But, in truth, Mandeville's European concern derives more from the body of material on which he based his text than on versions of his text itself.

Mandeville's Travels purports to be an account of a journey to the Holy Land, but the listener/reader is led off to Turkey, Tartary, Persia, Egypt, India, and, of course, the empire of the Great Khan. In the process, the work gives an account of the customs and mores of the people Mandeville encountered. The account is as "accurate" as any of the others we have examined, for, intermingled with his almost theoretical dependency on real travel writers, is the usual array of legends — accounts of monsters, Alexander's lost tribes, Amazons, Prester John, gold and spices, and the search for Paradise and the ideal state. "Mandeville" becomes a stand-in, even a sobriquet, for a European male persona.

Mandeville creates himself within the text as a "character" of fictional reality — even providing his alter ego with a shield, as in a British Library manuscript copy.[94] As with Polo, circumstances of confinement force him to pen his narratives, but, in his case, arthritic gout is substituted for Polo's incarceration. The writer attempts to make the fictitious character real by giving him a place of birth, St. Albans in England. He tells us with great precision that he embarked on his travels on September 29, 1322. But the "fiction" is circumscribed within the larger design; at the end, we are again reminded of his departure date and told that he has now returned home. Beginning and end mark the two halves of the shell in which Mandeville's narrative is encased, and both have their locus at home, in the realm of the "normal." "Home," therefore, marks the contextual center against which the exotic and macabre may best be understood by his medieval audience.

After our readings of previous sojourners, Mandeville's hyperboles seem relatively tame. Alongside Polo's "trees that bear flour," he finds "trees that bear poison."[95] In a land of much warfare, Mandeville observes God's grace in fish that come ashore voluntarily and "offer themselves to be killed without any compulsion."[96] We note that we are observing here the refinement of the travel narrative, where it is not enough simply to relate marvels; rather, the marvels must reveal the moral dualism in life itself.

All of the misfits of the medieval bestiaries are represented in Mandeville, almost as if he is intentionally seeking to convey a total picture of European beliefs. Moseley, depending mainly on the British Library Egerton text, has translated Mandeville"s observations as follows:

There are many different kinds of people in these isles. In one, there is a race of great stature, like *giants*, foul and horrible to look at; they have *one eye only*, in the middle of their foreheads. They eat *raw flesh and raw fish*. In another part, there are ugly *folk without heads*, who *have eyes in each shoulder*. . . . In yet another part, there are *headless men*. . . . In another isle there are ugly fellows whose *upper lip is so big* that when they sleep in the sun they cover all their faces with it. In another there are people of small stature, *like dwarfs*, a little bigger than pygmies . . . when they must eat *they suck their food through a reed or pipe*. In another isle there are people whose *ears are so big* that they hang down to their knees. In another, people have *feet like horses*. . . . In another isle there are people [who] are hairy . . . another isle where the people are *hermaphrodite*. . . . There is still another isle where the people have only *one foot, which is so broad that it will cover all the body and shade it from the sun.* . . . There is another isle where *people live just on the smell of a kind of apple.*[97] [Emphasis added]

I have quoted this at some length because it demonstrates something of Mandeville's intentions. He wishes to render every mythological belief in the context of his "discovery." The above quotation therefore lists, in order, the giants whom Alexander defeated in India; the Monoculi, also noted as Ulysses' Cyclops; the Alexandrian Raw-Meat-Eaters, usually shown in medieval illustrations holding a bowl and a piece of flesh; the Plinian Blemmyae of the Libyan deserts and the Plinian Epiphagi of Nilotic or Indian origin; the Amyctyroe, with prominent lips; the Pygmies, said by Homer and Herodotus to exist in Africa and India; the Straw-drinkers who, according to Pliny, live in Ethiopia; the Panoti or "all ears," who utilize their ears for flying; the Plinian Hippopodes, or "horse-feet," who, according to Pliny, live near the Baltic; the Androgini, possessing the genitals of both males and females who, again according to Pliny, live in Africa; the one-legged Sciopods of India, who lie on their backs, using their enormous feet to shelter themselves from the sun; and the Astomi, or Apple-Smellers, again according to Pliny, who dwell near the Ganges and exist by smelling flowers and fruits.[98]

The "elsewhere" where the monsters are located, notably "India" and Africa, would be transposed or at least searched for in the New World. Indeed, Friedman, from whom I have taken some of the preceding explanations, has written that:

The actual inhabitants of the New World did not fit easily into the categories of most of the Plinian races, but there was one figure with whom they were identified. This was the hairy wild man or savage man, not an original Plinian monster but a descendant of several, who begins to appear more and more frequently in European art and literature of the Middle Ages.[99]

This new creature is a kind of composite of Mandeville's monsters. He is described and drawn as nude and hairy, with a club in his hand.

This was, in large measure, an image that European illustrators foisted on the Native American Indian. Friedman has offered an illustration of two Indians supporting the shield of Charles V.[100] The male strides forward truculently — naked, with protruding lower lip, club in hand, and genitals dangling. The female seems more composed, albeit a trifle seductive, with her own genitalia hidden behind the escutcheon, but with her bare breasts prominently displayed. They are both extremely hairy, their barbaric hirsuteness in contrast with the cultivated plain and the mountain scenery in the background. In light of the unbridled sexuality that their postures suggest, Charles' armorial bearings, especially with its suggestion of the Christian cross, become a suitable allegory for understanding the European New World encounter. It explains the need for the serious debate between Sepúlveda and las Casas over whether Indians are "men" or "beasts"? Do "natural born" slaves exist, Sepúlveda asked, as Aristotle had contended? It is interesting to note that the misnomer "Indian," which includes a whole category of misunderstanding (since in the medieval period, "India" could mean Africa, India, or other parts of Asia), was not very helpful in dispelling the falsehoods that had been imposed on Native Americans.

Unrestrained sexuality, as suggested by the illustration, brings us to another issue with which Mandeville, as reporter, recorder, and synthesist, is concerned. This is the ever-present issue of loose morality, which usually hinged on medieval men's concepts of woman's place in the world and their refusal to accept any other alternative. Consequently, virginity is emphasized and praised. In the Egerton text of the travels, edited by Malcolm Letts, Mandeville affirms with some relish that, in one place he visited, "it is a full perilous thing to take the maidenhood of a maiden."[101] Mandeville also feminizes the very negative conception of Anthropophagi who consume their own parents. The introversion of standard European values means that these women make "mickle sorrow when that [their children] are born, and mickle joy when that they are dead."[102] In the Bodleian text, at least some explanation is given: "When they come into this world, they come to much sorrow and travail, and when they go out of this world they shall go to the joy of Paradise."[103]

As might be expected, Amazons pose a serious problem, since they are totally independent of males. Mandeville relates the familiar story of the "Land of Women," adding, a trifle contritely, "no man can live there, only women. This is not because, as some say, no man can live there, but because the women will not allow men to rule the kingdom." Preference for the company of their own gender forces a life-style on the Amazons that borders on what Mandeville concludes is crude female exploitation: "Beyond the water live their lovers to whom they go when it pleases them to have bodily pleasure."[104] The language here suggests a definite disapproval of such a liberated life-style.

Quite naturally, Prester John's empire is *de rigeur* for any medieval traveler. Prester John is extolled, having "many countries under his rule, in which are many noble cities and fair towns." Nevertheless, we are categorically informed, in keeping with the pragmatic political realities that Polo also recognized, that Prester John is not as wealthy as the Great Khan. Prester John is, however, a Christian, living in the midst of a land of "wonders." Situated nearby is Paradise, which is itself in close proximity to the Gravelly Sea (most likely a desert), "a vast sea of gravel and sand, and no drop of water in it." From nearby mountains, "flows a large river that comes from Paradise . . . full of precious stones."[105]

Within this idyllic setting, where spiritual well-being and physical abundance prevail, there is the expected hint of evil, the serpent of the Garden of Eden. In Mandeville's account, a mysterious fruit tree exists, from which none dare eat, for it represents a deceptive phantom. Mandeville pinpoints the dualism of good and evil, appearance and reality, coexisting side by side. Thus, the story of Prester John is improved and given a larger significance. In addition to moving in and out of his sources "with complete confidence," as Moseley has asserted,[106] Mandeville is also able to expand the scope of his account.

Columbus possessed a copy of Mandeville's travels, and, on his second voyage, according to Andrés Bernáldez, Columbus sought the rich city of "Catayo," which lay "near the lands of Prester John of the Indies, in the district which dominates and looks towards the north, and in that direction which the admiral sought it."[107] Mandeville cannot be considered merely an Old World romancer, for his authority profoundly affected New World exploration.

For medieval Europe, Prester John's kingdom and the khan's empire stood, above all, for abundance in spices and precious metals. I have tried to show that these were the physical *sine qua non* for Paradise. Prester John's *Letter* had related the story of the gold-digging ants, "the size of young dogs," that "dig for the purest of gold and bring it to light."[108] In the Nicobar Islands, Mandeville likewise recounts, even though the inhabitants "have heads like dogs" (the Alexandrian Cynocephali from India) and "go quite naked," "[e]ach one of them carries an ox made of gold or silver on his brow."[109] Similarly, in Silba (Sri Lanka), near a lake formed from the tears of Adam and Eve after their expulsion from Paradise, there are precious stones, under the constant guard of crocodiles and snakes. Nearby, more "pearls and precious stones are found."[110]

More successfully than any of the other voyagers, I believe, Mandeville is able to impose a grander design on his "plot." The horrible monsters, and even the depraved Amazons and hermaphrodites, offer us, by contrast, a glimpse of Paradise. Even though Mandeville is quick to add, "Of Paradise I cannot speak properly, for I have not been there," he nevertheless hints at its possibility.[111]

One such allusion to Paradise occurs in Mandeville's treatment of the theme of plenty and abundance. Of what is now Sri Lanka, he notes, "Here are two summers and two winters in a single year, and harvest also twice a year. And at all times of the year their gardens are full of flowers and their meadows green."[112] His most exalted language, rich in descriptive detail, is reserved for these intimations of perfection. Perversions like cannibalism do still exist, because humans are often incapable of striving for any real perfectability. One example is the people of "Melk" (Malacca): "There is no drink they like so much as man's blood, and *they call it God*"[113] [emphasis added]. Even in their depravity, Mandeville seems to recognize an inner need for some kind of spiritual ideal.

Mandeville does drink from the waters of Paradise, the fabled Fountain of Youth. To this he attaches his personal imprimatur, "I, John Mandeville, saw this well, and drank of it three times." He adds, with what is truly an awe-inspiring note of faith, "Ever since that time I have felt the better and healthier, and I think I shall do until such time as God in his grace causes me to pass out of this mortal life."[114]

Peter Martyr, the official historian to the papacy, had written about an island in the New World near Hispaniola, "celebrated for a spring whose waters restore youth to old men."[115] A very literal interpretation of this phenomenon caused Ponce de León and de Soto, among others, to seek it. Such hints at the pursuit of immortality afford us a kinder interpretation of the hard and often cruel men who invaded the New World, just as these indications of the idyllic suggest, for Mandeville, a larger context within which the journey may be understood.

From the start of Mandeville's "action," we are gradually led to the concept of Paradise. At an early stage in Egypt, there is the merest reminder of proximity to the eternal. The Nile, he tells us, "comes from the Earthly Paradise and flows through the deserts of India."[116] The notion is not as farfetched as it sounds, for the "visual" representation of the world that Mandeville describes was a very credible one at this time. In such a depiction, Moseley has concluded with reference to a T-O map, that "The Earthly Paradise is logically (and symbolically) enough at the top."[117] It should be noted that Mandeville's geographical *Weltanschauung* became the basis for the Catalan Atlas (1375) made by Abraham Cresques, the Bianco map (1434), and Behaim's globe (1492), which stood in the Nuremburg Rathaus until the early sixteenth century.

Mandeville does not devote too much time to describing the Old Man of the Mountain and his false Paradise. Instead, he is intent on relating to us the possibility of fulfillment in a real Paradise. Naturally, this Earthly Paradise cannot be reached, as Mandeville also testifies. But, for one who has not visited it, he certainly evokes a startling word picture of "the highest land on earth . . . so high it touches the sphere of the moon," "encircled by a wall [of] ever burning fire, which is the flaming sword that God set up before the entrances that no man should enter." This is the correct and typical view of medieval man, and yet Mandeville's language introduces a sense of awe. From the spring issue four rivers. One, the Ganges, has "many precious stones . . . and much gold in the gravel." The second is the Nile, which medieval maps had shown running south to north and linking up with the Ocean Sea. Third is the Tigris, so called "after an animal of the same name" and, fourth, the Euphrates, where "many good things grow."[118] Although most of the material is "borrowed," when put together by Mandeville, the whole constitutes a kind of personal anthology in which, in M. C. Seymour's words, "he "accurately incorporates much, indeed most, of medieval knowledge of the world."[119]

In the Hakluyt edition of Mandeville's work, three major texts are translated — the Egerton Text (British Library), the Paris Text (Bibliothèque Nationale), and the Bodleian Manuscript. Despite variations in the narrative and even the inclusion of sections not common to all, they still show how the pilgrimage to the edge of the world directly leads to a search for human perfection. Prester John and the Great Khan become symbolic expressions not merely of the virtuous god/king but also of possibilities that extend beyond a Paradise of the other world and lead us back to this. In the final sense, *Mandeville's Travels* sets off on a search for the perfect state, a quest that would later be undertaken in Sir Thomas More's *Utopia* (1516), Tomasso Campanella's *City of the Sun* (1602), Francis Bacon's *New Atlantis* (1627), and James Harrington's *Commonwealth of Oceania* (1656).

Particularly, through Marco Polo and John Mandeville (and, of course, emanating from Pliny, the Alexander romances and medieval belief), the entire paraphernalia of European belief was transferred to the New World. Thus, the peoples of the New World and Africa became known to Europe through the travel literature of another domain. The old stereotypes were merely consolidated and given a new application. The printing press aided in disseminating these particular ideas about the non-European world, partly spurred on by Turkish encroachments on the eastern border of Europe (particularly Hungary and Austria), where Suleyman the Magnificent sought territorial expansion at the expense of Charles V. The two main purveyors of medieval belief were the Spaniards and the Portuguese, although the French, the Dutch, and the English contributed their own store of fabulous expectation.

We have already noted that Columbus sought monsters and found them in Hispaniola. Later, he would inquire about these among the "cannibal" Caribs. He also sought and found the flip side to this — the Earthly Paradise. This search did not end in 1493. Later conquistadors sought both El Dorado and the Fountain of Youth — two phantoms, as I have suggested, of European lore first implanted on the East of Prester John. Indeed, both George Boas in *Essays on Primitivism and Related Ideas in the Middle Ages*[120] and George P. Hammond in "The Search for the Fabulous in the Settlement of the Southwest,"[121] have demonstrated how these ideas persisted well beyond the perimeter of Hispanic influence and, indeed, by the sixteenth and seventeenth centuries, had become part of a total European world view.

All of this mistaken lore was synthesized into the New World "Wild Man," who was first an "Indian" and later a "Negro." The consequences were twofold. First, the "Wild Man" was seen as badly in need of "civilization," so no means should be spared to accomplish this. Second, the "Wild Man" obviously inhabited a "wilderness," which belonged to no one and had to be tamed. Both conquistador and colonist accepted *in toto* the apparent need to redeem the Wild Man, but the idea of an empty wilderness that was specifically provided for God's Chosen was peculiar to North American colonial endeavor.

As seen, the concept of the Wild Man was a reality from the Middle Ages. Lewis Hanke has ably summarized its prevalence and wide dispersal:

They were depicted on the facades of churches, as decorations for manuscripts, and in tapestries, as ferocious beings of wild men rending lions barehanded or smashing their skulls with trees or mighty clubs. Wild men served as jamb figures on the facade of the fifteenth-century San Gregorio monastery in Valladolid in which Las Casas lived during the 1550 disputation with Sepúlveda. The wild man motif was much used in Spain, crossed the Atlantic with Spanish workmen, and is seen on the facade of the Casa del Montejo in Yucatan, built in 1549. Wild men also supported the arms of Charles V in Tlaxcala.[122]

Hanke stated that it was therefore not surprising to read that the inhabitants of the New World were blue in color with square heads.

Above all, Wild Men needed a god. Because they were not privy to European Christianity and thus were unable to recognize a Judeo-Christian god, they were especially prone to associate the male European newcomer with a deity. This belief is seen at its historical best in the Cortés/Montezuma encounter, when Montezuma presumably saw Cortés as a returning god.

The European-as-God became a recurrent theme in literature. Witness, for instance, the character of Caliban (itself a corruption of "cannibal") and his attitude to Prospero, or, even more ridiculously, his ardent desire to view the jesters, Stephano and Trinculo, as gods. Note also how Crusoe imposes on Friday all of the stereotypes of a previous age; Friday is seen as wild, untutored, un-Christian, and his first action is to recognize Crusoe as "master" and kiss his foot.

From public forum to the church and later publicized by the printing press, the Wild Man became the inhabitant of the New World. Because the indigenous people were unaware of this, their reactions tended to be in sharp contrast to these expectations. Nonetheless, they were often interpreted in such a way that any action on their part suggested elements of the "wild" and the "savage." Thus, while their domain in the New World was, ironically, "Utopia," they were simultaneously the bearers of this new "fiction" foisted upon them, namely the "Noble Savage."

Perhaps, in our new environmental zeal, we are again imposing on indigenous peoples the reverse aspects to our own shortcomings, thereby once more enforcing a newer savage nobility on them. Events have come full circle, whereby the mythologies of Europe, partly accepted even by New World indigenous peoples, become part of the agreed-upon discourse through which we again try to come to terms with our environment. Our inherited language and the burden of our history still force us to assume old patterns of verbal, visual, and viewed responses, which deprive us of any real or intimate understanding of others or of ourselves. We are still "new" in this New World, both to the land and its people.

Chapter 4 _____

African Voyages:
"Discovery" of Europe

Up until now, we have concerned ourselves with "encounters" primarily between European and "others" — Asians, Arabs, and Africans. We will now intentionally invert our order and examine how Africa has engaged in contact. We shall attempt to view this from an Afro-centric perspective, accepting with little question what Africans say about themselves, and noting, as we did with Europeans, that "movement" — the physical passage from x to y — results in new ways of interpreting the world.[1] Of course, a new centering point is established with Africa as its hub. Beyond lies the unfamiliar, the strange, the macabre. Here we cannot rely on conventional travel accounts. Instead we must extrapolate from folkloric and historic accounts the major issues of African contact and learn how this contact acted as a transforming agent in global culture. Therefore, new "facts" and "fictions" may be utilized to put forward an equally plausible argument to answer a different question — who discovered Europe? Various arguments, some a trifle tongue in cheek, may be marshalled. As we examine the anthropological argument and place it side by side with African "mythology," an equally strong case may be made for African "discovery," if only to argue that both African and European viewpoints eventually become absurd. Nevertheless, since Africans "encountered" Europeans at various stages of the prehistorical and historical record, they too can make a very plausible case for "discovery." The rebuttal may be made that Western scholarship does not accept all of what is offered here, but that is just the point. We have so far gone along with the idea that the wildest Western imaginings constituted sacrosanct fact. It seems only fair to marshal a counter-argument that, simply put, turns the tables.

There are six ways in which contact between Europe and Africa can be synthesized around our basic concept of physical movement:

1. Prehistoric examinations reveal that, if life began in Africa, then the earliest links obviously occur there. African myths can be selected to demonstrate two important aspects of primordial human experience — origin and migration.

2. Africans intermingled with Native Americans in what later would be called the New World. They had traveled from earliest times, later embarking on similar encounters with other peoples of the world. A common endeavor of reaching out thus links Africans and Europeans.

3. The next important association occurs with real historical linkages, from the earliest Egyptian period, 5,000 years ago. Egypt, Nubia, the Bible, and the Classical past all reinforce one another and become relevant.

4. From the eighth century until well into the fifteenth, the African presence has been noted, not only in the flowering civilizations of the African continent itself, but also in the part that Africa played, through the Moorish conquest, in inventing and revitalizing Europe, thus making the Renaissance possible.

5. African expansionism, of course, manifested itself most clearly in the post-Portuguese exploration period. Africans, from the sixteenth century onward, lived in Europe and contributed, as Afro-Europeans, to Europe. By the eighteenth century, there were African writers, lecturers, essayists, and professors, affecting European life and letters.

6. The major movement of the slave trade transferred Africans to Europe, the Middle East, and the New World. In varying degrees, Africans took aspects of their culture with them; these are particularly manifest today in Cuba, Haiti, Brazil, New Orleans, South Carolina, and the English-speaking Caribbean.

Africa, then, in these six ways, underwent its own encounter with Europe. By the twentieth century, population movements were taking people of African origin back to Africa, to Europe, and other parts of the world. Thus, the entire drama is almost cyclical, in that the culture changes and is changed, refurbishes and is refurbished.

Any attempt at discussing the European encounter in the New World first necessitates an examination of the enormous role that Africa has played. Hitherto, cultural historians have admitted to a small degree of interaction during the Moorish Conquest, but this ignores the fact that the entire New World experience, as we know it today, would have been impossible, were it not for African participation.

In the following sections, we shall therefore look at the nature of African cultural experience as it relates to the larger human drama of "movement," human origins, and migration, as well as Africa's contribution to the cultural synthesis that fed both the Classical and the Renaissance European past. We will show that the African presence in world affairs did not begin with European travel accounts or the Portuguese West African exploration. We will use anthropological information better to understand the nature of African archetypal travel and contact. The process has been a long one and goes back to a time when our world was less divided and our cultures more interdependent.

PREHISTORICAL PROTO-JOURNEYS

Who discovered Europe? We do not usually ask this question since, imprisoned as we are by Euro-centricity, we tend to think of Europe as the original source. The anthropological record tells us something different, although, in the 1890s, the major focus was still on Europe. In the mid-1800s, Neanderthal Man was found in France and Germany. Later, *Homo erectus* was identified as Java Man and Peking Man, but Charles Darwin suggested that Africa would reveal the earliest remains of human ancestry.[2] Darwin's prediction came true. In 1924, at Taung, South Africa, a six-year-old child, the so-called "Taung Baby," was found and identified by Raymond Dart. Later, the fossil would be given the name *Australopithecus africanus* (Southern African Ape-man). The name indicated that the fossil was in the direct line to later hominids, including *Homo sapiens*.

Dart's discovery met with great hostility. Few in the European world wanted to admit even the vague possibility that human beings could have originated in Africa. For the next few decades, however, locations in southern, eastern, and northeastern Africa produced additional specimens of the human family tree. There were two branches of the australo-pithecines — *Australopithecus africanus* and an extinct *robustus*. Louis Leakey and his wife, Mary Leakey, continued the search in Olduvai Gorge in present-day Tanzania. By 1959, the skull of *Australopithecus robustus* (Robust Ape-man) had been found, perhaps the earliest form of the family "Hominidae," which included *Australopithecus robustus*, *Australopithecus africanus*, and *Homo sapiens*. The Leakeys' find was a specialized form that had lived all over eastern and southern African between 1 million and 2 million years ago.

In 1964, Leakey established that *Homo habilis* (Tool-making Man) from Olduvai Gorge (actually another australopithecine) was another ancestor of humans on the African continent. *Homo habilis* was between 1.8 and 1.2 million years old. Other finds from the famous "Bed 1" and "Bed 2" of Olduvai Gorge confirmed that *Homo erectus* (erect man), about 1.5 million years old, had a common ancestor in the australopithecines.[3]

For anthropologists, the East African Rift Valley opened up new sites that, as Donald Johanson has pointed out, could be dated. From Taung northward through Olduvai Gorge and Laetotil, up through the area around Lake Turkana, and northeast to Hadar, fossils of the oldest variety, as demonstrated by potassium-argon dating, have been identified.[4]

Additionally, in the fall of 1981, Desmond Clark, Tim White, and Johanson himself identified the remains of what was possibly another branch of human ancestors, going back beyond 4 million years. This was the famous find at Afar involving *Africanus afarensis*. Johanson has stated that the striking feature of the find was that "Lucy" walked upright, although she was too small to be termed a human being. But she was bipedal, "ancestral to humans," and, thus, the first voyager.[5]

Simply put, the Leakeys refused to accept the Lucy find as a truly distinct australopithecine. Anthropologists have differed as to whether *africanus* and *robustus* represented two separate species. Others have suggested that the split showed racial or even gender differences. Still others have argued that *robustus* was a type of genetic dead end, whereas *africanus* was the true ancestor of modern humans. All that we need note is that the oldest forms of human evolutionary life have been found in Africa and that this area thus marks the cradle of human life and the starting point of all movement.

Anthropologists have further concluded that the australopithecines utilized tools that were fashioned from stone and that, in all probability, they were hunter-gatherers. They had made several important steps toward evolving as *Homo sapiens*. First, they had switched from forest and tree life to open country and savanna dwelling. Second, they cooperated in hunting, thus mixing a carnivorous diet with their previously herbivorous pattern. Third, this change opened up for them new physical and cultural possibilities, since now, obviously, their time was not solely devoted to stalking a single monotonous activity.

One common point of agreement among anthropologists is that the australopithecines did not leave Africa. Thus, if australopithecines did not coexist with the first humans, then the first humans evolved from them, there on the African continent, and literally walked into and out of the continent.

Evidence collected thus far shows that even the beginnings of early human family life were in Africa. In *Lucy's Child*, Johanson has detailed how he went to the Olduvai Gorge, finding the "First Family" who lived near the lakeshore some 1.8 million years ago. They existed in a band, searched for food, and fashioned crude tools.[6] Now we are in definite contact with people who made the first journey.

From the confinement of eastern and southern Africa, groups migrated north and west to Europe, eastward to Asia, and, some 30,000 years ago, across the Bering Straits to America. Over land bridges established during the Ice Ages, humans followed the herds as far afield as various Pacific islands, Australia, and New Zealand. *Homo sapiens* evolved between 40,000 and 100,000 years ago.

How then does one answer the question, "Who discovered Europe?" Part of the response lies in the evolution and dispersal of humans who originated in Africa. The French priest, Jean Baptiste Siméon Teilhard de Chardin, after years of research in the Far East, bluntly responded by asserting that the African continent was the main birthplace of humans. Richard Ardrey has cited the favorable conditions in east and southern Africa; this environment, he contended in *African Genesis* "presented the planet with man."[7] Some have gone further, placing the flake stone tradition in Africa and arguing that the Oldwan tool, used for preparing meat and exploiting plant resources, was an indigenous African technology exported to other parts of the world. Richard Leakey stated in the first volume of the UNESCO *General History of Africa* that "the evidence available could suggest a migration of the handaxe people from Africa into Europe and Asia."[8]

Since we seek a "discoverer," we could, quite logically, suggest that all identification begins with the small semihuman from Afar. Lucy and her descendants are not only ancestors but also proto-voyagers who embarked on global travel that would eventually result in new racial groupings, national identities, and language variation. Their "text" lies in the skeletons that the anthropologists have so painstakingly reconstructed.

CREATION AND THE JOURNEY TOWARD HUMANNESS

To understand the concept of "Lucy," one of the first hominids on earth, we should not merely examine the anthropological record but also try to interpret what Africans themselves, in their oral literature, have to say about their origins. Like other people in the world, they use "myth" (actually creation accounts that are group-sanctioned) to explain their concepts of how humans originate. At another level, such "myth" also attests to the human journey out of Africa.

A Fon account explains creation this way:

Before anything at all was made, Mbere, the Creator, made man out of clay. He took clay, and he shaped it into a man. This was how man began, and he began as a lizard. This lizard, Mbere put it into a bowl of sea water. Five days, and this is what happened; five days passed with him in the bowl of water, and he had put him there, inside it. Seven days passed; he was in there for seven days. And the eighth day, Mbere took a look at him, and now the lizard came out; and now he was outside. But it was a man. And he said to the Creator: "Thank you!"[9]

Mbere is substituted for the woman for Afar, and the entire process of human evolution and development is rendered in metaphorical terms. Human beings, therefore, invent gods in order to explain their world, while gods, in turn, create humans, in order to define their own divinity. For the Berbers, "In the beginning, there was only one man and one woman and they lived not on the earth but beneath it."[10] This is another version of creation that is closely linked with the cycle of vegetation and growth.

In a way, all the accounts point toward the same end, genesis and exodus, but in proto-symbolic form. They sound as if they concern themselves with specific group issues, but, in reality, they are giving cosmic renditions of prehistorical events that are situated out of time. Creation accounts demonstrate how the world is given form and how humans are oriented in the world. Cosmogonic accounts thus express a philosophical and theological view of the world, through the use of order and sense, and are often dramatized in ritual.[11]

Dualisms, at the center of the creational force, help identify and maintain balance. Among the Dogon (Mali), Nommo is contrasted with Yurugu, who lives mateless in the wilderness, a kind of ultimate other. The creator deity creates an egg, within which are androgynous twins, the earth's ancestors. One frees himself from the egg, and it becomes necessary for the creator deity to sacrifice the other, in an effort to counterbalance this. The earth, no longer perfect, thus comes into being.[12]

Unlike anthropology, creation accounts do not present an ascent toward the human order but recall a previous time when humans, co-existing with gods, brought about their own imperfection or their final separation from perfection. Perhaps, because these accounts predate anthropological investigation, the view has to be solemn. Humans do not evolve; instead, they *devolve* from divine status. In a curious way, these accounts retell *homo*'s separation from *robustus* and, in turn, show how *homo* changes from being merely the inheritor of humanity to being the progenitor of all life.

Both the Fon human and the unnamed Dogon man and woman exist *out of time* in a remote place. The difference is surely that the Afar woman is *in time* and our modern methods of potassium-argon dating place her even more securely there. But this fact does not in any way suggest that any particular version has a greater preponderance of the truth. They both express truths; creation accounts do so in universal terms, and anthropology and prehistory in human words.

According to Ulli Beier,[13] the Fulani believe that Doondari created the world from a drop of milk. This is surely the main point about all the creation accounts from Africa: Human beings direct the drama of creation, inventing the creator and the order of "creation." As a consequence, gods in the African context are humanized. In a Kono account, at the beginning of time, only Sa (Death), with his wife and daughter, existed. In a Maloxi account from Zambia, Nyambe "lived on earth with his wife, Nasilele, long, long ago." At the very beginning of time, these could be considered solitary australopithecines who existed in a timeless realm.

African oral belief recognizes that life on earth is human-centered. In a way, this means that accounts are not overly concerned with an emerging cosmos. Molefi Asante has argued that few African creation accounts describe "the universe emerging out of chaos."[14] Human creation by gods was enough to explain the world; thus, E. Bolaji Idowu has asserted that, for the Yoruba:

Someone who has made a careful study of all the material which our sources afford will have no hesitation in asserting that Olódùmarè [Creator God] was the origin and ground of all that is. This is the fact which impresses itself upon us with the force of something incontrovertible. From all the evidence which we gather from the traditions, the Yoruba have never, strictly speaking, really thought further back than Olódùmarè, the Deity.[15]

In the Western world, there exists a sharp distinction between creationism and evolution; in the African world, the gods initiate the process of "evolution," so there is no opposition. Humans come from gods and embark on an archetypal journey through various, clearly distinct phases.

"Let there be humans" is the essence of the African account of creativity, played out in countless forms throughout the continent. Such a cosmic drama places humans at the center of all things; they are triumphant and whole but never perfect. There is no Eden and no Fall, although Western interpretations have sometimes lent this view to the creation accounts.

Because the contact between gods and humans is never severed, African religions constantly invoke gods as participants in human affairs. The chain and ladder symbolize physical ways in which the evolution from God is most effectively shown. Gods utilize these to maintain their link with humans and, conversely, humans establish this image as a reminder of their own evolution from gods.

An examination of peoples anywhere in the world will reveal a similar storehouse of folk belief and oral narrative. But what we are attempting to assert is that, in Africa, the oral account of human genesis and exodus is actually a way of interpreting, in symbolic form, what we understand from the anthropological account. In other words, we can take the prevalence of certain motifs in African "myth" (the creation accounts) and "legend" (journeys) as indicators that African groups, collectively considered, understood the nature of human evolution, development, and migration — the archetypal journey toward humankind.

Herman Baumann in *Schöpfung und urzeit des menschen* (1936)[16] identified specific cosmic occurrences in the cosmic cycle. He pointed to the Great Flood, the Collapse of the Firmament, the Big Fire, and Death as cataclysmic experiences. These can also be used to explain not merely human experience in Africa, but also the actual scripted details of what happened in the physical world at large. The "Great Flood" could well constitute ancient recollections of what followed after the Ice Ages; the "Collapse of the Firmament" may represent some primordial earthquake, resulting in enormous loss of life; the "Big Fire" might indicate volcanic eruptions or vivid descriptions of areas of intense heat; finally, "Death" may represent not just physical death of a person or even an etiological explanation for the group, but may instead attempt to describe the ultimate "death" or separation of one group from another as they went their ways. Granted that these occur in traditional oral accounts of "other" peoples, they may well, in view of the anthropological record, take on a proto-mythic quality for all.

African oral accounts therefore involve two specific paired themes: Creation and Separation; Birth and Death; evolution and dispersal; indeed, Genesis and Exodus. We will now discuss the second aspects, whereby humans moved out of Africa into a vaster global landscape, in what may truly be described as the primal archetypal voyage that defines all others.

HUMAN EXODUS

Humans in creation accounts are always made to undergo a passage of time, a type of womb-like gestation, which could well reflect the movement out of Africa. Mbere puts man in a bowl, and, in the Berber account, the two humans are said to "live not on the earth but beneath it."[17] As humans disperse, the attempt is made to explain how the progression occurs. Maria Leach has described the process thus: "When the hero is man rather than a god, myth becomes legend."[18] Chronologically, "legend" occurs after creation, after evolution, thus relating the *human* drama. For our purposes here, dispersal is paramount.

Jan Vansina has reminded us in his study of oral tradition that "there is no such thing as absolute truth, and no one can formulate an 'unchanging law of history' on the basis of our knowledge of the past. The truth always remains beyond our grasp, and we can only arrive at some approximation of it."[19] There are different types of "approximations" within the accounts themselves, and still others that divorce oral "versions" from scientific "certainty." Somewhere, in between the two, we can perhaps locate an important element of "truth."

Typically, the accounts that best describe human migration are the numerous ones within hero-quest stories, which Joseph Campbell has subdivided into tales of departure, initiation, and return. "Departure," on a grand scale, is a moving away from the familiar, from one's own people; "initiation" is the manner in which the "hero" becomes used to dealing with a foreign, even antagonistic, landscape; "return," in the grand scheme, is not only a going back to the familiar (although this does occur), but also a reentry into a newer group understanding.

Placide Tempels, in *Bantu Philosophy*, has explained why the "hero" is triumphant. He possesses *muntu* or living, personal force, "the force or the being that possesses life that is true, full, and lofty."[20] Tempels has also asserted that the human "is the dominant force among all created visible force."[21] Thus, this "hero," unlike Campbell's culture heroes, stands for and symbolizes a primal human being.

When this human being embarks on the journey, which is not personal, tribal, or even racial, (s)he cannot be defeated, for this is the factual account of successful evolution. The vital force in humans, living or dead, "can directly reinforce or diminish the being of another man," as well as of inferior "beings" or "forces" — what Tempels has summed up as "animal, vegetable, or mineral."[22] Humans are therefore in a unique position of dominance and are subsequently held responsible. As Giambattista Vico asserted, the accounts do not really moralize but instead project, in seemingly theoretical terms, what is obviously pragmatic.

Humans exist, paradoxically, in a mortal world where there is no death. John Mbiti has commented:

The dying person is being cut off from human beings, and yet there must be continuing ties between the living and the departed. Relatives and neighbours come and bid farewell to the dying man and to mourn his departure, and yet there is continuity through his children and through the rituals which unite the two worlds.[23]

This is part of what Claude Lévi-Strauss termed the "complete range of unconscious possibilities." To comprehend the union of this concept, one must go beyond anthropology, beyond history, and "beyond the conscious and always shifting images which men hold,"[24] toward an African account that helps put these aspects of the journey into focus.

TUTUOLA'S TEXT AND THE JOURNEY

Amos Tutuola's *The Palm-Wine Drinkard*, published in 1953, offers an excellent means of understanding how genesis and exodus occur in African literary form. At the same time, Tutuola showed us how "speech accounts" may be transformed into "writing accounts."

In literal terms, the plot is about a palm-wine drinker who sets out to find his dead palm-wine tapper. He seeks him in various places, only to discover, when he does find him, that the dead are not allowed to return to the living. Still, the palm-wine drinker is given an egg with which he saves the world.

Even in skeletal outline, we can note the enormous gift Tutuola has given African literature. Since he was himself not part of a tradition of written literature, he wrote down, simply, in a new spoken English, what was actually a compilation of Yoruba folk utterance. Above all, he combined two major elements of the journey — physical movement and spiritual growth.

At the beginning, we are in a primeval period, certainly out of time, discovering the paradoxical situation of a living man who is about to seek Death's town. Like Orpheus, Hercules, Ulysses, Aeneas, indeed Dante himself, this hero's quest leads him through a variety of crucial encounters. The landscape is bare, except for:

Many wild animals and every place was covered by thick bushes and forests; again, towns and villages were not near each other as nowadays, and I was travelling from bushes to bushes and from forests to forests and sleeping inside it for many days and months, I was sleeping on the branches of trees, because spirits etc were just like partners.[25]

Tutuola is a "natural," a virtually unschooled writer, who spent most of his working life in a fairly menial position with the Nigerian Broadcasting Corporation, being scorned by the "real" writers of contemporary Africa. But his first "novel" introduced into African fiction what no other writer had managed, by taking the raw stuff of oral accounts and shaping it into literature. In the above reference, note how timelessness is rendered: Drinkard exists in a primordial time amid animals and forest. Like a pre-Lucy hominid, he sleeps "on the branches of trees." Most importantly, he coexists, not merely with the seen *physical* reality of his environment, but with the equally seen *spiritual* reality. However, the "I"-narrator is very human. In a forerunner to this work, Tutuola wrote of an encounter with Ghost, "I replied with fear that I was a human-being."[26]

Tutuola unconsciously incorporates three traditions into his palimpsest. First, there is the "oral," specially "edited" for presentation in written form. Second, there is the "vernacular," using other writings in his native Yoruba, especially those by writers like D. O. Fagunwa. Third, there is the overall theme of human origin and dispersal, into which the entire "plot" is situated.[27]

At the "oral" level, several good examples of Yoruba tales are actively interwoven. For instance, Tutuola borrows one account of a vain young woman who marries a Skull, another about magic food, and yet another about the quarrel between Heaven and Earth. The last story is often used in Yoruba folklore to explain the vulture's outcast status; Tutuola, however, places it at the very end of his "novel," and has a slave take a sacrifice to the sky. This action causes rain to fall, and Heaven and Earth are reconciled. The oral account is thus altered to fit the general thrust of Tutuola's narrative.[28]

At the "vernacular" level, Tutuola tries out what he knows has "worked" best in the written literature. Since 1949, Fagunwa's works had been much admired by Yoruba readers and, in 1968, Wole Soyinka translated from Yoruba Fagunwa's *The Forest of a Thousand Daemons*. We may note Fagunwa's influence on Tutuola. Thee is Fagunwa's direct appeal to the reader, his use of Yoruba proverbs, and the complete accommodation of the spirit world with the human world. Tutuola thus borrows part of his own view of the African world from Fagunwa, who seemed to him even closer to the roots of African culture.

Referring to Tutuola's earlier manuscript, Bernth Lindfors has summed up:

Certainly there are striking similarities in some of the events recounted. For instance, in the course of fighting with a fierce ghost in the First Town of Ghosts, Tutuola's Wild Hunter breaks his cutlass on the adversary's body and The Ghost calmly repairs it and returns it to him so they can resume their battle; Fagunwa's Akara-Ogun is offered the same courtesy in his duel with Abako. . . . Next the Wild Hunter is victimized by a ghost who mounts and rides him as a horse; so is Akara-Ogun.[29]

Tutuola does not use Fagunwa only as an indicator of the direction he is pursuing, however. He integrates the experiences that Fagunwa relates only as "adventures" into his own larger creation of a literary work about a human journey through death toward a new life.

In such a grand scheme, Tutuola best shows us his total African approach when his hero enters Deads Town. There, "As soon as the dead man who was asking us questions saw us moving he ran to us and said that he told us to go back to my town because alives could not come and visit any dead man in the Deads' Town, *so he told us to walk backward or with our back and we did so*[30] [emphasis added]. The act of walking backward (we are reminded unwillingly of European monsters), away from Deads Town, attempts to retrace prehistory and history, going back to an immediate past. Indeed, the entire section about the dialogue with the Deads is an attempt, in written literature, to establish contact with the ancestors. Since we are discussing an Africa that mothered humankind, we are actually naming the ancestors of the human race itself. Walking backward is an impossible task, for it is not possible to reclaim the pristine state of the human race, back before the palm-wine tapper fell from his tree, before he had the opportunity to tap the wine of life. Tutuola writes that "both white and black deads were living in the Deads' Town."[31] It is a kind of graveyard of the universe.

Ancestors may, however, provide aid and succor. This comes in the form of an egg, which the hero has to guard first from the Deads, who attempt to bother him and his companion; then from the creature who captured the egg, the hero, and his wife in a bag; then from the hungry creature's stomach and from mountain creatures. Tutuola is relating the task of preserving life from omnipresent death and the need to make the journey outward, which will indeed preserve the egg of the world. He is also adding to our understanding of the concept of the journey.

In the Yoruba creation account, a firm link is established between creator and created, palm tree and wilderness:

When Olódùmarè and certain divinities resided in the heavens above, the earth was like a marsh and wasteland. He provided him [the actual Creator God] with some soil, a hen with five toes, and a pigeon. . . . The hen spread the soil, the waters were driven back, dry land appeared. . . . The first trees were the palm.[32]

Tutuola changes the order, gives new properties to some items associated with the creation account, and *invents* a new narrative structure.

African narratives may thus be interpreted to help explain all human origin and dispersal. Equally, creation accounts among various African peoples help inform us about the nature of the cosmos and even indicate how a proto-African people may have become the parents of all mankind. Written accounts, such as Tutuola's, define the novel in Western form and simultaneously demonstrate how African cultural forms remain relevant to the world at large.

The Yoruba world view that Tutuola relates will later help "civilize" the New World, particularly in the forms of *candomblé* and *macumba* in Brazil, *santería* in Cuba, and *vodun* in Haiti. Since these religious syntheses have become a way of life for millions of New World people, of all racial persuasions, may we not also contend that Africans demonstrably civilized the New World?

THE DOGON UNIVERSE AND THE MANDINGO ATLANTIC VOYAGES

African creation accounts, therefore, show us important stages in human development. We have examined some at the cosmic level, which deal with human genesis and exodus, and we have noted how, in the text of at least one African writer, they are brought together. African creation accounts may also help us to understand the world at other levels and from another viewpoint. For instance, the Dogon people describe a cosmography whose aspects were unknown to the European world until a century ago. Similarly, the Mandingo people relate an account of two trans-Atlantic voyages. In both instances, we note how Africans continue the process of "discovery" through their knowledge of astronomy and of its possible applications in travel.

Because African culture is never theoretical nor abstract and because it always addresses itself to the functional, we look to the oral tradition for a variety of phenomenological explanations. As we attempt to interpret oral belief, we also discover anthropology, philosophy, and religion. Equally, we have utilized legends to tell us about population dispersal. Out of the total African *Weltanschauung* emerges "history," "geography," "literature," and many of the other ways in which the West has clothed its comprehension of the world. An African historian, D. T. Niane, has stressed that the West limits its understanding of oral literature because it is "all too often considered merely from the historical and literary points of view" or even as just quaint.

A powerful creation account from the Dogon culture reveals not only sophisticated concepts of ethics and astronomy but also a total world view that permeates their arts. Their village plan, in the form of a human being, incorporates the Nommo (the first created humans). A typical village "physiognomy" includes, at the head, the houses of the smithy and the men's houses; at the chest, the houses of leaders; at the hands, the women's houses; at the genitals, a mortar, which feeds the body, and an altar, which feeds the spirit. Finally, at the feet are the shrines that enable humans to interact with gods. From this architecture, any sculpture becomes a representation through which the Dogon consciously use a spiral form to symbolize "the continual expansion of the universe."[33]

In *Conversation with Ogotemmêli*, Marcel Griaule has showed that the Dogon concept of the universe is based on two phenomena: the vibration of matter and the movement of the whole cosmos.[34] The original life germ is a seed that, through internal vibration, bursts and reaches out to the entire universe. At the same time, this changing matter moves along a helical path. The Dogon thus express through continuous spiral movement, the conservation of matter:

In addition, this motion, which is represented graphically by a zig-zag line on the walls of sacred places, is said to symbolize the perpetual alternation of opposites — right and left, high and low, odd and even, male and female — and to reflect a principle of twinship which, ideally, should rule the reproduction of life.[35]

Dogon and other African ethnic groups therefore translate their reality into an ultimate "vital force" that permeates all things. In 1844, Friedrich Wilhelm Bressel "discovered" that Sirius probably had a binary star, but this was already known to the Dogon and had been rendered in their "mythology." Bressel made his assumption because Sirius seemed to wobble through space. Indeed, the companion to the Dog Star was not verified until 1862, when astronomers saw the very small "dwarf star," later called Sirius B.[36] But Sirius and Sirius B may be found in the Dogon seed and in the arrangement of their villages. Germaine Dieterlen has explained it in this way: "The Universe as a whole issued from an infinite smallness, created by the 'word' (*so*) of a single god, Amma; this is symbolized today on Earth, by both the fonio seed (*digitaria exilis*,

Dogon *pō*), and in space by a satellite of Sirius, the star Digitaria (*pō tolo*)."[37]

In "African Observers of the Universe," Hunter Havelin Adams has concluded as follows:

The Dogon say the "po tolo" (Sirius B), though invisible, is the most important star in the sky. It is the egg of the world, the beginning and ending of all things seen and unseen. The period of its orbit around Sirius (the visible one) is counted twice, that is, 100 years, corresponding with their concept of twin-ness, principles of imperfection/ perfection; singularity/duality; disorder/order; male/female; and human/divine. These principles of twin-ness are very important, for through their antagonistic yet complementary character, which the entire philosophical, social, and territorial organization of the Dogon reflects, a systematic knowledge of the nature and purpose of human existence is revealed to the initiate.

Sirius B is not only the smallest type of star in the sky, it is also the heaviest. It consists of a metal the Dogon call "sagala," which is a little brighter than iron and so heavy that all earthly beings combined cannot lift it (the Dogon know of 86 fundamental elements)! They say there is another star besides "po tolo" orbiting Sirius called "emme ya," which is larger than it but four times lighter and travels along a greater trajectory in the same direction and in a period of 50 years. This star "emme ya" (sun of women) has a satellite called "nyan tolo" (star of women).[38]

This is not a view with which Carl Sagan agrees. In *Broca's Brain*, he has devoted some time dispelling the belief that "myths" can reflect science, arguing that the Sirius B account might have been told to the Dogon at an earlier time by a missionary. Sagan has insisted that when "Griaule made mythological inquiries in the 1930's and 1940's, he had his own European Sirius myth played back to him."[39] But Griaule's work is convincing in its account of Dogon philosophy in terms of the total existence of the Dogon people, showing that "Dogon religion and Dogon philosophy both expressed a haunting sense of the original loss of twin-ness. The heavenly Powers themselves were dual, and in their earthly manifestations they constantly intervened in pairs."[40] To do what Sagan has suggested, the Dogon people would have had to reconstruct every aspect of their mythology as it applied to the universe and to daily life and then compel everyone to accept the new beliefs. This would clearly be an impossible task. In any event, we merely seek to show that it is plausible that this type of intricate knowledge of the stars may have helped Africans in their westward peregrinations.

In the same manner that a creation account from the Dogon explains distant cosmic events, an oral account from the Mandingo of Mali tells us about nearer historical occurrences. Ibn Fadl Allah Al-'Umari was a fourteenth-century Arab traveler who visited the court of the *Mansa* (Emperor) of Mali, then a large West African kingdom that extended to the coast. There he heard Mansa Kanku Musa give an account of his predecessor, Mansa Abu Bakr:

> He did not believe that the ocean was impossible to cross. He wished to reach the other side and was passionately interested in doing so. He fitted out 200 vessels and filled them with men and as many again with gold, water, and food supplies for several years. He then said to those in charge of embarkation, "do not return until you have reached the other side of the ocean or exhausted your food or water." They sailed away. Time passed. After a long time, none of them had returned. Finally one vessel, only one, returned. We asked its master what he had seen and heard: "We sailed on and on for a long time until a river with a violent current appeared in the middle of the sea. I was in the last vessel. The others sailed on and when they reached that spot they were unable to return and disappeared. We did not know what had happened to them. For my part, I came back from that place without entering the stream."[41]

Al-'Umari published this around 1342, in Cairo, as *Masalik al-absar fi Mamalik al-amsar*. It was reprinted in 1927 in Paris; J. M. Cuoq published a French translation in 1975 and Basil Davidson's *The Lost Cities of Africa* (1958) includes an English version.

Yet the account has not received its deserved attention, although, M. Hamidullah, in a 1958 article, borrowed a conclusion from M.D.W. Jeffreys' 1953 article, which had asserted that the "river with a violent current" was probably the Amazon.[42] C. L. Riley has confirmed in *Man Across the Sea* that this possibility exists.[43] After all, ocean currents can conceivably take ships westward across the Atlantic. Returning home might well be difficult, or it might not pose a problem, given a knowledge of ocean currents that may have been passed on to Columbus.[44]

A number of textual points make this account quite credible. First, even within the translation, certain oral techniques of the African *griots* or oral historians are apparent. The repetition, for instance, of "he" lends a rhythmic quality to the entire piece. Moreover, the sentences that all build up to the climactic "They sailed away" are very much in keeping with other surviving texts of African oral literature. Equally, as in any genuine oral account, the words are carefully used to contribute to the approximation of space and time. "After a long time, none of them had returned" is an excellent way of creating suspense for listeners, for they hang on the words, perhaps hoping for a different meaning. Reading the text is obviously different. The use of dialogue not only helps to authenticate the orality of the piece but also places it firmly within a tradition in which drums and masks help interpret the drama. Finally, these are the historical truths of a *griot*-king. Mamadou Kouyaté, one of the best-known *griots*, has affirmed that when reciting the history of one of the greatest Mali emperors, Sundiata:

I teach kings the history of their ancestors so that the lives of the ancients might serve them as an example, for the world is old, but the future springs from the past. . . . *My word is pure and free of all untruths; it is the word of my father's father.* I will give you my father's words just as I received them.[45] (emphasis added)

Merely on literary grounds, the account passes the credibility test. We noted with the Dogon that cosmic truths lay buried within metaphor, but here it is different. This Mandingo account is intended for a more general audience, to acquaint them with their history, indeed to tell the *mansa* and his people of the great valor and supreme abilities of their ancestors. Thus, in the final analysis, it is most appropriate for Al-'Umari to have *heard* of the achievements of one *mansa* from his successor.

In *The Black Discovery of America*, Michael Bradley has asserted that the intellectual climate of Mali was suitable for such a venture, since "beyond doubt, the Mali geographers possessed a knowledge of the distribution of lands and waters upon the earth more accurate than that of any European mariner of the time."[46] Moreover, J. Devisse and S. Labib have pointed out in the UNESCO *History of Africa* that "Navigation had certainly existed for a considerable length of time in all the coasts of Africa." Their conclusion is that Africans had, quite naturally, been curious about the sea and that activities described by the first European navigators prove that "a certain area of the sea, both to the west and to the east, had been mastered by the Africans."[47] In "Traditional African Watercraft," Stewart C. Malloy has found that western and central Africa alone formed part of an interlocking trade network that ran from the Mediterranean to West Africa and inward to Lake Chad.[48]

As if to support this, G. E. de Zurara has quoted the cautious reply given by one of the sailors whom Prince Henry had conscripted to explore the coast of West Africa:

How could we go beyond the boundaries set by our fathers? And what benefit can the Prince derive from the loss of our souls as well as our bodies, for it is obvious that we would be committing suicide? It is plain to see that there are neither men nor inhabited places beyond this cape [Cape Bojador]. . . . The currents are so strong that no ship which rounded the cape would ever be able to return.[49]

Yet, after several efforts, Portuguese caravels did go and return. Is it possible that they learned about the currents off West Africa from African sailors? Does this not have real relevancy when we realize that European New World exploration was preceded by Portuguese African exploration? And what, indeed, did Columbus himself learn on his voyage to Guinea? Samuel Eliot Morison, at least, has admitted that Columbus' West African apprentice voyage impressed him and must have helped to improve his seamanship.[50]

The oral account of the Mandingo voyage ends not with failure but with a second attempt. After the *mansa* heard about the first voyage: "He then ordered 2000 vessels to be fitted out, 1000 for himself and his men and 1000 for food and water. He then appointed me [Mansa Kanku Musa] his deputy, embarked with his companions, and sailed away. That was the last we saw of them, him and his companions."[51] The other end of the saga would occur in the African New World presence, long before Columbus, as the continued "discovery" of Europe by Africa was also played out in the New World. For instance, when Balboa and his party arrived at the northern section of the Isthmus of Panama, they identified Africans who "only live in the region one day's march from Quarequa, and they are fierce and cruel. It is thought that negro pirates of Ethiopia established themselves after the wreck of their ships in these mountains."[52] We can safely ignore the generic use of the term "Ethiopia" for Africa, as well as the stereotypical view of them as "fierce and cruel." But we cannot ignore a Black presence: Las Casas identified Blacks when describing an expedition by Vasco Núñez, as did Gonzalo Fernández de Oviedo and Antonio de Herrera. Herrera also alludes to a shipwreck of Black "Ethiopians."

Mandingo oral accounts, both internally and externally, indicate that African voyages to the New World did take place, and Spanish written accounts confirm that Blacks were living there when Europeans arrived. One need not pursue the matter any further: Africans anticipated Europeans in New World encounters and may have come even in pre-Christian times, as both Leo Wiener and Ivan Van Sertima have suggested.[53] In *Cosmos*, Carl Sagan has categorically concluded that:

Four hundred years before Eratosthenes, Africa had been circumnavigated by a Phoenician fleet in the employ of the Egyptian Pharaoh Necho. They set sail, probably in frail open boats, from the Red Sea, turned down the east coast of Africa up into the Atlantic, returning through the Mediterranean. This epic journey took three years.[54]

By the sixth century B.C., the circumnavigation of Africa by Africans had already been completed. It would take the Portuguese almost 2,000 years to duplicate this feat.

It matters little which African expedition, out of several possible ones, was encountered by the Spaniards. What seems more relevant is that African technology, knowledge of the stars and ocean currents, and navigational skills had brought Africa and Europe together. Can we then assert, as the Afro-centrics might, that Africans first created Europeans and then anticipated their presence in the New World?

EGYPT, NUBIA, THE BIBLE, AND CLASSICAL EUROPE

Most directly, Africa may be said to have "discovered" Europe from the eastern and western ends of the Mediterranean. At the eastern end, Egypt and Nubia directly influenced the culture of ancient Greece. At the western end, African armies moved across the Mediterranean from as early as Hannibal's time (some scholars have asserted that his elephants came from Nubia) and as late as the eighth century, with the Moorish invasion.

Recently, Egypt has again become the locus of an intense scholarly debate. To what extent — if any — did Egypt influence the culture of Greece and hence of Europe? Cheikh Anta Diop, a Senegalese historian, has argued quite convincingly that:

For us, the return to Egypt in all domains is the necessary condition for reconciling African civilizations with history, in order to be able to construct a body of modern human sciences, in order to renovate African culture. Far from being a reveling in the past, a look toward the Egypt of antiquity is the best way to conceive and build our cultural future. In reconceived and renewed African culture, Egypt will play the same role that Greco-Latin antiquity plays in Western culture.[55]

Diop has argued that "Egyptians perceived themselves as Blacks."[56] This point is where the major argument usually centers. The dispute is not easily settled, but, for Diop and many other historians, Egypt is the point of origin for all African civilization, where any discussion of human encounter must be initiated.

A second issue is the extent to which a Black Egypt influenced the growth and development of the rest of the world. Many writers have cited Herodotus, who argued quite categorically about practices "borrowed by Greeks from Egypt"[57] or, more emphatically still that "It was the Egyptians too who originated and taught the Greeks to use ceremonial meetings, processions, and liturgies."[58] In fact, Herodotus himself saw the Egyptians as "the most learned of any nation of which I have had

experience,"[59] who "keep to their native customs and never adopt any
from abroad."[60]

Herodotus' account of Egypt is found mostly in Book Two of *The
Histories*, written after his visit there between August and December,
around 460 B.C. His account was, therefore, based on personal
experience. He wrote about what he had seen and directly observed; for
instance, he described the Nile flood, Memphis, and the Pyramids. He
did not go beyond the First Cataract, so he was unable to relate much
about the Nubian influence on Egypt.

Herodotus did confirm the Nubian conquest of Egypt under Shabaka
(Herodotus calls him Sabacos), one of the Nubian kings of the Twenty-
Fifth Dynasty. Although the account is given in the manner of a legend,
independent historical investigation confirms that Neferkare Shabaka was
the second of five Nubian kings after the foundation of the Nubian
dynasty around 747 B.C.[61]

Diop has gone on to establish a firm association between an
indubitably Black Nubia and Egypt, which is sometimes even oddly
classified by scholars as the "Middle East":

As a matter of fact, the Negro characters of the Ethiopian or Abyssinian race have been
sufficiently affirmed by Herodotus and all the Ancients; there is no need to reopen the
subject. The Nubians are the accepted ancestors of most African Blacks, to the point
that the words Nubian and Negro are synonymous. Ethiopians and Copts are two
Negro groups subsequently mixed with white elements in various regions. Negroes of
the Delta interbred gradually with Mediterranean Whites who continually filtered into
Egypt.[62]

Diop has then shown that several customs, such as circumcision, were
handed down to the Semitic Middle East; likewise, kingship concepts,
cosmogonies, social stratification, and even matriarchy were passed on
from Egypt to the rest of Africa.[63]

The issues of the Blackness of ancient Egypt, its nurturing within the
African continent, and its influence on that continent and Europe have
become a rallying cry for contemporary Black nationalists. One of the
pioneers, Yosef A. A. ben-Jochannan ("Dr. Ben") has contended for
years, in books like *Africa: Mother of Western Civilization* and *Black
Man of the Nile and His Family*, that "ancient Libyans were Black," that
Judaism "had its real birth in Africa,"[64] and that Greek Philosophy "got
its beginnings from the Egyptians and other indigenous Africans of the
Nile Valleys and Great Lakes."[65] Dr. Ben's work is fiercely militant, and
its tone has consequently caused much of it to be discarded, despite some
careful scholarship.

Chancellor Williams has made an equally strident case in his books. In *The Destruction of Black Civilization*, he has contended that there has been a deliberate attempt to erase the African imprint from Egyptian history and that:

The Asians and their Afro-Asian offsprings set about to . . . destroy everything left by the Africans that indicated African superiority; . . . but where the temples, monuments, etc., were of such beauty and durability that destruction was less desirable than claiming the achievements as their own — in these cases, African inscriptions were systematically erased and replaced with Asian and new Egyptian inscriptions that gave to themselves the credit for whatever achievements there were.[66]

Whatever may or may not be the truth of this, what must be patently obvious is that it has become impossible to speak dispassionately of the influence of Egypt on Africa or, for that matter, Europe and the Western world.

Two important academicians have been Molefi Asante, who has utilized the Egyptian past to support his concept of Afro-centricity, and Maulana Karenga, who has used the philosophy of ancient Egypt as a way of understanding God. For Asante, the five Kemetic concepts of Beginning (Tep), Extensions (Pet), Festival (Heb), Circle (Sen), and Crowning Glory (Meh) "must be seen in the light of general African cultural developments," and this "has meant that the influence of Kemet continues unabated even in the language and behavior of African Americans."[67] For Karenga, in *The Book of Coming Forth by Day* (usually known as *The Book of the Dead*), "one finds theology and ethics, a philosophical anthropology and eschatology, hymns of praise and declarations of innocence from offenses to God"[68] that have become most relevant for African Americans in the twentieth century.

Originally, these writings consisted of the Coffin Texts (from c. 2000 B.C.), Pyramid Texts (from c. 2400 B.C.), and other works, including hymns to Ra, the sun god. In *Pharaohs and Mortals*, the authors have stated that the long spells of the Coffin Texts frequently incorporate "a conversation envisaged between the dead man or woman and a divine being."[69] In another instance, that of "The Instruction of King Amenemhat I," the authors have cited the lines, "When you lie down, guard your heart yourself, for no man has adherents on the day of woe"[70] as an example of how ancient Egyptians sought to reconcile the conflicting claims of humans, gods, and Pharaohs. What is most intriguing in the works of Asante and Karenga is how the interpretation shifts to include the African American search for identity in the twentieth century.

The African Presence in Early Asia has identified African influence in
ancient Sumer ("the formative civilizing influences of early West Asia"),
in Arabia and Sumeria, and in India where:

The original inhabitants were dark-skinned and closely resembled the Africans in
physical features. They founded the Indus Valley Civilization which, according to
historians, was one of the world's first and most glorious. Aryan tribes invaded India,
destroyed the Indus Valley Civilization, and employed a cunning, deceptive religious
ideology to enslave the indigenous people. Those who fled to India's forests and hills
later came to be called "tribals." As these native Indians were gradually overcome,
captured, and enslaved, they were kept outside village limits and "untouchability" was
enforced upon them. These people became "untouchables."[71]

All of this represents the modern Black academic push to subvert what a
recent White scholar, Martin Bernal, has termed the "Aryan Model,"
which, Bernal argues in *Black Athena*, replaced the "Ancient Model" as
conscious European propaganda. We now turn to this important
discussion in order to examine further associations between Africa and
Europe and the extent by which these became another stage in the
progression of Africa toward Europe.

Bernal has published two volumes of his projected four, all entitled
Black Athena.[72] In this groundbreaking work, Bernal has argued for a
new "model," a new understanding, of the origins of European culture.
He has asserted that the contention that Greek civilization arose on its
own, with little influence from the neighboring Middle Eastern and
African cultures, makes little sense. This assertion, the so-called "Aryan
Model," Bernal has claimed to be an invention of the nineteenth century.
The "Ancient Model," he has argued is truer and more relevant: Greek
and Roman civilization were both tremendously influenced by ancient
Egyptian thought.

It little matters whether ancient Egyptians were of African, Indo-
European, or some mixed stock, although much of the debate has
centered on this. What is more significant is that Egypt is geographically located in Africa, did influence Greek culture, and was, in
turn, affected by African civilizations, particularly Nubian culture, to its
south.

Because the Parthenon has come to symbolize the origin of all
European civilization, it follows that those who were outside its
controlling influence must, of necessity, be uncivilized and unlearned.
This outside group would account for the majority of the world —
Chinese, Africans, Indians, and, of course, Native Americans.

Obviously, if we are to go beyond this absurdity, which would banish a major portion of the globe to cultural obscurity, we need to think more clearly about what constitutes civilization and about how various cultures, including Greek culture, do not simply arise from nowhere but instead represent a product of cross-fertilization.

Bernal has been staunchly committed to this argument. He has claimed that European scholars have rewritten their history, embracing a kind of mythical Greece, so that they could deny the influence of Africa and Asia. Greek revisionism, he has asserted, grew out of nineteenth-century European politics to justify its colonial policy. Greece was invented as the fountainhead of democracy, science, and philosophy, because Europeans could not possibly suggest the truer version — namely, that Greece was a product of African and Asiatic invention — while justifying colonial overlordship.

The argument in favor of a non-African origin for Greek civilization takes into consideration only the fact that Europeans from the north moved south and conquered the Aegean peoples. As a result of this, early fusion was directly linked to Europe and had nothing whatsoever to do with ancient Phoenecia or Egypt. This is the only model that most of us were taught and grew to accept. But it is an exaggerated one, as Bernal has noted:

This leads us back to the quarrel which dominated European intellectual life during the 18th century: that between the Ancients and the Moderns. As mentioned above, the crux was the issue of whether the Moderns were now morally and artistically superior to the Ancients, and its centre was on the moral and artistic qualities of the Homeric epics; it should be remembered that Homer was seen by the Ancient Greeks as a cultural "founding father." From the 15th to the early 17th century the Egyptians had represented true Antiquity, but at the same time the authority of Egypt had been used by innovators to challenge the ancient authorities of Aristotle, Galen, etc. In this respect, then, it had what one might call a double image. In late-17th- and early-18th-century France, the progressive aspect was dominant: Egypt, with its identification with the France of Louis XIV, was clearly on the side of the Moderns.[73]

Bernal has painted a view that the Greeks themselves accepted. Greeks, he has argued saw their own past in completely different terms. Egyptians and Phoenicians came to Greece, established colonies, and brought their culture. Around 1500 B.C., in the Aegean of the Bronze Age, these two influences permeated Greek society and changed it.

There was another and even more pressing reason that Egypt as source was rejected by Europeans. Once the Rosetta Stone enabled scholars to decipher hieroglyphics, Europeans concluded that Egyptian civilization, which they still little understood, was one of artisans, not of scribes. When scholars turned toward Phoenicia for verification, Bernal has argued, they did so at the end of the eighteenth century, in a climate that was distinctly both anti-African and anti-Semitic. Politics, therefore, dictated that both Africa and Asia had to be rejected as the fertilizing influences of Europe. Bernal has contended that:

The men who destroyed the Ancient Model and those who established the Aryan one swept the board clean and began *de novo*. Why then did 19th-century ancient historians not fit into [this] . . . pattern? The answer would seem to be in what they perceived to be the enormity of the anomaly in the Ancient Model, which made any other model — or no model at all — preferable. The only internal reason for the Aryan Model's success was its power to explain the Indo-European basis of the Greek language. Thus, there was an exchange between this undoubted advantage and the need to deny the Greek tradition on the one hand and the many traces of Near Eastern culture in Greece seen by earlier scholars on the other. In short, the fact that the Ancient Model was replaced by the Aryan one does not in itself give the latter any superiority.[74]

Bernal's argument, both here and in interviews, has been that the "Aryan model" was put forward by a racist European society that sought to justify its own superiority.

Bernal has also argued for Egyptian influence from an etymological approach. Classicists have conceded that they can pinpoint the origin of as many as half of the words of Ancient Greek in a proto Indo-European language. Bernal has attempted to show that some of the derivations not accounted for may be found in Coptic and in the languages of ancient Egypt and Ethiopia.

Archaeological evidence has been found on the island of Thera, near Crete, the destruction of which probably gave rise to the Atlantis legend. Bernal has agreed with some archaeologists who have investigated the survivals of the island, which was destroyed by a volcanic eruption in 162 B.C. There, the Bronze Age city of Akrotiri has been found, containing, some excavators have argued, artifacts that reveal close links with Ancient Egypt. Critics have contended that there may be evidence of contact with Egypt but no sign of Egyptian influence in architecture, pottery shards, or art. Bernal, however, has claimed that, in some paintings, the depiction of palm trees, geese, and sailing vessels all belong to the Egyptian world.

Arguments go back and forth but center around the issue of whether the Aegean was "colonized" by Egypt or whether it merely absorbed (as would be natural) some cultural influences from Egypt. It scarcely matters whether the Egyptians physically colonized the area and thus spread their cultural influence. What is more important to note is the extent of the cultural presence of Egypt in the second and third millennium of the pre-Christian era. Because it is here that we can state that, whether through conquest or contact, Egypt effectively introduced culture to early Greece and thus became largely responsible for whatever Europeans have chosen to dub their Greek heritage.

Nubia thus becomes of intense interest because it establishes Egypt's link with sub-Saharan Africa. Recently, archaeologist Bruce B. Williams, who has authored five volumes on his Nubian excavations,[75] and museum curators Timothy Krendall and Emily Teeter,[76] who have long researched the issue, have sought to show the distinctive nature of Nubian culture. They have argued for a distinct culture in Black Nubia that goes back some 6,000 years, passing various phases. They have shown that the first period, between 3800 B.C. and 3100 B.C., extended from the First Cataract, near Aswan, south to the Second Cataract. Excavations on this period have revealed an incense burner. This object Williams has categorized thus:

Not as a provincial imitation of some unknown Egyptian monument but as the first self-evident pharaonic monument from the Nile Valley, the first unequivocal representation of a pharaoh in his person, the first definite linking of the pharaoh's figure with the Horus falcon, palace facade, and boat that later became the sacred bark, the first self-evident representation of an event linked with the royal sacrifice, and the first datable monumental-ceremonial object that compares with the slate palettes and maceheads of Egypt.[77]

Beatrice Lumpkin has dated this at about 3300 B.C. and, more importantly, has identified "a seated figure wearing a crown known from later Egyptian times."[78]

After the period of Egyptian domination, lasting from 2000 to 747 B.C., Nubian kings began to rule Egypt, after King Plankhy's successful entry into Thebes. During this twenty-fifth dynasty, between 747 B.C. and 656 B.C., Nubians did not merely copy the Egyptians but introduced new forms of art and architecture. During the next period, the Nubian kings retreated further south, ruling from Meroe. Thus, the famous kingdom of Kush developed a culture that was unrelated to that of the Mediterranean and was instead distinctly African, influencing Egypt with its own formative style.[79]

An exhibition at the Oriental Institute Museum in Chicago between February 4 and December 31, 1992, assembled important information that succeeded in classifying Nubia as an independent culture. Nubia emerged around 3800 B.C. and established its own culture and kingship around 3100 B.C. The culture, curator Teeter has stated, was "sophisticated"; Williams has argued that the discovery of the incense burner suggests that, because of the decoration of a seated king with a crown, this is one of the earliest pharaonic symbols and that kingship may well have originated in Nubia long before it did in Egypt.

Nubia, therefore, assumes great importance in our study for a number of reasons. First, whatever we may eventually agree about Egyptian civilization, we must also affirm that Nubian civilization most probably predated it and, in any case, profoundly influenced it in many important ways. Second, the history of Nubia and the artifacts that have been found speak to a high level of culture. Nubia was an equal trading partner with Egypt, providing gold, ebony, ivory, skins, and feathers. These, the Chicago scholars have pointed out, found their way into the pyramids of some of the most famous Egyptian kings. Third, Nubia itself possessed more pyramids than Egypt and therefore not only influenced Egyptian pyramid architecture but, in addition, described a regal and stately culture. Finally, these researchers have noted the Nubian conquest of Egypt and its reunification under the Nubian pharaohs as "a renaissance in art and learning." They have pointed out that, during the Roman period, "Nubia was in contact with the classical world and was the conduit through which Rome learned about Northeast Africa and the upper Nile." Features of Egyptian pharaonic culture, ancient deities, art, and architecture, were all preserved in Nubia after they had disappeared in Egypt.[80]

After the Assyrian invasion of Egypt in 656 B.C., when the Nubians moved further south, Nubian kings continued to maintain their culture. Between 200 B.C. and 300 A.D., Meroe became the center of the culture. Indeed, Nubia became a contact point between the Greek/Roman world, on the one hand, and Central Africa and the Nile Valley, on the other. Nubia "provided the corridor by which Africa and the classical world met." The *Nubian News* newsletter from the Museum of Fine Arts in Boston has summed up the achievement:

For more than six thousand years, ancient Nubian civilization flourished (6,000 B.C.— 350 A.D.). This sophisticated and unique culture is characterized by its own artistic development, central organization often led by a king, and, at one particular period, a type of writing called Meroitic. Nubians created some of the earliest ceramics in the ancient world, as well as magnificent stone colossal sculptures. At one point in their long history they built pyramids for their kings, and for over sixty years they successfully ruled Egypt.[81]

Chancellor Williams has related Nubian independence more directly to

Black America, showing yet again how intellectual ideas travel. He has written:

Nubia, therefore, revolted and became independent during the same period of general collapse at the center. But the compelling reasons, as stated elsewhere, appear to have been resistance not only to the increasing Asian power in Upper Egypt but also to the African and Afro-Asian pharaohs whose integration policies promoted the spread of this foreign power in what had been an important region of their homeland. It was black separatism and racialism without apology. It was even something more than a resistance movement against the political domination of foreigners and the social degradation of the blacks that always followed, but it was a stubborn resistance to the extinction of the race itself through amalgamation. These were the first of the race for whom black was in fact beautiful, and not just a catching slogan of the day.[82]

We need only note that Nubia has become a concept that has been justified by Afro-centric scholars. As such, like many other ideas, it "journeys" to the New World.

By 570, Nubians had been converted to Christianity, and Axum became an early center. As late as 1240, Nubia provided the German town of Magdeburg with the statue of an African which over the years

Very certainly became a Nubian, even down to the lineage cuts upon his forehead. Facing his stern and yet warmly protective gaze, you know that you are looking at a man from Nubia, a Nubian crusader in the chain mail likewise worn in Nubia then, but a Nubian, moreover, very clearly regarded as a friend and ally.[83]

According to Basil Davidson, this was a decision consciously made at a time before racism was rampant. When Frederick II led the sixth Crusade in 1227–1229, he wished to commemorate his religious allies in the twin kingdoms of Nubia. Davidson has argued that there was an earlier Maurice (was he a Moor?) and that he was supplanted by this new Black, the Nubian St. Maurice. Europe had thus accepted the images that Africa exported.

Black saints have survived in the contemporary mind. Recently, a musical video by the popular singer Madonna featured San Martin de Porres as an African Americanized Black man wrongly accused of rape. Equally, the Egyptian influence often appears in rap songs and even Michael Jackson's video, "Remember the Time," combines love lyrics with historical invocation. Thus, at both the academic and popular level, Egypt and Nubia persist in contemporary American discourse, if sometimes merely as fantasy.

An important point worth emphasizing is that two versions of Egypt, one positive and the other negative, have become part of the African American inheritance. This is particularly interesting for our study, since it shows that Africa's "discovery" of Europe was changed and altered to suit European whims and, ironically, in turn, was later used to influence Africans. In *Rasselas* (1759), Dr. Samuel Johnson had no compunction about celebrating the glories of Egypt. Indeed, although this Egypt was observed from the comfort of Johnson's study, it was nevertheless invested with the accepted qualities of learning and achievement. Prince Rasselas, never too patient with European values, extols the Egyptian/ African world of intellectual accomplishment. But, if we are to go along with the most cogent arguments that Bernal has advanced in *Black Athena*, then we have to recognize that a second Egypt was concocted in the nineteenth century, when European imperialism could no longer accept the former superiority of one of its own colonies. Despite the cultural presence of Africa through Egypt and Nubia, African Americans have therefore inherited the post–nineteenth-century version of events. "Discovery" does not ensure acceptance, as was realized, in a different context, in 1992.

Add to this the logic of the Bible, particularly regarding the imprisonment and enslavement of the children of Israel in Egypt. For christianized African Americans, this meant having to reject Africa even further, since, by siding with the enslaved, they demonized Pharaoh and romanticized the Israelites. Marc Connelly's *Green Pastures*, particularly in the popular film version of 1936, reinforces this point. De Lawd, played by Rex Ingram, is a lovable jocular fellow, presenting expensive ten-cent cigars to those he likes like Noah. When visiting earth, he encounters all the "sins" of post-Prohibition America, especially excessive drinking. First, he sends a flood, but, in a reversal of the biblical account, De Lawd dispatches Moses, a famous "tricher," to Egypt. There Moses performs conjuring tricks that so impress Pharaoh that he sets the Israelites free.

Clearly, the African American audience was expected to rejoice in the death of the Black Egyptian Pharaoh's first-born, and to empathize, even sympathize, with Moses' craft and cunning. At the very roots of Bible literature and Christian belief lies denunciation of Egypt as a land of evil and horror, on which African Americans (like the Israelites) must turn their backs in order to seek the Promised Land. It is almost impossible to avow Christianity and not reject Egypt. Egypt is anathema to Judaic and later Christian belief. Once African Americans had placed themselves in the position of the freed Israelites, who literally turned away from Egypt to gain freedom, they almost by definition had to reject Egypt.

Whites could intellectually reject a historical Egypt without denying themselves a cultural origin. For Blacks, the denial of Egypt was no mere allegory but a definite divorce from their own African past. Only through a new approach, by carefully reconstructing a newer version of Egyptian historical reality, could Afro-centrists hope to interest Blacks in reviewing Egypt and restructuring Africa.

Here then is the essential difference between the two Africas encountered in African American liberation. On the one hand, older writers, such as the eighteenth-century African American poet, Phillis Wheatley, opted for the rigid biblical stereotype of Africa as something negative. Indeed, this was the only way that the Senegalese-born poet could visualize Africa in her poetry, if she were to project herself as cultured, Christian, and Western. She turned away from Africa, the archetype of barbarism and horror, to the West the embodiment of civilization and happiness. Denunciation of the African/Egyptian past was a way of both including such writers in the good graces of European and Euro-American readers and, at the same time, freeing them from a heritage that they might have found restrictive and reprehensible.

In the twentieth century, Langston Hughes projected a differing view of another Egypt. Even as an eighteen-year-old poet, he depicted Egypt as the originator of civilization in "A Negro Speaks of Rivers." For Hughes, the Nile was the symbol of this new Egypt, the very origin of the human race at a time, in his words, "when dawns were young."

Of course, both Africas are "relevant," in the sense that both versions are part of the "propaganda" that artists utilize.[84] But "belief" in one or the other has less to do with individual poetic preferences and more to do with responses to the given value systems of specific historical periods. Phillis Wheatley wrote at a time, before Charles Darwin and Alfred Wallace, when the order of the biblical world had not been challenged in the West. After the work of Sigmund Freud, new alternatives became possible, and, even though African American writers have remained curiously conservative when it comes to Christianity, they have been open to new interpretations of intellectual apprehensions of the world. The second Egypt found in the work of Hughes is therefore the new response. The "Egyptian gloom" is banished, and instead Egypt is put forward as culturally relevant for all, particularly for African Americans.

The Bible has often been seen as a source that justifies the status of Africa not merely as a receiver of culture but also as a provider. References are often made, in accordance with popular African American conceptions, to the very origins of human thought in African experience. Thus, in "A Negro Speaks of Rivers," Hughes included the entire world past as part of Black heritage, as the young poet cried out that his race created the pyramids. In *Moses, Man of the Mountain* (1939), Zora Neale Hurston's hero is Black, speaks a Black dialect, and leads Black people to the Promised Land. Indeed, this work even states that :

This worship of Moses as the greatest one of magic is not confined to Africa. Wherever the children of Africa have been scattered by slavery, there is acceptance of Moses as the fountain of mystic powers. This is not confined to Negroes. In America there are countless people of other races depending upon mystic symbols and seals and syllables said to have been used by Moses to work his wonders.[85]

Hurston, incidentally, was referring here to the so-called "Sixth and Seventh Books of Moses," which are still secretly read in Germany as the "Schwarz Buch Moses," because Moses, the Black Egyptian, was supposedly able to bring about miracles. Note how the mythology of the Egyptian/African past was first altered (distorted?) and then shipped to Europe and the New World, where it has been heard by New World Africans in a totally new form.

It is often argued by Afro-centrists that God himself is Black. "The Church of the Black Madonna" in Detroit, founded during the 1960s by Reverend Albert Cleage, proclaimed just such a message. Although neither the Peace Mission Movement of Father Divine nor the "United House of Prayer for All People of Daddy Grace preached an extension of Africa into the United States, there were African elements in the ritual and worship, again demonstrating how ideas from and about Africa have influenced New World people.[86]

With Marcus Garvey's movement, we not only see Africanity but also note that both God and Jesus are Black and that part of Black liberation involves moving away from worshipping a White God. More directly, African Americans have appropriated the Middle East in the various "Black Jew" movements of Philadelphia, Harlem, and the District of Columbia. The Noble Drew Ali introduced North African Moorish concepts to America in "The Moorish Science Temple of America," founded in 1913.[87] This was a forerunner of Elijah Muhammed's Nation of Islam.[88]

In *Ethiopia and the Bible*, Edward Ullendorff has made the case for looking beyond Western versions of Christianity in order to understand different perceptions. He has written about the Queen of Sheba:

In turning to the Ethiopian version, we become at once conscious of a fundamental change of atmosphere; the emphasis is no longer on Solomon and his wisdom but on the Queen of Sheba and her nobility; no longer is Solomon exposed
to the wiles of the seductress ... but he himself assumes the role of
seducer.[89]

This is part of a connection that was mentioned earlier — the
Christianizing of Nubia and its surrounding areas. In this instance,
Ethiopia in general and Axum in particular are seen as vital parts of a
cultural bridge that extends from Nubia to the Mediterranean.

Ullendorff has shown how Ethiopia Africanized early Judeo-
Christianity. In rituals, David and the House of Israel entertain the Lord
with harps, lyres, and drums. The priests dance before the ark, lending
their own vigor to the message of the Bible, refusing to numb religion
with a cold Western hand.

Other African American scholars have examined the writings of
Homer, Hesiod, Ovid, Virgil, and, of course, Pliny and Herodotus,
in order to show that these Classical writers were influenced by
Egypt, Nubia, and Kush. This exercise seems almost pointless today,
since it seems scarcely possible that these writers could have ignored
Africa. These scholars have sometimes bent over backward to show
that Africa has always been a part of the world — that even the
name "Ethiopia" could derive from "Aethiops," a son of Vulcan, as
Pliny had suggested. William Hansberry has noted happily that "The
classics abound in references and allusions to Ethiopia, and the
Ethiopians,"[90] although Ullendorff has shown that "Moors and
Ethiopians and nations of barbarous speech" were cursed like the tribes
of Gog and Magog.[91]

Early pioneering work has uncovered not merely the presence of
Blacks in Classical literature and shown that, to a great extent, Blacks
existed in a world free from excessive concern with skin coloration.
Frank M. Snowden, in both *Blacks in Antiquity* and *Before Color
Prejudice*, has written much about how well even the ancient Greek gods
interacted with Blacks:

Homer tells us that the Olympians were fond of visiting the Ethiopians. Zeus,
followed by all the gods, went to feast with the blameless Ethiopians, where he
remained for twelve days. Poseidon also visited the distant Ethiopians to receive a
hecatomb of bulls and rams. At the end of the *Iliad*, Iris informs the winds that it is
not possible for her to remain but that she must return to the streams of Ocean in order
to participate in a sacred feast offered by the Ethiopians. Hence, the goddess makes a
special trip alone.[92]

As we have seen, however, a stronger, more nationalistic argument maintains that the still more ancient world of Nubia and Kush helped to invent Olympus itself.

Much of the Afro-centric literature on the Classical period has tended to adopt polarized views. George G. M. James' *Stolen Legacy* has argued that Plato did not author *The Republic* and that some of its source lay in the Egyptian *Book of the Dead*. He has concluded that the Greeks stole Egyptian philosophy, which was itself the result of the Egyptian Mystery system, secret knowledge of life and death possessed by the priests and pharaohs. Pythagoras, Socrates, Aristotle, and others all owe their fame to knowledge possessed by Egyptian priests.[93]

Versions of Egypt, as idea and reality, continue to be actively articulated by Afro-centrists. By attempting to return to a more ancient model, these scholars are seeking to make the African/Egyptian legacy one that penetrates directly into New World culture, having ramifications particularly for African Americans, who had previously been deluded by an invented Euro-centric concept. We do not have to agree with all that they say, only to note that the "ancient" model is as valid a reference point for understanding African cultural influences as the "revised" model of the nineteenth century. The new discourse continues to argue for the validity of Egyptian influence in Europe, in a reassessment that stresses the prevalence of African thought and belief in the process of global encounter in the New World.

INVASION: MOORISH PRESENCE IN EUROPE

Moors from North Africa invaded Spain and southern France, occupying various parts of these lands between 711 and 1492. Most of the invaders were Muslims, having themselves been converted in the great Islamic religious zeal following Mohammed's death; many were Islamized Africans.

During a period when Europe was in its own "Dark Ages," the Moors were a stabilizing force. Their architecture, especially in Andalusia, their aqueducts, houses, and life-styles were sources of constant amazement to visiting Europeans. In addition to the task of copying Classical Greek texts into Arabic (which were later translated back into Greek and Latin), Moors imported a civilization into Spain, through their pioneering efforts in astronomy and early medicine. Their legacy includes not only mathematics and science, but also their own creative works. Important writers of the period dealt with a number of themes, such as patriotism, religion, love, government, and duty. The work of these writers, still a little shrouded in obscurity, deserves to be better known, since again it reveals important aspects of the African contact with Europe. Above all, Moorish culture represented a synthesis between the Christian West and the Islamic East, reflecting a personal ease and familiarity with the new European scenario, as scholars adapted their new environment to their African continent of origin.

RISE OF MOORISH INFLUENCE

Moorish presence in Spain marked the westward cultural extension of the African continent into Europe renewing the import of both "travel" and "discovery." The historical and cultural importance lay in how the Moorish presence changed Spain, as well as the other areas with which it came into contact. At its zenith, an Islamic/Moorish/African presence physically existed in most of the Iberian peninsula, in southern Italy, in various Mediterranean islands, and, of course throughout northeastern Africa, extending eastward beyond Arabia. In Europe proper, the Moorish expansion was contained only by Charlemagne's empire to the north, the Byzantine empire to the east and areas occupied by Normans, Slavs, and Turkish peoples further north.[94]

As noted, Muslims were inveterate travelers, traders, and evangelists. They had spread out into Africa, long before the advent of Europeans into its eastern area, traveling down the coast as far as Madagascar. They had moved across the Sahara into the northern areas of West Africa and even partly penetrated into Central Africa. Moorish culture was a unique combination of basic African elements with a surface layer of Islam.[95]

After the death of the Holy Prophet Mohammed in 632 A.D., Islam began its initial expansion, until 661, under the first four caliphs. Under the Umayyads up until 751, they pushed into Northern Africa, past Egypt and Tripolitania, into the Maghrib. Under the Abbasids, the frontier moved to take in Sardinia in 825, Sicily in 878, Crete in 823, and, finally, the southern tip of Italy. The only serious threat to their expansion came not from Europeans but from the Mongols.

Today, the word "Moor" survives in contemporary nation-states like Morocco and Mauritania, where, in the latter instance, it was first utilized by the Romans. Here, the reference was to an area made up of modern Algeria and the northern portion of modern Morocco. Thus, even though the Islamized Berbers have been properly credited as the "Moors" of Spain, it must be noted that their culture embraced not just a single ethnic group in northern Africa. Indeed, any careful evaluation must take into account a number of factors: first, the movement of African peoples as they interacted with each other in the northern Sahara; second, a primary synthesis of these differing groups; third, a secondary synthesis of the new, unified, African group culture; and finally, a tertiary synthesis, with the advent of early contact with the two worlds of Europe — the pagan Roman empire, which had conquered North Africa, and the semi-Christian Hispanic fiefdoms, which the Moors later conquered.

The Berbers proper lived in what is now Algeria. Cave paintings in the Ahaggar area reveal that they were a domesticated people as early as 2000 B.C. They hunted game, raised cattle and traded with Phoenicians. Cato the Elder, the Roman orator, constantly warned, "delenda est Carthago" (Carthage must be destroyed), and his xenophobia helped bring about the destruction of the city by Rome in 146 B.C. Today, the ruins nevertheless still remain as a symbol of a once thriving North African civilization.

A Berber king allied himself with Rome and established Numidia. The currents of history thus indicate constant interaction between the Western and Islamic worlds. The Moors absorbed all this as well as the invasion of the Vandals in the fifth century, the conquest of Justinian in the sixth, and the eastern movement of the Arabs in the seventh. At one time, they resisted under the High Priestess Kahina, but eventually they settled down and accepted Islamic conquest.

Contact with the Iberian peninsula was not all in one direction before 711. Between 172 and 175 A.D., Moors crossed what would later be the Straits of Gibraltar and invaded the Roman provinces of Baetica and Lusitania, laying siege to Singlia Barba and Italica. By the end of the third century, the Roman emperor Diocletian, recognizing the inevitable historical, cultural, and geographical link, joined Diocesis Hispania to the new Provincia Mauritania Tingitana, administering it through delegates. Hence, Moorish presence in Spain between 711 and 1492 consolidated the cultural influences of the Roman empire, the Arab conquest, and the undergirding African synthesis.

The vagaries of history had also exposed northern Africa to Christianity. The decline of Egypt around 3000 B.C. coincided with the rise of Kush. With the fall of Meroe, the last great Kushite state, Axum rose and was converted to Christianity. By the first century, the various North African states were part of the Roman Empire. Under the influence of "Fathers" of the Church, such as St. Augustine (himself a North African), the region had become a center of Christianity. By the end of the fourth century, lands to the west of modern Libya were also part of Rome's western empire, while those to the east were part of the Byzantine Empire (ruled from Constantinople). Thus, at the beginning of the millennium, North Africa had already been subject to western and eastern influences.

Up until the death of Mohammed, Islamic raids into the area had been pushed back by the Berbers, but the *jihad* proved too powerful. By the eighth century, Morocco had been conquered, and the Christian Berbers of the coast had begun to be converted. The inland Berbers resisted and withdrew to the Sahara; today, their descendants are the Tuaregs.

At first, Arabs maintained only a small garrison in North Africa, but, by the mid-eleventh century, the westward movement of the Seljuks had caused a new wave of immigrants. The pastoral Berbers were conquered and partly assimilated into Islamic culture. Further south within the continent, contacts persisted between northern Africans and their southern neighbors; the Sanhaja Confederation of Berbers (in what is today Mauritania) formed the main link between the old kingdom of Ghana and the north. Later on, Arabs explored these same trade routes and, by the eleventh century, Muslim ministers and advisers were at the court of the Ghanaian king. Arab and Islamic influence pushed even further into Mali and Songhai. Mansa Musa made his famous pilgrimage to Mecca in 1324, and, under Sunni Ali (1464–1492) and Askia Muhammad (1493–1528), Islam flourished in Songhai, with Timbuktu becoming an important center of learning that was renowned for its famous library. In Kanem-Bornu, the Zaghawa nomads were displaced by the Islamic Saifawa. Berber influence therefore facilitated the spread of Islam, and the Arabs, who traveled on foot, donkeys, and later camels, continued to maintain a southern African contact that was first initiated by the Berbers.

As Islam spread over northern Africa, it came into contact with Christianity, but Muslim Arabs did not see this as conflict. For instance, when they drove the Byzantines out of Egypt, they rewarded the Copts by appointing upper-class members of that group as district governors to collect taxes and take charge of irrigation and agriculture. They recognized the Monophysite Coptic Church as the true church of Egypt and forbade Christian Copts from adopting Islam. Instead, they raided the Berbers of Libya, enlisting them into the army and admitting them to a community of "muslims," that is, people who had made their "islam" or submission. By 670, Arabs had established a garrison just south of Carthage, and, by 705, Carthage had been conquered and the Romano-Berber princes defeated. Byzantine Africa had become part of the Arab Empire and was now known as the province of Ilfriqiya.

Therefore when in July 710 the first "Moorish" party crossed the Straits of Gibraltar, they did so under the leadership of an African

Berber, Tarif ibn-Milik, who landed with a complement of four ships and 400 soldiers. As Jan Read has argued in *The Moors in Spain and Portugal*, this expedition was concerned with reconnaissance and initiated a series of landings that took four years, until 714. Read has shown how al-Andalus, encompassing both Portugal and Spain, first came under the sway of the North Africans; this presence lasted through various emirates and caliphates until 1002. By 1017, Christians had begun to fight back, but the power and influence of the Africans lasted well into 1492, when Grenada finally fell to Isabella and Ferdinand. Neither the Inquisition nor expulsion of Moors, however, could effectively end the influence of a 300-year occupation.

In order to identify the true Moors, it is necessary to explore a plethora of names that historians have left us. For instance, "Mozarabs" were Christians (some Moors) living under Muslim rule; "Moriscos" were Christians (some Moors) who had converted to Christianity, especially after 1500; "Mudéjars" were Muslims (including Moors) who lived under Christian rulers; and, finally, "muladí" were Muslims (including Moors) who had converted from Christianity to Islam. One cultural by-product was "Aljamiado literature," in which the Spanish language was converted to Arab script; the earliest text, "Poema de Yúçuf," circulated clandestinely, like most of this type of literature, at the height of the oppression of Muslims by the ever-encroaching Christians. Behind these various terminologies and the even more generic term "Muslim" lies the varied account of the Moorish influence from North Africa.

Historians have had difficulty in assenting to the simple fact that:

The invaders were not purely Arab, including as they did numerous Berbers from North Africa and people of mixed Arab and Berber descent [for], in the first place the Moors were simply the inhabitants of western Islam, or the North African Maghrib. Again to apply the world "Muslim" to al-Andalus and its inhabitants is to underrate the contribution of the very large numbers of Mozarabs or arabicized Christians, who helped to give al-Andalus a character distinct from the Islam of the East.[96]

The Moors were, therefore, an interesting example of old-world African cultural synthesism. They were, in large part, Africans who had absorbed some Islam and, later on, either coexisted easily with their Christian subjects or themselves took on aspects of Christianity. The blend of three cultures — African, Arab, and European — helped give Andalusia its distinctive flavor. This has never been stressed enough.

It should be noted at this point that the Berbers did not easily accept Arab overlordship. As early as 698 A.D., the Berbers, led by their prophetess, Kahina, defeated the Arabs at Carthage. As Rolf Reichert has noted, they pursued the Arabs as far as Barqa and were only pushed back by the arrival of new Arab reinforcements. During the counterattack, Kahina was killed.

As already noted, the movement of peoples from the western and eastern parts of Africa was part of an Islamizing force that can be traced from Syria through Egypt (640–642) and into northern Africa (Ifriquiya) by 670. The Governor of Tangier, Tariq ibn-Zayad, himself a Berber, sailed from North Africa with an African force 7,000 strong. He gave his name Jabal Tariq (Gibraltar, i.e., the mountain of Tariq) to the tiny strait he crossed.[97]

Under Roderick, the Duke of Baetica, Visigothic Spain, which was already factionalized, attempted to repel the invaders, but the Africans, joined by Jews in southern Spain, moved north, past Córdoba and into Lisbon and Toledo. Soon they had pushed farther north, occupying Narbonne in 717 and Autun in 726. By 732, they had reached Bordeaux and Tours in the western part of present-day France.

As Jan Read has pointed out, only after the initial success of Tariq did eastern Muslims under Musa ibu-Nusayr attempt the crossing. In June 712, with a force of 18,000 men, Musa arrived and assisted the African force in pushing farther north, finally linking up with Tariq at Talavera. The jealousy between the two generals, Arab and African, was great. Nevertheless, after a stormy meeting, they again combined forces. In 714, Tariq and Musa went to Damascus but received little support for what they had done.

Yet the importance of this new African contact with Europe through Spain cannot be overstated. It brought not merely Muslim beliefs as is commonly asserted, but African thought to the European continent. This occurred not only thanks to African Berbers who had crossed over to Spain in large numbers, but also to the eastern Muslims who had interacted and married Africans, "a process that was to be hastened and accentuated in al-Andalus," as Read has added "already racially complex as the result of successive invasions and settlements from the eastern Mediterranean and northern Europe."[98]

Conflicts between Arabs and Africans, as well as disputes among Arabs, would eventually lead to the downfall of al-Andalus. First, the Arabs preferred to live in towns, whereas the Africans generally inhabited the mountain areas, where they intermarried with converted Christians or *muwallahs*. Second, the Africans always saw North Africa as home and resented the treatment that Arab governors had meted out to them there. In 740, a Berber army descended on the Arabs and did great damage, reinforcing a similar uprising by Berbers in North Africa. Later on, the Berbers linked up with the Kalbites, who came originally from Yemen, against the Qaysites, originally from the north of Arabia Early rulers reflected the compromise that had to be achieved between Africans and Arabs. For instance, 'Abd-al Rahman, the founder of the Umayyad dynasty that ruled for 300 years in al-Andalus, had an African mother. He seized Córdoba in 756 and began the construction of the Great Mosque there.

Berber history therefore does not show a meek acceptance of Arab or Muslim norms. Given their wide exposure to several parts of the known world their restiveness again asserted itself in the ninth century. The Berber Fatimid family asserted its independence by conquering a state that extended past Egypt to Syria and Arabia. Cairo was the Fatimid capital, with its imposing palaces and exquisite mosques. Although the Berbers were forced out of Egypt by the Turks in the twelfth century, they maintained their rule in the Maghrib.

Islam, sometimes in union and sometimes at odds with Berber aims, was, a catalyst. Two reform movements propelled the Berbers toward Spain. The al-murabit (Almoravid) was a military and religious brother-hood that in 1061 came under the leadership of Yusuf ibn Tashfin (d. 1106), himself a Berber chief. After conquering Morocco, the Almoravids invaded Spain in 1086, conquering and subjugating the area between the Tagus and Ebro rivers. Not until 1147 was the dynasty overthrown by a second reform (and again Berber) movement.

This, the al-muwahhid (Almohad), was led by Muhammad ibn Tumart (1080–1130), but the founder of the dynasty was a Berber, Abd al-Mumin (d. 1163), who conquered Morocco (1140–1147), and ruled Spain and part of Portugal after 1154. His successors aided the sultan Saladin against the Crusaders. The dynasty ended in 1212, with their defeat at the Battle of Navas de Tolosa against the united might of Castille, Aragon, and Avarre. Almohad power declined, ending in Spain in 1232 and in Africa in 1269.

Just as the Arab/Berber movement was divided, so too was the Christian/Iberian effort on the part of the kings of Asturias, Leon, and Castile, and the rulers of Portugal, Navarre, and Aragon-Catalonia. The latter dreamed of the Reconquista but were able to realize it only with the disintegration of African and Arab unity. Although the Kingdom of Granada persisted as a tributary state until 1492, Edward Scobie has concluded in a recent study that:

It is not for their military conquests in Europe that the Moors are remembered. It is the culture and learning which they gave to European countries at a time when there was darkness and nothing elevating in the arts and sciences of a country that was to claim falsely in later centuries to be the cradle of the civilization of the world. That this civilization was first given to them by the Africans who remained in European countries for several centuries is still shrouded in perjuries, half-truths, mythologies, and/or total omissions.[99]

These Africans who influenced Europe for seven centuries and more, represent another important way in which the two continents touched each other and another significant aspect of the Africa invention of Europe. One must, however, add that they too were driven on by their fantasies. For them, the legendary wealth of Solomon lay in Toledo, offering reason enough for Tariq to sack and conquer that city.

OVERVIEW OF MOORISH ACCOMPLISHMENTS

The Crusaders used the term "Moor" disparagingly. They applied it to non-Christian, usually Muslim, peoples who were Berber, Bedoin, Yemeni, and, of course, Africans from Mauritania. To the Muslims, the Christians were all "Franks," the people originally ruled by Charlemagne.[100]

As the Crusaders retreated, the Latin kingdoms crumbled. May 1291 marked the end of the Crusades. The grand ideals had flagged, and the great militarism had weakened. The Crusaders had fought with and often betrayed each other. In the final analysis, the Crusaders succeeded only in driving an enormous wedge between Christians and Muslims, and vice versa. Francesco Gabrieli has contended "when medieval Muslims write of Christian beliefs or observances they create a grotesque caricature . . . based on misconceptions that can only be equalled in Christian accounts of Islamic beliefs and practices."[101]

With the fall of Byzantium, Sicily, for instance, fell to the Arabs and was later seized by the Normans. Byzantine, Norman, and Christian influences exist today in the rituals, the architecture, and the music of the Sicilian church. Norman architecture itself was influenced by Muslim art, as seen in the palace of Palermo. The *Koran* and the Bible were almost interchangeable there for a century. This tolerance would not last, and there finally emerged a single authority that was Western and Christian. But the actual foothold for Muslim and African cultural penetration occurred in Spain, and there Africans and Muslims brought a level of cultural flourishing not witnessed since Roman times. Al-Andalus was the focus of a world extending eastward to Sicily and southward to North Africa. The Alhambra in Grenada still represents the magnificence of the era; it is a monumental piece of architecture, almost the reproduction of Paradise on earth.[102]

In Córdoba, the capital of Muslim Spain, the caliph combined the power of spiritual and lay leader from the tenth century on. Córdoba possessed wealth and abundance, far beyond anything in Christian Europe. Under Muslim rule, Christian, African, Jew, and Muslim not only coexisted but drew from each other's cultures. Because of the cross-fertilization of these four civilizations, Córdoba, like other cities in Muslim Spain, retained and could provide a veritable storehouse of multicultural ideas, once Europe moved out of its Dark Ages. As Joseph Roucek and Thomas Kiernan have put it:

Scholars from all over Europe, stimulated by the renewed contact with Arab and classical thought, came to the schools of Toledo. Among them were Robert Anglicus, the first to translate the Koran, Adelbard of Bath, Michael Scot, and Daniel Morley. Latin translations of the works of Aristotle, Euclid, and others were exceedingly hard to come by, and making them more available was, in fact, one of their major objectives.

In Moorish Spain, the intellectual climate was such that it was almost natural for the Moslem philosophers to function as a liaison between the Hellenistic and Christian worlds. . . . Since Moorish Spain was a reflection of Oriental and African Islam in terms of theological inquiry, its own intellectual ferment could not help but stimulate Christian minds.[103]

Medieval musical instruments, for instance, were of Moorish origin. Christians who lived under Muslim rule, the *mozarabs*, bequeathed elements of music that still survive in present-day Spain. Architecture, poetry and manuscript illustration all owe their origin to the African/Muslim presence in Spain. Arabic and African languages provided many words in the Spanish language. The sciences of Greece, India, Persia, and even China were translated into Arabic. Later, they were retranslated into Latin to help fuel the Renaissance, when teachers and scholars from all over Europe came to learn from the North African Moors.

For 600 years, Spanish princedoms fought against the Moors and the Muslims. For later Spaniards, the *Reconquista* was the last of the Crusades that sought the total obliteration of the foreigner — here the Moor. Alfonso of Castille reconquered Toledo in 1085 and, for many, this was the re-assertion of Visigothic might. In reality, this was not the case, but the myth developed that contemporary Spanish authority had received a kind of sanction from old Visigothic Spain. Assistance came to the Muslims from North Africa, and indeed, at one time, Muslim Spain existed as a satellite of Northern Africa.

Once Seville and Córdoba had fallen, only Granada seemed unbeatable. Finally, in 1492, a mass expulsion of Jews and Moors followed the victory of their Catholic Majesties. So fervid was the emotional climate after the Moorish expulsion that the leader of the Inquisition, Tomás de Torquemada, convinced their Catholic Majesties that it was their pious duty either to expel the Jews or to force their conversion. According to some historians, about 200,000 remained in Spain as *conversos*, who, along with the Moors, would later assist Spain during its Golden Age. In 1523, the Córdoba mosque was made into a cathedral. The Inquisition made sure that only Moriscos or Conversos (converted Jews) were tolerated. But even this basic attitude lasted for only a short time, and soon more expulsions took place.

Nevertheless, the African Moorish influences on Spain and Portugal have not been eradicated. Today, Moorish influences continue to exist in Black America. Many African Americans see the Moorish past as theirs. They associate with it in dress, by taking on Moorish-sounding names, and, in one important instance, by following the calling of the Noble Drew Ali. A comment by a conservator of the Metropolitan Museum of Art, during the joint Al-Andaluse/Granada exhibition, also revealed the continuing European fascination with the Moors. As he put it, "we are dealing here with the stuff of Paradise."[104]

AFRICAN/EUROPEAN SIXTEENTH-CENTURY CONTACT

In the late fifteenth century, African/European contact shifted or seemed to begin all over again, thus marking (this time from the African viewpoint), yet another "discovery." Surely, we may contend that the first Africans who walked ashore from Portuguese slave ships "discovered" Europe. We are, after all, merely displaying the same sort of arrogance as Prince Henry's navigators, who sailed down the West African coast, naming places according to their fancy and bringing Africans back to Europe.

Earlier, Italians had attempted a similar excursion. Two Genoese brothers, Ugolino and Vadino Vivaldi (or Vivaldo), set out in two galleys in 1291, with the intention of going to the "Indies." When they stopped off in the country of the Moors (Morocco), they vanished. Although Ugolino's son, Sorleone, sought him in Africa, the quest was in vain. The story of the Vivaldi brothers faded into European myth. It was even said that they had reached Ethiopia, the country of Prester John, and were there taken prisoner.[105]

The Genoese had first been forced to seek the sea-route to the East, since their very landscape, with its backdrop of mountains, always forced them to look seaward for expansion. In addition to the confinement of Genoese life, constant factionalism pitted one warlord against another.

The Vivaldi brothers had a definite plan, they thought. They would sail westward from the Mediterranean, through what would later be called the Straits of Gibraltar, south along the African coast, and around the Cape toward India. They had a compass and new maps made weather-proof by their sheepskin design. But the information on the maps was limited. While the Mediterranean, coastal Spain, and even the northern coast of Africa were drawn in detail, no one in thirteenth-century Europe knew what lay beyond.

Africans, as noted, were not in this unfortunate position. From the early years following Mohammed's death, the very West Africans whom Italy and later Portugal set out to explore had been linked to the Berbers along donkey and camel routes. The Berbers traveled between the southern (and northern) Mediterranean and the northern and western parts of Africa. Later on, in addition to goods and news, they would also carry the Koran. But, from the earliest times until now, they have represented the great desert travelers, linking two parts of Africa, one that was more in contact with European Christianity and Arab Islam, and the other, on its own, developing and maintaining important areas of African cultural independence.

Today we know that the empire of Ghana (seventh to eleventh centuries), Songhai (eighth to sixteenth centuries), Kanem-Burnu (ninth to nineteenth centuries), Mali (eleventh to seventeenth centuries), and the Zenj city states in East Africa (eleventh to sixteenth centuries) were all thriving cultural centers. In addition the cultural centers at Benin, Oyo, Nok, Timbuktu, Zimbabwe, Kush with its center at Meroe (tenth century B.C. to third century A.D.), and Axum (first to eighth centuries) reveal, in detail, the heights to which African civilizations had risen.[106] The point is surely that Africa was not asleep or dead, awaiting European "discovery" by Mary Kingsley, David Livingstone, Henry Morton Stanley, Cecil Rhodes, and others. Europe created the illusion, as it did in the New World, that the continent was "dark," because this mythology had to be announced in order to justify, first, African enslavement and second, African colonization.

From the viewpoint of Europe, Africa became the home of Prester John. The continent was associated with the legend of the priest-king who was fending off Muslims. After his mythical location shifted from India, it was found in Ethiopia, before being moved to the New World. The African Prester John, somewhat like Mansa Musa of Mali, who was known to Europe because of his fourteenth-century pilgrimage to Mecca, was wealthy, religious, and Western-oriented. In the 1375 Catalan Atlas, Mansa Musa is depicted seated on a throne, wearing traditional European regal clothing complete with orb, scepter, and crown. He is the "Lord of the Negroes of Guinea," a little like the earlier representation of Prester John.

As in the case of the New World, African peoples were considered as "barbaric" and in dire need of Christianity. The European motivation was the same in both cases. To justify the slave trade from Africa to Europe, Africans had to be dehumanized. They were therefore subjected to stereotypes that stemmed more from European social preoccupations than from African reality. Like New World inhabitants, Africans were also described as shiftless and lazy, amusing and rhythmically gifted.

The Portuguese began their explorations of the African coast as early as 1433, when caravels reached Cape Bojador. By 1444, N'uno Tristão had reached Cape Bojador, at the same time that Diní Dias had arrived at Cape Verde. Tristão reached the Gambia River in 1446 and was followed by Fernão Gomes in 1469, who explored along the area of what was promptly termed the "Ivory," "Gold," and "Slave" coasts. As early as 1482, the Portuguese constructed a castle at São Jorge da Mina, the same year that Diogo Cão reached the mouth of the Congo River. Six years later, in 1488, Dias reached the Cape, and, four years later, Vasco da Gama rounded it, pushing on to India with the aid of an Arab pilot.[107] Initial African contact had ended, and, like Native Americans, Africans would now be redefined.

Significantly, the Portuguese exported the identical mythology to Africa that the Spaniards would do to the New World. As far as Europe was concerned, Africa's "discovery" simply predated the New World's; therefore both areas were natural repositories for European invention. Diogo Gomes' descriptions of Africa paralleled later European accounts of the Americas. There was the same distance between "perceiver" and "perceived." The landscape was large, almost gargantuan. Thus, Gomes wrote of the Gambia "we saw the broad mouth of a river three leagues in width . . . and from its size correctly concluded it was the river Gambia."[108]

As with Columbus' and post-Columbian accounts, otherness was projected on the people encountered. In the Gambia, "many canoes full of men . . . fled at sight of us." Some people, however (since contact had

to be made), were termed "friendly." Wherever Europeans ventured, all
the people seem to have had a similar social structure, whereby Euro-
pean-type monarchs were easily recognized as lesser kings or chiefs. In
this instance, "their chief was called Frangazick, and was the nephew of
Farisangul, the great Prince of the negroes."[109] The names were the
result of overheated Portuguese imaginings, utilizing corruptions of
"Frank" and Arab-sounding words; they never existed.

The European exportation of one pervasive myth was abundantly
evident. Not only did the explorers seek gold, but also they invented its
discovery. The Gilded Man, the early Portuguese account continued, was
indeed in Africa. Captain Diogo Gomes continued:

I questioned the negroes at Cantor as to the road which led to the countries where there
was gold, and asked who were the lords of that country. They told me that the king's
name was Bormelli ... that he was lord of all the mines, and that he had before the
door of his palace a mass of gold just as it was taken from the earth, so large that
twenty men could scarcely move it. ... The nobles of his court wore in their
nostrils and ears ornaments of gold. They said also that the parts to the east were full
of gold mines.[110]

In this way, Africa, like the New World, was "named" and "owned."
Only people who came from outside and were totally oblivious to ethnic
realities could allocate names that merely signified trade or the
possibilities of material wealth. Prince Henry the "Navigator" set out on a
serious and deliberate attempt not at collaboration, but at conquest. Little
by little, as his caravels pushed farther south and then east, he sought not
only the spice routes but also the more immediate satisfaction of a
lucrative trade in gold, ivory, and slaves — the very names given to the
coast.

Prince Henry's trade in human bodies from Africa began as early as
1441, when the Portuguese first made a slave raid into African territory.
Of course, given the mores of the time, this was not as dastardly as it
sounds. The European ethos permitted the capture and enslavement of
those defeated or conquered. The permanent name "Slavs" is ample
testimony to this. In the case of Africa, however, Europe expanded its
hegemony, and, from 1441 through 1505, between 140,000 and
170,000 captives were forcibly taken to Europe. This was the first
African slave trade, justified because these so-called "Moors" were
considered prisoners of war.[111]

Africans were often employed in the households of famous or titled
Europeans. They were status symbols and, of course, regarded as
oddities. As with the later trans-Atlantic slave trade, they were considered

to be "owned" and could be sold or given away as presents. With the hypocrisy typical of the entire period of the later trans-Atlantic slave trade, much of this was do:.e as part of a supposedly civilizing and Christianizing mission. Jan Albert Goris has mentioned that some Africans were often baptized and then "freed" amid great pomp and ceremony.[112]

These same Africans integrated themselves into European society, and some, like the sixteenth-century poet Juan Latino (c. 1516–c. 1594), became leading intellectuals in Europe. Latino married the daughter of a Spanish nobleman and composed several volumes of verse in Latin. He identified himself in his poetry with Spain and the Catholic Church and paid little attention to his African origins. His *Epigrammatum Liber* was written to celebrate the birth of Prince Ferdinand in 1571; the *Austriad* narrated the victory of Don Juan of Austria at the Battle of Lepanto; a year later, in 1574, Latino published *Translatione*, praising the filial devotion of Philip II; and, in 1585, he produced a short panegyric dedicated to the Duke of Sesa, who had died in 1579. There also exists an elegy to Pope Pius V. The most that we learn about his African past from his verse appears in occasional wry comments on his skin color, such as these lines to Philip II: "For if our Black face, O King, displeases / Your ministers, a White face does not please the men of Ethiopia." Like most of these early Afro Europeans, Latino was in the process of trying to become as accepted as possible.[113]

According to Dunzo Annette Ivory's study of Blacks in Spain between 1500 and 1700, Spanish playwrights, in particular, created many portraits of these new Blacks, especially portrayals of scholars, soldiers, saints, and nobles. These Afro Europeans are rendered in terms of the Spanish background, so one glimpses little of their origins. Indeed, this is to be expected, since the Spanish dramatists themselves knew nothing about Africa. But we do note that some Blacks organized themselves into *cofradías*, which, by unifying them, enabled them to be supportive of each other's physical and spiritual welfare. Ivory has added that the majority of Blacks were assimilationists, but their music, dance, and instruments influenced Spanish culture.[114]

Albrecht Dürer, the German painter, made two sketches of Africans he met, suggesting that their presence was significant.[115] Although one cannot be certain of exact dates, it is believed that he drew in charcoal his famous "Portrait of a Black Man" in 1508. Dürer probably made his sketch sometime during a visit to Venice, between 1505 and 1506, although it has been suggested that he could have made his sketch in Nuremberg, a major trade center, as late as 1515. Certainly from as early as 1504, he had begun to follow a tradition of showing one of the three wisemen a Black. His "Adoration of the Magi" of that year probably drew on a real-life Black model. Dürer's later unnamed Black Man is a portrait of a serious-looking older person that follows this tradition. The subject wears an undershirt and a loose-fitting jacket, giving him a kind of regal elegance. His features are angular, and he has a receding hairline and an untrimmed mustache and beard. The sketch captures him as a real person, free from sentimental stereotype.

An instance of the African female presence in Europe may be noted in Dürer's "Portrait of Katherina," executed in 1511. Here Dürer drew on his real-life contact with the "Moorish" servant of a Portuguese factor, João Brandão. As Dürer himself commented in his diary, between March 16 and April 5, 1521, "I drew a portrait of his Negress with metal point," suggesting that his use of this particular process aided him in achieving an almost photographic preciseness about the portrait. After this we continue to see Africans as objects of European art and writing, equally during the seventeenth century. Aphra Behn's *Oroonoko* (c. 1688) is a good example of how Africans could even be distorted as "noble" for the cause of abolition.

Several other Africans should be mentioned, because they contributed to the eighteenth-century intellectual and cultural climate of Europe, particularly in their efforts at dismantling the slave trade.[116] One might contend that their presence not only lent reality to the debate but also provided both its moral conscience and its impassioned oratory. Among them should be mentioned Ottobah Cugoano (b. 1748?), Olaudah Equiano (1745–1780), Ignatius Sancho (1729–1780), and Phillis Wheatley (1753–1784). They were all first-generation Africans who described their early recollections of life on the continent and their later memories of Europe and/or America. Woven through these two types of recollection the narrative sought to establish an authoritative voice for the writer as a different kind of traveler from those so far examined.

Most significant about these writers was not only their adoption of Europe, but their easy adaptation of themselves to the English language. Beneath their accounts, there runs a definite understanding of the European mind of the time, especially the way they argued their antislavery cause from a biblical viewpoint. Their texts, whether purely "documentary" or "imaginative," sought to captivate their readers in what was for them a pioneering experience — creating a new "format" in a new "medium."

Indeed, the new form best expressed itself in what today is often termed the "slave narrative." But this expression, in many respects, is restrictive, ignoring the wider manifestations of the art these writers embraced. Above all, they sought to be morally sound, to deliver sermons in writing, while ensuring that they were neither long-winded nor dull. The writers tried to transfer the "sound" of an oral literature (which, in hindsight, some of them could have only vaguely recalled) while combining this with an urgent "sense" of argument, reason, and good debate.

In many respects, the very *functional* thrust of their arguments meant that they remained part of an African traditional continuum, whereby all art was relegated to the nondecorative and useful. Literature had to have a purpose, therefore, in that it sought to achieve in its design certain elemental and basic aims that celebrated life itself. Whereas *oral artists* were concerned with rituals such as birth, initiation, marriage, and death, the *literate scribes* had to invent a new "ritual," making out of pressing contemporary matters the occasion for their creative urges. Social issues, particularly as they affect group awareness, have continued to be the major concern expressed by Black artists.

When Francis D. Adams and Barry Sanders contrasted Equiano's 1789 biography with "the travel adventure book that delighted eighteenth century readers,"[117] they were in fact helping us to realize that the work of eighteenth-century African writers can and should be compared with Jonathan Swift's *Gulliver's Travels* and Daniel Defoe's *Robinson Crusoe*. Indeed, therein lay much of their achievement — the ability to marshal a serious argument while at the same time entertaining, to take the partly recollected rituals of "another" past culture and transform them into the well-recalled beliefs of contemporary Europe. In this way, they truly acted as agents of synthesis.

Sancho was another case in point.[118] His *Letters* (1782) sound quite affected in parts; he was enamored of the works of Laurence Sterne and used every opportunity to sound like him. But one episode stands out very clearly, in which Sancho discusses a reference to an unhappy Black female in *Tristram Shandy*. By writing about her, particularly because Sancho was more often concerned with the small issues of existence as a Black grocer in Westminster, Sancho displayed his emotion, his empathy, and his concern.

A major problem is that it was often difficult for Sancho to describe the emotional without an overt display of feeling. This is indeed one of the major differences between Sancho and the other Black writers of the period. He had never personally experienced slavery, and his treatment of it tended to be a little too sentimental and overzealous. We must not conclude, however, as Paul Edwards has done, that Sancho's letters "point clearly to his almost complete assimilation into 18th century English society."[119] This is surely the most important distinction of these writers. They did not opt out. Instead, they were natural outsiders; their texts provide us with interesting glimpses of life in Europe and America, as seen from the viewpoint of the minority. None of them could have done more than exist on the fringes of European society as odd curiosities.

We can be reasonably certain that they were all aware of their unique position in society. In one of his earliest letters, Sancho referred to himself by using the derogatory term "negur." Even more pointedly, in his *Thoughts and Sentiments* (1787), Cugoano accusingly related the fate of Atahualpa at the hands of Pizzaro and his men:

As soon as the signal of assault was given, their martial music began to play, and their attack was rapid, rushing suddenly upon the Peruvians and with their hell-invented engines of thunder, fire, and smoke, they soon put them to flight and destruction. The Inca, though his nobles crowded round him with officious zeal, and fell in numbers at his feet, while they vied one with another in sacrificing their own lives that they might cover the sacred person of their sovereign, was soon penetrated to by [sic] the assassins, dragged from his throne and carried to the Spanish quarters.[120]

Cugoano easily identified both Africans and Indians as victims, a noteworthy accomplishment at the time, since such a concept would have been anathema to any writer claiming to project a Euro-centric perspective or, for that matter, simply attempting to appeal to a European audience.

In connection with the problem of identity, no easier example exists than Phillis Wheatley, whose work clearly shows her ambivalence toward being both an "Ethiope" and a Bostonian White. Two lesser-known writers highlighted the problem even more — Jacobus Eliza Johannes Capitein (1717–1747)[121] and Anton Wilhelm Amo (c. 1700–1743), both from Ghana. In both instances their total cultural confusion led to some very odd behavior. For instance, Capitein defended his dissertation written in Latin, that proved that slavery was not contrary to Christianity. Later on, as pastor at Elmina in Ghana, he translated the Ten Commandments into Fanti, but "failed to mention that also servants and slaves should rest on the Sabbath."[122] He was too zealous even for the missionaries who sent him.

Amo was brought up by German royalty,[123] but, as a recent biographer has put it, "'There is a great deal of mystery surrounding Amo's first dissertation on "The Rights of an African in Eighteenth Century Europe,"'" which, in any event, has disappeared. Amo had been considered a rising star in the Enlightenment and, possibly, this work was too hard-hitting. The facts show that Amo left the University of Halle rather abruptly, and, when he reappeared in academic life at the University of Wittenburg, he no longer pursued the topic of an African's rights," as Marilyn Sephocle has related.[124] Indeed, by 1751, he had returned to Ghana, where he worked as a goldsmith until he died.[125]

These Black eighteenth-century writers and academicians deserve our attention because they too traveled away from "home" but, in reverse, toward the "center" of cultural activity. We have noted that, in some instances, we find a dislodgment but the writers generally remained free from too many sweeping generalizations that might paint themselves and their original cultures in overly warm tones. True, realism was not their forte, for they were writing to instruct and to entertain. But, considering that for them the journey was inverted, in that the more they moved away from "home" the closer they came to the "center," we have to be struck by their fearlessness. Few questioned the status of Europe as the apex of cultural being, because they were all incipient colonialists intent on acquiring the skills of the colonizer. At this distance in time, however, we should not be too judgmental, since their word remains as a testament to the tensions involved in being both "separatists" and "integrationists."

AFRICAN VOYAGERS

One could argue that the presence and influence of Africans in the Americas has constituted another type of "discovery," apart from anything else that has been considered. Africa has persisted in various ways as myth and reality, New World life. In truth, Africa entered into the consciousness of the New World, especially America, as a synthesis, since the very terminology presupposes that disparate groups of people have already been merged together Thus, in the New World context, "tribe" has been submerged and a new concept has arisen — namely, a continental "Africa," both imagined and substantial. Because both "Europeans" and "Africans" were only hazy notions in the old worlds of Europe and Africa, their New World manifestation indeed involved the birth of a novel concept.

Africans arrived in various stages. First as noted there were pre-Columbian Africans, such as, but not limited to the Mandingo. They were the first representatives of the African continent who arrived in the New World, and, even though we still know little about them, enough evidence has been presented in terms of their impact on Mayan and Aztec culture to conclude that trans-Atlantic journeys, even if in only one direction, were successfully accomplished..

Second, various Africans came with the conquistadors. We may note particularly Estabanico, an intrepid explorer who journeyed with Cortés and was among the first Old World explorers to reach the Pacific and travel through the American Southwest. These Africans were to a large extent Europeanized, in that they had been brought to Spain and Portugal from the time of Prince Henry's early explorations down the coast of Africa.

Third, Africans also came to the New World as settlers. The early settlement in Jamestown (1607) included a number of Africans, often wrongly described in the history books as "slaves." In addition, many Africans established permanent free enclaves in various parts of the New World, particularly in Surinam, Jamaica, and Brazil. Today, in Surinam, the Djuka and Saramaka survive as testimony to the earlier presence of free Africans, as do the Maroous in Jamaica. In Brazil, Palmares existed as an independent territory for several years, even though the Dutch tried several times to destroy it. In no small measure the presence of Africans remains as part of a viable cultural continuum, showing how their trans-Atlantic movement globalized African impacts and influence.[126]

Fourth, after slavery was abolished, some African groups came to the New World as indentured laborers. Among these the Kru, under strict control by their own kinsfolk in Africa, worked for various periods. Some returned to Africa, while others stayed. During the time that they were employed in the New World their fellow Kru visited to inspect working conditions.

Fifth, in the present century, Africans have continued to influence the New World and American culture. They have come as students and workers. Some, like Kwame Nkrumah, the first president of Ghana, studied in America and then returned to Africa.[127]

Fifth, the vast majority of Africans came to the Americas as slaves, but in most cases, they were not merely cultural spectators. Indeed, their presence brought about tremendous change in the Americas. Frank Tannenbaum has stated in *Slave and Citizen* that:

The Negro, by his presence, changed the form of the state, the nature of property, the system of law, the organization of labor, the role of the church as well as its character, the notions of justice, ethics, ideas of right and wrong. Slavery influenced the architecture, the clothing, the cooking, the politics, the literature, the morals of the entire group — white and black, men and women, old and young. Nothing escaped, nothing, and no one.[128]

This slave past has been the most prominent in literature. As previously noted, from the earliest writings by poets such a Phillis Wheatley and

Jupiter Hammond, Africa had become not a place, but what the Sierra Leonean poet, Davidson Nicol, would later call "a concept." Thus, Wheatley, for instance, denounced the Africa of her own mind as a "pagan land," "benighted," from which she had been mercifully snatched to receive the benefits of Christianity. Wheatley was simply buying into part of the mythology. After all, demonization was utilized to justify slavery. Robert Hayden's "Middle Passage" shows the extent to which Christianity was offered as an appropriate exchange for enslavement.

Real and invented aspects of the African presence continue to permeate American life. From Europe came the idea of the Noble Savage, part "Indian," part "African." Aphra Behn's *Oroonoko* (c. 1688) portrayed an African with European features, who was endowed with the name of a South American river, helping to contribute to the general confusion. Rousseau's Noble Savage did not need tutoring: Émile learned everything from the natural world. Supposedly, therefore, this composite African/ Indian possessed qualities superior to those of the learned European, but to take the logic of this too far was clearly dangerous.

At the same time, however, the African was certainly not seen by Benjamin Franklin and Thomas Jefferson as being superior — this honor they reserved to some extent for Native Americans — but as being distinctly inferior. In *Notes on Virginia*, Jefferson described Blacks as "inferior to the whites in the endowments both of body and mind,"[129] adding that he had not been able to identify any Black person who "had uttered a thought above the level of plain narration."[130]

Jefferson roundly denounced eighteenth-century Black writers like Wheatley as being mere hacks. Franklin was even more severe, coming down strongly against the importation even of dark-skinned Europeans and especially of Africans. He asked, "Why increase the sons of Africa by planting them in America, where we have so fair an opportunity, by excluding all blacks and tawnies, of increasing the lovely white and red?"[131]

Despite these grave reservations by the "Founding Fathers" of the nation, Africans still continued to make inputs into American cultural life. Africanisms flourished best when they could exist physically apart from European domination. A good example exists in Seminole society, where escaped Black slaves joined the Creek group and sought refuge in the Everglades.

In the United States, there are two excellent examples of this African cultural persistence. The first may be noted in the Sea Islands off the coast of the Carolinas and Georgia. Darwin Turner's *Africanisms in the Gullah Dialect* has pointed to the preponderance of African language

forms that have survived among the Gullah people. Until recently, they
lived outside Euro-American cultural domination and, as such, their
cooking and basket weaving, their rituals and language, have preserved a
fair degree of African influence. DuBose Hayward's *Porgy* (1925) and
George Gershwin's *Porgy and Bess* (1935) are both attempts at relating
aspects of Gullah culture in literature, opera, and film.

Another important African survival is to be found in New Orleans.
After the Haitian revolt against France, some slavemasters fled there with
their slaves. John Blassingame has shown in *Black New Orleans* how
Africans took their musical instrumentation to New Orleans and often
"carved figures on their stringed instruments and used hollowed-out
pieces of wood with animal skins stretched over them as drums."
Blassingame has added that the presence of these Blacks in New Orleans
actively carried on Africanisms that survive to this day, particularly when:

African religious rites were fused into one — voodoo, the worship of Damballa or the
snake God. The king and queen of the voodoo sect in New Orleans were "Dr. John" and
Marie Laveau, who exacted blind obedience from their followers. Claiming a
knowledge of the future and the ability to heal the body and to read the mind, Dr. John
and Laveau exercised great control over the blacks. Slaves bought charms and amulets
in order to control their masters, obtain money, gain success in love, insure good
health, and to harm their enemies.[132]

Today, *Vodun* has been reinforced by the growing presence of Haitians
in New York and Miami. Thus, the African traditions undergo change
and new mergings, but still continue to affect American culture.[133]

In addition to Gullah survivals and *Vodun*, Santería must be mentioned. Santería is a blend of Yoruba religion and Roman Catholicism.
Originally taken in its pure African form to eastern Cuba, synthesis
occurred because of the need for survival. The names of Christian saints
were substituted for African gods, but the African gods continued to be
worshiped in Yoruba (or Lucumi, as the language was known in Cuba).
Interestingly, the African religion was passed on to White Cubans. In
turn, they brought it with them to south Florida, from where it has spread
to Chicago, New York, and the West Coast.[134]

Africa, therefore, exists as reality in the United States. If more concrete
evidence is sought, surely no better example could be found than in the
Yoruba settlement of Oyotunji in South Carolina. There a number of
African Americans have erected a village that conforms to Yoruba-style
archi-tecture. They speak Yoruba, dress Yoruba-style, and engage in the
rituals of Yoruba belief. The entire social structure of the village is
modeled along Yoruba lines, with a king, a council of elders, priests of

various ranks, schools for children, and various temples for the worship of Yoruba gods.[135]

Africa has continued to influence American cultural life. Throughout the eighteenth and nineteenth centuries, Africa was seen not so much as a place but as part of a polemical debate. It later became the ultimate reference point for Black nationalism and an alternative to what America seemed to offer, both during and after slavery.

Because Blacks had not been accepted within American society, the American Colonization Society, founded in 1817, came to stand for an alternative that no less a figure than Abraham Lincoln put forward on August 14, 1862, to a group of African Americans. He warned them that their color was an inescapable yoke: "Go where you are treated the best . . . for the ban is upon you." He seemed to blame their very presence for the Civil War, arguing that "without the institution of slavery and the colored race as a basis, the war could not have an existence." Lincoln concluded to his Black countrymen:

It is better for us both, therefore, to be separated. I know that there are free men among you, who even if they could better their condition are not as much inclined to go out of the country as those, who being slaves could obtain their freedom on this condition. I suppose one of the principal difficulties in the way of colonization is that the free colored man cannot see that his comfort would be advanced by it. You may believe you can live in Washington or elsewhere in the United States the remainder of your life [as easily], perhaps more so than you can in any foreign country, and hence you may come to the conclusion that you have nothing to do with the idea of going to a foreign country. This is (I speak in no unkind sense) an extremely selfish view of the case.[136]

Among Blacks who sought alternatives to America were Paul Cuffee, Daniel Coker, Lott Cary, and John Russworm.[137] They attempted to establish settlements in West Africa and, except for Cuffee, all perished in the attempt. Cuffee visited Sierra Leone in 1811 and 1815; he took thirty-eight Blacks on his second trip but died before a grander scheme could be implemented by the American Colonization society.[138] Other relatively unknown but rather successful attempts at settlement were made. For instance, Black Americans remain to this day in Semana in the northern portion of the Dominican Republic, where they live as farmers and entrepreneurs.

Early colonization efforts were directed mainly at Sierra Leone, although later in the nineteenth century, the focus shifted to Liberia. Alexander Crummell emigrated to Nigeria in 1855, Martin Delany visited both Liberia and Nigeria in 1861, and Henny McNeal Turner followed in 1880.[139] They were all bitter men, with beliefs compounded of an intense rejection of America and a desire to Europeanize and Christianize Africa. For instance, Delany spoke of "the Moral, Social, and Political Elevation of Ourselves, and the Regeneration of Africa"[140]; Crummell saw Africa as "the victim of her heterogeneous idolatries. Darkness covers the land, and gross darkness the people"[141]; Turner, completely repudiating American values, cried out against the United States, but more in frustration than in anger: "We were born here, raised here, fought, bled, and died here, and have a thousand times more right here than hundreds of thousands of those who help snub, proscribe, and persecute us, and that is one of the reasons I almost despise the land of my birth."[142]

These early pioneers to Africa never fully expressed their real motives — their simultaneous desire to live in America and their desperation at having to seek refuge in Africa. Instead, they constantly stressed the very myth from which they themselves had suffered in the United States — that Africans were barbaric and in need of a guiding hand. By proclaiming Africa as a redemptive goal, they were able to preserve their own status, at least seemingly so. They could now (and this is a generalization, although not an unfair one) assume the role of colonizer and accept some of the mythology endorsed by Europe and White America.

One instance that lay outside the scope of the designs of the American Colonization Society and that brought Africa once more into American life was the *Amistad* incident. The *Amistad* was a vessel that was taken over by Africans off the Cuban coast and drifted ashore at New Haven. The Africans were defended by John Quincy Adams in a famous case of 1841. Mostly Mende and Temne people from Sierra Leone, the Africans asserted that they had been "kidnapped," were free people, and should be returned to Africa. The U.S. Supreme Court, in March 1841, set a legal precedent by agreeing with them.[143]

The African presence thus asserted itself yet again. These were real Africans who lived temporarily in New Haven. They petitioned the court not for something mythical but for their freedom. During the time that they lived in America they became well known, appearing at various benefits to raise money for their expenses and defense. When they left for Africa, having won their case, they once more showed how African issues have continued to touch on America.

For Marcus Garvey, Africa was a rallying cry, a threat to remove the Black workforce from America. Garvey's vision, however, went beyond just a physical return: African Americans would use Africa as a way of discarding the influence of both Europe and America. In August 1920, Garvey addressed the First International Convention of the Negro People of the World and attacked the barbarity and senselessness of the White world's internecine conflict. Garvey, while conceding that America was a great democracy, acknowledged that it shared its racism with Europe, for, in both parts of the world, Blacks were daily demeaned. The only sensible alternative was for Blacks to opt out, in order to protect their interests, as Garvey put it. Separatism was no hastily conceived solution; Garvey was arguing instead that the connections, the long march from Africa, the "discovery" of Europe, had not worked. Blacks, he said, had to be separated "mentally and physically," so that they could "win out by evolution."

Africa offered the possibility of starting human life all over again. Fifteen years later, Garvey reasserted this view of Africa as Paradise: "Africa is today a new country — new from outlook, new from consciousness, new from environments and conditions." As such, Africa represented a projection of the future or, as Garvey termed it: "Africa has registered the indication of approaching time"[144] with its promise of perfectability. Such a transcendent vision of the world meant that the image of Africa had again altered. No longer was it a continent to be saved. Instead, Africa would become the means through which economic power could be gained for African Americans. Again, this messianic interpretation had little to do with the reality of Africa.

W.E.B. DuBois took Garvey's advice and went to live in Ghana in his final years. But earlier on, he had had serious misgivings. "Africa," he pronounced in *Dusk at Dawn* (1949), "is, of course, my fatherland. Yet neither my father nor my father's father ever saw Africa or knew its meaning or cared overmuch for it."[145] Moreover, he worked assiduously to help obtain Garvey's deportation. His bias seems all the stranger, if only because DuBois' father was Haitian and thus ought to have been more closely attuned to the African realities of the New World.

When Claude McKay wrote about Africa, his sentiments were always the outpourings of fantasy. In his poem "Africa," the continent was the one that "brought forth light," "when all the world was young," "an ancient treasure-land." In "Outreach," according to this Harlemite from Jamaica, it was a place from "whence [his] fathers came," but in the poem "Enslaved," Africa is the "Black Land disinherited."[146]

McKay's imagery gives away an underlying suspicion. Africa is likened to a "dim bed" or "dim regions," where people sing "jungle songs." In a way, of course, this is a revival of the Noble Savage theme. McKay composed a trifle naively, but this is understandable. He knew nothing of African reality and assumed that images of Africa should be

dark and benighted, even as he condemned those who castigated the
continent in this way. Again, we note the dual inheritance already
mentioned.

Countee Cullen was little different. "Heritage," his much celebrated
poem, questions the African heritage and does so by reciting an
accumulation of stereotypes. As in works by McKay, there is reference to
the jungle — "Jungle boys and girls in love." As in McKay, there is a
blend of apparently laudable qualities, borrowed from romantic European
literature. For Cullen, Africa was a mixture of "copper sun" and "scarlet
sea," with all that the images suggest about the very sunlight being
exchanged for *copper* (pidgin English for money), and the marine
landscape being sold like a *scarlet* woman. Even when Cullen attempted
to be his most laudatory, he fell back on the clichés of "strong bronzed
men" and "regal black/Women." For Cullen, Africa was theoretical,
removed — "a book one thumbs listlessly."[147]

When Walt Whitman attempted to incorporate a cultural mix in his
poetry, the African presence remained a footnote, an afterthought, usually
expressed in negative superlatives. Whitman was striving for globalism
when he wrote in "Salut au Monde," "I am of Adelaide, Sidney,
Melbourne / I am of London, Manchester, Bristol, Edinburg, Limerick."
But how was globalism accomplished when he tacked this on a few lines
further? "You Hottentot with clicking palate! You woolly-hair'd hordes! /
You human forms with the fathomless ever-impressive countenances of
brutes!"[148] Whitman was suggesting that the African became part of the
American epic only as a distorted "savage," "heavy-lipped" — negative
monstrosities that perhaps only affirmed greater humanity for the other
races mentioned.

Africa has continued to be important in the national imagery of the
United States, as it moved over the color line. Carl Van Vechten's *Nigger
Heaven* (1926) set the wrong precedent for the Harlem Renaissance,
utilizing all the stale racial stock of the American psyche. Van Vechten's
novel, which in part initiated the Harlem Renaissance, is replete with
stereotypes: lazy studs, shiftless layabouts, amusing childlike oafs. The
irony is that African American writers did not hesitate to replicate these
stock figures.

McKay continued these same stereotypes in his first novels, *Home to
Harlem* (1928) and *Banjo* (1929). In both novels, McKay's major
character is intentionally set up as an antithesis to Ray, a thinking,
intellectual individual. Both Jake and Ray suggest that, as French
négritude poet, Léon Damas, would say later on, "emotion is Black."[149]
Of course, to argue this is to place oneself and the race on whose behalf

the writer speaks on very dangerous ground. It can, after all, be argued that those who possess an abundance of "emotion" may well be defective in "intellect."

Langston Hughes, despite his later visit to Dakar, also expressed Africa in this mystical manner. His early poem, "The Negro Speaks of Rivers" alludes to the Euphrates "when dawns were young," to the "singing of the Mississippi," and to the pyramids of the Nile. But regarding the Congo, Hughes could only state, "I built my hut near the Congo and it lulled me to the sleep." Hughes may be forgiven for thinking of Africa as a place not of houses but of huts, not of activity but of torpor, since he was only eighteen when the poem was written. Still, the poem does express an attitude of the time.[150]

African American oral literature has always reserved a place for Africa. In the story of the Signifying Monkey, for instance, the animals of the tale (an elephant, a lion, and a monkey) clearly owe their presence in the account to a remembered African past.[151] Furthermore, the monkey is a trickster, like the African spider, hare, and tortoise. One difference in the oral account, in which the monkey tricks the lion into fighting the elephant, is that listeners in the New World situation would interpret the monkey's actions not merely in jest, not merely as the weaker overcoming the stronger by use of his wits, but as a direct corollary with the situation of the Black underclass in American society. African folktales, therefore became altered and, in the process, acquired racial overtones that they did not have in their original context.

Another example of how African American folklore has sustained the presence of Africa appears in the recurrent motif of slaves who either swim or fly back to Africa. Toni Morrison took up the theme and used it as the end of *Song of Solomon* (1977). Likewise, in *Beloved* (1987), Morrison borrowed another African belief that probably originated to account for the high rate of infant mortality. An "abiku" is a child that keeps returning to its mother's womb. Prayers must be said to prevent it from going away again or from continuing its cycle of birth and death. Beloved herself is such a creation — she has, however, returned both to the "womb" and to her new home in America.

Slave narratives, which have been most popular in the nineteenth and twentieth centuries, are generically New World African. They depict the condition of enslavement and cry out against the harshness of servitude, yet their audience is the White reading public, and their purpose is to redress racial inequity.

Arna Bontemps attempted to resuscitate the slave narrative in *Black Thunder* (1936), which gave the account of Gabriel Prosser's uprising in 1800. Denmark Vesey's 1822 revolt in Charleston was the source of a motion picture, *A House Divided*. Nat Turner's revolt in 1831 has captured a great deal of attention. Turner supposedly dictated his memoirs to a White minister, the Reverend Thomas R. Gray, who afterward published them; William Styron recreated the account in his controversial novel, *The Confessions of Nat Turner* (1967). In Gray's version, Turner was suitably contrite and claimed to have been acting under the command of voices that had bade him to lead the insurrection. This instance demonstrates the problem not just with Gray's version of what Nat Turner said but with most slave narratives. Did the writers themselves actually compose their work or were they aided by well-meaning Whites?

If slave narratives were intended only to help speed up the abolition of slavery, then emancipation would have spelled their demise. But the genre persisted. Booker T. Washington's *Up From Slavery* (1901) took over from Frederick Douglass' *Narrative* (1845), in that they were both personal accounts, not about individuals, but about their times. Both advocated a cause and set forth remedies to correct conditions.

Indeed, it may be argued that a great deal of Black biography does just this. It moves away from personal reminiscences (or at least downplays them), in order to make statements that apply to the community at large. In this way, Malcolm X's *Autobiography* (1964) and Eldridge Cleaver's *Soul on Ice* (1968) are both "slave narratives." Although written in the twentieth century, both works follow the pattern of the slave narrative. They relate public events in relation to the narrator, address themselves to a White audience in order to initiate change, and, above all, put forward solutions to remedy the situation.

Slave narratives are African-American in origin, not because of their topics, but because of their format. Basically, they are a combination of personal praise poem and masquerade verse. The personal African liturgy lavished praise on the singer himself, at least seemingly so, since the "I" (even when referring to a king or to cattle) often was assumed by the praise-singer. Masquerade verse was utilized at festivals when provocative issues could be lam-basted. These verses can be found in most oral African traditions. In them, little is sacred. They attack transgressors and often condemn authority figures. Carnivals in Brazil, New Orleans, and the Caribbean make use of this African format, incorporating it, with song and dance, into parades.

Africa has been further mythologized in Black religion. This is not the place for a lengthy discussion, but suffice it to say that as early as the period of slave insurrections, leaders often claimed to receive their authority from God. Although, as in Nat Turner's case, this was assumed to be a Christian God, instances of African prophets deriving their authority from indigenous African beliefs are manifold.

A type of "mystical" Africa has survived, particularly in the deification of Black religious leaders who utilized Judaism, Islam, or Christianity to proclaim "authority." Both Father Divine and Daddy Grace established themselves as African kings — I would suggest in a very distorted way — but, nevertheless, this persona offered the justification for their authority. When Father Divine spoke of his "kingdom" or Daddy Grace of his "House of Prayer," they were both establishing territories within which they and their followers could function in an apparently sovereign manner.

Prophet F. S. Cherry and the Noble Drew Ali (Timothy Drew) sought to incorporate, respectively, Jewish and Islamic forms of worship. Of course, both choices may be justified within the strictest African frame of reference, but each "converted" African authenticity into a nationalist vision, thereby further distorting the image of Africa. For instance, Prophet Cherry's group claimed that Jesus was Black (a claim taken up later by Reverend Albert Cleage in the "Church of the Black Madonna" in Detroit in the 1960s). On the other hand, for the Noble Drew Ali, Blacks were "Asiatics," "Moors," "Moorish Americans." This group did not, however, incorporate only Islam (as Elijah Muhammed would later do), but took in all major world religions. Any examination of African influences in African American life must thus consider the distortions that, however well-intended, have moved Africa further into a mythical frame of reference.

Finally, Africa has been "returned" to African Americans and Euro-Americans via Europe. At the turn of the century, Pablo Picasso and Henri Matisse experimented with forms from Ivory Coast sculpture. Igor Stravinsky utilized ragtime music and jazz in "serious opera." André Gide wrote *Voyage au Congo* (1927), while anthropologist and folklorist, Leo Frobenius, put together a monumental collection of African folklore. The effect was to force U.S. intellectuals to take a serious look at the African past of Black Americans, and to make Blacks themselves strive to incorporate African elements into their work. In the former connection, Nancy Cunard must be mentioned, although she seldom is. The wealthy heiress of the English steamship company openly flouted the prevailing norms, became a Communist, and lived openly with her Black lover in a Harlem hotel in the early 1930s. Her claim on our attention is that she compiled *Negro* in 1934, an anthology that brought together some of the best writers on both sides of the Atlantic, in the cause of putting forward a universal view of the Black world. Her work is all the more remarkable because she was able to recruit people like Ezra Pound to her cause and especially since she herself disapproved of the earlier Harlem Renaissance movement as too bourgeois. In 1935, George Gershwin and DuBose Hayward produced *Porgy and Bess*, partly based on the street ballads of the Gullah people.[152]

Two White American writers should be specifically mentioned — Eugene O'Neill and Vachel Lindsay. O'Neill, both in *The Emperor Jones* (1920) and *All God's Chillun Got Wings* (1924), tried to be as serious as possible regarding the African/African American theme. O'Neill's problem was that he could not, given the severe limitations of his time, construct credible portraits. Although Paul Robeson himself played Brutus Jones in both the stage and screen versions of *Emperor Jones*, Robeson's presence merely served to underscore the simplicity of the era.

Jones lacks the capacity to move us. We see him as a crook, who has the brutish personality his first name implies. Throughout the play, he is moved, not by noble causes but simply by greed. His sorry actions, especially as controlled by an English trader, make Jones seem simplistic and stereotypical. Furthermore, because Jones is a mere bully, intent on exploiting the "natives" of some mythical "West Indian" island, he loses the audience's empathy. We can no more easily believe in his potential for goodness than we can in the crude props that constitute the island — drums in the distance and the picture of Jones regressing to a "savage" condition.

Lindsay's "Congo" is an exercise in the easy acceptance of the trite and the macabre. His idea of the Congo combines all that is negative in popular Euro-American belief: Blacks are shallow but rhythmical, sexual but superficial. In their posturings, they become examples of both the grotesque and the absurd, frightening and laughable at the same time. Ironically, the European contact with Africa leads to an ultimate rejection of Africa itself, one, we must stress, that was shared by both Black and White writers alike.

Even Richard Wright felt that, in many ways, it was impossible to empathize with Africa. Even though Wright was treated in Ghana as a distinguished visitor and offered all the hospitality that Head of State Kwame Nkrumah could give, he still yearned for the boulevards of Paris.

Emotionally, from within, he cried out, "They were Black and I was Black, but my color did not help me." Finally, he had to resort to a bit of intellectual nonsense to explain his relationship with Africa: "One does not react to Africa as Africa is. . . . One reacts to Africa as one is, as one lives."[153] Wright could never clearly empathize with the physical reality of Africa. Instead, it represented for him the cultural monsters of his American upbringing, which, in turn, presented an impediment to his understanding.

Once more, Africa has entered into American consciousness. This has happened in two ways. First, when Nelson Mandela was freed from prison, his liberation took on symbolic overtones. Americans mentally replayed their own campaigns for the civil and human rights of Blacks, their own long period of history when segregation was the law of the land.

Mandela's first visit to the United States, therefore, was not merely that of an imprisoned South African. His presence represented the validation of virtue, of ethnic and national pride. Black and White Americans could use his visit as a way of saying that their own nightmare of legalized racism was over. Mandela's presence became, in other words, another way in which the African subconscious, always a few levels beneath the national consciousness, revealed itself.

Second, at the academic level, Africa is also reasserting itself. After the agonizing debates over Black Studies in the 1960s, the issue is still here and still unresolved. How can we incorporate large segments of the population into the curriculum? How can American schools reflect the community's culture as so-called "multiculturalism"?

Despite all the negative attacks, multiculturalism attempts to provide an answer. Simply stated, multiculturalism challenges the old conceptual framework that "American" and "European" education are synonymous. If this is a new country with needs that differ vastly from Europe's and with a polyethnic population, then a national curriculum must address the varying ethnicities in our midst.

Africa is therefore an appropriate topic for incorporation into the curriculum, partly as "myth," since the myth has been validated by African American culture and partly as "reality," since we need to return to sources to fully understand origins. "Africology" as subject or "Afrocentricity" as method are only two among many approaches under the vast banner of multiculturalism. But we must begin if the curriculum is ever to be affected in any degree so that it reflects the heritage of at least one important sector of the population.

Multiculturalism intentionally attacks the longstanding model that puts forward a White, male, heterosexual monolith. Clearly, to advance such a version as the only model has become a little ridiculous in our time. The victims of European oppression have had a different history, and someone must acknowledge that we have all so far been too absorbed in the history of the victor. The cultural record must express different views and, in so doing, point out negative and unsavory aspects that have been accepted for too long. Thus, multiculturalism provides a challenge, in that the global scenario is ripe for a different and bolder experiment. Through a new approach to a more holistic curriculum, we can reclaim all our pasts, thus giving new meanings to New World culture and forever laying to rest the European fantasy that imposed "discovery" on both discoverer and discovered. Perhaps, through the subversion of this concept, its folly can become more manifest, and we can lay claim to a new understanding of a final reality when "myth" is finally expelled. Perhaps, in this way, the experience of Africans in the New World can become the supreme arbiter that will allow all to engage in a final reconciliation. Myth might then give way to a new understanding of reality, and we may thus complete our cycle of eternal sojourning, having been fully restored with a new faith. Only then will the journeys, physical and intellectual, end in a final triumph of the human spirit.

Notes

CHAPTER 1

1. Christopher Columbus, *Libro de las profecías*, trans. Delno West and August Kling (Gainesville: University of Florida Press, 1991), 107. For a good discussion of biblical references, see Samuel Eliot Morison, *Christopher Columbus Mariner* (New York: New American Library, 1955), 19.

2. See Claudius Ptolemy, *The Geography*, trans. and ed. Edward Luther Stevenson (New York: Dover, 1991). Also see Claudius Ptolemy, *Cosmography: Maps from Ptolemy's Geography* (Wigston, U.K.: Magna Books, 1990).

3. See Pierre d'Ailly [Petrus Aliacus], *Imago Mundi*, trans. Edwin F. Keever (Wilmington, NC: privately published, 1948).

4. Paolo dal Pozzo Toscanelli cited John Boyd Thacher, *Christopher Columbus: His Life, His Work, His Remains*, 3 vols. (New York: G. P. Putnam's Sons, 1903), vol. 1, 348–380; for letters, see vol. 2, 306–316.

5. Pope Pius II, *Historia Rerum Ubique Gestarum* (Venice, 1477). See Thacher, *Columbus*, vol. 1, 308–316, 319.

6. Christopher Columbus, *Selected Documents Illustrating the Four Voyages of Columbus*, trans. and ed. Cecil Jane. 2 vols. (London: Hakluyt Society, vol. 1, 1930; vol. 2, 1933), vol. 1, 27.

7. Kirkpatrick Sale, *The Conquest of Paradise* (New York: Alfred A. Knopf, 1990), 134.

8. Charles Bricker, R. V. Tooley, and Gerald Crone, *Landmarks of Mapmaking* (Amsterdam: Elsevier, 1968), 22–23.

9. J. B. Harley and David Woodward, *The History of Cartography*, 2 vols. (Chicago: University of Chicago Press, 1987), vol. 1, 287.

10. Harley and Woodward, *Cartography*, vol. 1, 334.

11. Patrick Gautier Dalché, *La "Descriptio Mappae Mundi" de Hughes de Saint-Victor* (Paris: Études Augustiniennes, 1988), plates 1 and 2, 83.

12. Harley and Woodward, *Cartography*, vol. 1, 287.

13. Ibid., 334.

14. Rodney W. Shirley, *The Mapping of the World* (London: Holland Press Cartographica, 1984), 1–2.

15. J.R.S. Phillips, *The Medieval Expansion of Europe* (Oxford: Oxford University Press, 1988), 218.

16.   For good background information, consult Leo Bagrow, *History of Cartography* (Chicago: Precedent, 1964), especially plates 27–39, p. 72, and map No. 42; also, see Daniel J. Boorstin, *The Discoverers* (New York: Vintage, 1985), 150, 162.

17.   "Beowulf" in *Anglo-Saxon Poetry*, trans. R. K. Gordon (London: J. M. Dent and Sons, 1954), 74–75.

18.   "Seafarer" in *Anglo-Saxon Poetry*, 76–78.

19.   Columbus, *Selected Documents*, vol. 2, 104.

20.   Richard Hakluyt, *The Principal Navigations, Voyages and Discoveries of the English Nation* [1589] 2 vols. (Cambridge: Hakluyt Society, 1965), vol. 1, 2.

21.   Helena Flavia Augusta cited in Hakluyt, *Principal Navigations*, vol. 1, 1–2.

22.   Thomas Wright, ed., *Early Travels in Palestine* (New York: A.M.S. Press, 1969).

23.   Wright, *Early Travels*, 21.

24.   Ibid., 415–416.

25.   Columbus, *Selected Documents*, vol. 1, 24.

26.   Flavius Josephus, *The Complete Works of Josephus* (Grand Rapids: Kregel, 1981), 180; see also Columbus, *Libro*, 88.

27.   Gordon Speck, *Myths and New World Explorations* (Fairfield, WA: De Galleon, 1979), 63–67.

28.   George P. Winship, ed., *The Journey of Coronado* (New York: Allerton, 1922), 1–2.

29.   Peter D'Anghera Martyr, *De Orbe Novo*, trans. Francis Augustus MacNutt, 2 vols. (New York: Burt Franklin, 1970), vols. 1 & 2.

30.   Winship, *Coronado*, 1–2.

31.   A great deal has been written on these imaginary islands. See W. P. Cumming, R. A. Skelton and D. B. Quinn, *The Discovery of North America* (New York: American Heritage, 1972), 41.

32.   See, among other references, Cyrus H. Gordon, *Before Columbus: Links Between the Old World and America* (New York: Crown, 1971).

33.   Winship, *Coronado*, 1–2.

34.   Walter Raleigh, *The Discoverie of the Large, Rich and Bewtiful Empyre of Guiana* [1596] (Amsterdam: De Cap, 1968), 13–16. A modern version exists in Richard David, ed., *Hakluyt's Voyages* (Boston: Houghton Mifflin, 1981), 460–464.

35.   Germán Arciniegas, *Germans in the Conquest of America* (New York: MacMillan, 1943), 140, 152.

36.   Raleigh, *Discoverie*, 11.

37.   Alvar Núñez Cabeza de Vaca, *The Narrative of Cabeza de Vaca* (Barre, MA: Imprint Society, 1972), 155.

38.   Ibid., 47.

39.   Ibid., 258.

40.   Ibid., 217.

41.   See Gerald Holton and Duane H. D. Roller, *Foundations of Modern Physical Science* (New York: Addison-Wesley, 1958), 42.

42.   Phillips, *Medieval Expansion*, 216.

43.   Carl Sagan, *Cosmos* (New York: Random House, 1980), 20.

44.   Columbus, *Selected Documents*, vol. 2, 28.

45.   Ibid., 30–32.

46. Cited by Ernle Bradford, *Christopher Columbus* (New York: Viking, 1973).

47. Columbus, *Libro*, 10.

48. Ferdinand Columbus, *The Life of the Admiral Christopher Columbus by His Son Ferdinand*, trans. Benjamin Keen (New Brunswick: Rutgers University Press, 1959), 20–22.

49. See Bartolomé de las Casas, *History of the Indies* (New York: Harper & Row, 1971); also see Thacher, *Columbus*, vol. 1, 301–316.

50. Thacher, *Columbus*, 304.

51. Ibid., 305.

52. Ibid., 301.

53. Ibid., 306.

54. Ibid.

55. Ibid., 312.

56. Ibid., 313–316.

57. Fred F. Kravath, *Christopher Columbus, Cosmographer* (Rancho Cordova, CA: Landmark Enterprises, 1987).

58. Ibid., 109.

59. Ibid.

60. Columbus, *Selected Documents*, vol. 1, 14.

61. Lewis Hanke, *All Mankind Is One* (De Kalb: Northern Illinois University Press, 1974), 84.

62. Kravath, *Columbus*, 112–113. Also see an excellent evaluation of Chinese exploration in Walter Albert Chan, *The Glory and Fall of the Ming Dynasty* (Norman: University of Oklahoma Press, 1982), and C. P. Fitzgerald *The Chinese View of Their Place in the World* (Oxford: Oxford University Press, 1966).

63. Martyr, *De Orbe*, vol. 2, 204.

64. *Beowulf and the Finnesburg Fragment*, trans. John R. Clark Hall, rev. C.L.R. Wrenn (London: George Allen & Unwin, 1954), 58.

65. *Beowulf*, 84.

66. J.R.R. Tolkien and E. V. Gordon, eds., *Sir Gawain and the Green Knight* (Oxford: Clarendon Press), 1952.

67. Bruce Dickins and R. M. Wilson, *Early Middle English Texts* (Cambridge: Bowes and Bowes, 1957), 51–57.

68. Francis MacNutt, ed., *Fernando Cortés: His Five Letters of Relation to the Emperor Charles V*, 2 vols. (Glorieta, NM: Rio Grande Press, 1977), vol. 2, 262–263, n.1.

69. Bartolomé de las Casas, *In Defense of the Indians* [c. 1552], trans. Stafford Poole (De Kalb: Northern Illinois University Press, 1974), 45.

70. See references to Sebastian Münster, *Cosmographica*, in Cumming, Skelton, and Quinn, *Discovery, passim*.

71. Cumming, Skelton, and Quinn, *Discovery*, 44.

72. Peter Jackson and David Morgan, eds., *Mission of Friar William of Rubruck* (London: Hakluyt Society, 1990), 4.

73. John Block Friedman, *The Monstrous Races in Medieval Art and Thought* (Cambridge, MA: Harvard University Press, 1981), 9–21.

74. Pliny, *Natural History*, ed. H. Rackham, W.H.S. Jones, and D. E. Eichholz, 10 vols. (Cambridge: Harvard University Press; and London: William Heinemann, 1967), vol. 2, 517. For a good "general" account of Amazons and of Francisco de

Orellana, see José Toribio Medina, *The Discovery of the Amazon* (Mineola, NY: Dover, 1988). This book includes translations of Gonzalo Fernandez de Oviedo's account (as told to him) and Gaspar de Carvajal's own version.

75. Pliny, *Natural History*, vol. 2, 517.

76. Ibid., 517, 251–533.

77. Ibid., 251.

78. Ibid., 479.

79. Ibid., 479–481.

80. Ibid., 513, 517.

81. Ibid., 519, 521.

82. Ibid., 521, 525, 527.

83. Christopher Columbus, *The Journal of Christopher Columbus*, trans. Cecil Jane (New York: Bonanza, 1960), 135.

84. See Columbus, *Libro*, 24.

85. Paul Turner, *Selections from the History of the World* (Carbondale: Southern Illinois University Press, 1962), 11.

86. Pliny, *Natural History*, *passim*.

87. Samuel Purchas, *Hakluytus Posthumus*, 20 vols. (Glasgow: James MacLehose Sons, 1905), vol. 2, 27.

88. Stephen Greenblatt, *Marvelous Possessions* (Chicago: University of Chicago Press, 1991), 163, n. 43.

89. Martyr, *De Orbe*, vol. 1, 64.

90. Friedman, *Monstrous Races*, 15.

91. Martyr, *De Orbe*, vol. 1, 315.

92. Transilvane, Maximilian, "The Epistle of Maximilian Transilvane," in Richard Eden, *The First Three English Books on America* (Birmingham, 1885), 247–248.

93. Eden, *First Three Books*, 248.

94. Columbus, *Selected Documents*, vol. 1, 14.

95. Ibid., 12, 24, 26.

96. Friedman, *Monstrous Races*, 11–12, 15–16,.

97. Ibid., 7.

98. See Eden, *First Three Books*, 251–252.

99. Seneca, *Selections*, ed. Umberto Moricca (Turin, Italy: I. B. Paravia, 1947), 258–261. (English translation by O. R. Dathorne)

100. Columbus, *Selected Documents*, vol. 2, 92.

101. Ferdinand Columbus, *Admiral*, 18.

102. Salvador de Madariaga, *Christopher Columbus* (New York: Frederick Ungar, 1940), 81.

103. Plato, *The Timaeus and the Critias or Atlanticus*, trans. Thomas Taylor (New York: Pantheon, 1944), 63, 104.

104. Ibid., 238.

105. Ibid., 242.

106. Ibid., 148.

107. See Ignatius Donnelly, *Atlantis: The Antediluvian World* (New York: Dover, 1976), 1–30.

108. Ferdinand Columbus, *Admiral*, 17–19.

109. Euripides, *Plays*, trans. A. S. Way, 2 vols. (London: J. M. Dent and Sons, 1956), vol. 1, 51.

110. Madariaga, *Columbus*, 80–81.

111. See Columbus, *Libro*, 24.

112. Plutarch, *Lives*, ed. Alan Wordman (Berkeley: University of California Press, 1974), 215.

113. Ibid., 229.

114. Herodotus, *The Histories*, trans. Aubrey de Sélincourt (London: Penguin, 1972), 65.

115. Columbus, *Journal*, 27–28.

116. Columbus, *Selected Documents*, vol. 2, 148.

117. Samuel Eliot Morison, *The Great Explorers* (New York: Oxford University Press, 1978), 430.

118. Agatharchides of Cnidus, *On the Erythraean Sea*, trans. and ed. Stanley M. Burstein (London: Hakluyt Society, 1989), 173.

119. Friedman, *Monstrous Races*, 199.

120. Leonardo Olschki, *Marco Polo's Asia* (Berkeley: University of California Press, 1960), 232.

121. Sir John Mandeville, *The Travels of Sir John Mandeville*, trans. and intro. C.W.R.D. Moseley (London: Penguin, 1983), 116.

122. See William Blake Tyrrell, *Amazons: A Study in Athenian Mythmaking* (Baltimore: Johns Hopkins University Press, 1991).

123. Eden, *First Three Books*, 251–252.

124. Samuel Eliot Morison, *The European Discovery of America: The Southern Voyages 1492–1516* (New York: Oxford University Press, 1974), 368.

125. Eden, *First Three Books*, 251. Also Morison, *European Discovery, Southern*, 369.

126. Eden, *First Three Books*, 252. Also Morison, *European Discovery, Southern*, 369.

127. Marco Polo, *The Description of the World*, ed. A. C. Moule and Paul Pelliot, 2 vols. (London: George Routledge & Sons, 1938), vol. 1, 122. Also see Theodore de Bry, *Discovering the World*, ed. Michael Alexander (New York: Harper & Row, 1976), in which some text and illustrations are reproduced; also see R. A. Skelton, *Explorers' Maps: Chapters in the Cartographical Record of Geographical Discovery* (London: Routledge and Kegan Paul, 1958).

128. Morison, *European Discovery, Southern*, 550.

129. Columbus, *Selected Documents*, vol. 1, 116.

130. Martyr, *De Orbe*, vol. 1, 274. For a good introduction to Prester John, see C. N. Gumley, *Searches for an Imaginary Kingdom* (Cambridge: Cambridge University Press, 1987), 5–7, 101–103.

131. Morison, *European Discovery, Southern*, 502–515.

132. Mary B. Campbell, *The Witness and the Other World* (Ithaca, NY: Cornell University Press, 1988), 52.

133. Amerigo Vespucci, *Mundus Novus* [letter to Lorenzo Pietro de Medici], trans. George Tyler Northrop, 5 vols. (Princeton: Princeton University Press, 1916), vol. 5; also see Amerigo Vespucci, *Letters from a New World*, ed. Luciano Formisano (New York: Marsilio, 1992).

134.   Mandeville, *Travels*, 169.

135.   Ibid., 255.

136.   Columbus, *Selected Documents*, vol. 2, 104.

137.   Ibid., 36.

138.   Ibid., 36–38.

139.   See Michael Wood, *World Atlas of Archaeology* (Boston: G. K. Hall, 1985); also see two good works that relate this "encounter" empathetically from the viewpoint of the "encountered." These are William Keegan, *The People Who Discovered Columbus* (Gainesville: University Press of Florida, 1992); and Irving Rouse, *The Taínos: Rise and Fall of the People Who Greeted Columbus* (New Haven: Yale University Press, 1992).

140.   Jan Albert Goris and Georges Marlier, *Albrecht Dürer: Diary of the Journey to the Netherlands 1520–1521*, (London, 1971), cited by Jean Michel Massing, "Early European Images of America: The Ethnographic Approach," in *Circa 1492: Art in the Age of Exploration*, ed. Jay A. Levinson (New Haven: Yale University Press, 1991), 515–520.

141.   Ibid.

142.   Ibid., 515.

143.   Ibid., 515, 514.

CHAPTER 2

1.   Pliny, *Natural History*, vol. 2, 477.

2.   Ibid., 479.

3.   Ibid., 523.

4.   Ibid., vol. 10, 159.

5.   Ibid., 59.

6.   Ibid., 61.

7.   Columbus, *Selected Documents*, vol. 2, 40.

8.   D'Ailly, *Imago Mundi*, 16–18.

9.   Ibid., 28.

10.   Ibid., 30.

11.   For background information on some of these writers, see relevant portions of Rhys Carpenter, *Beyond the Pillars of Heracles* (New York: Delacorte, 1966); Fred F. Kravath, *Christopher Columbus Cosmographer*, as well as *The Penguin Companion to Literature*, vol. 2, ed. Anthony Torlby, and vol. 4, ed. D. R. Dudley and D. M. Lang (Harmondsworth, Middlesex: Penguin, 1969).

12.   This version of the *Koran* was translated with notes by N. J. Dawood (London: Penguin, 1990), 18:84–18:97, 302.

13.   Campbell, *Witness*, 65.

14.   For "Alexander's Letter to Aristotle about India," see Donald Davidson and A. P. Campbell, "The Letter of Alexander to the Great Aristotle," *Humanities Association Bulletin*, 23:3 (Summer 1972), 3–16; and Lloyd L. Gunderson, *Alexander's Letter to Aristotle about India* (Meisenheim am Glan, Germany: Anton Hain, 1980). My textual quotations come from Gunderson's version, entitled "Epistola," 140–156.

15.   Gunderson, *Alexander's Letter*, 140.

16.   Ibid., 144.

17. Ibid.
18. Ibid.
19. See Davidson and Campbell, "Letter of Alexander," 4.
20. Gunderson, *Alexander's Letter*, 144.
21. Ibid., 146.
22. Ibid., 145.
23. Ibid., 145–146.
24. Ibid., 155.
25. Ibid., 147.
26. Ibid., 148.
27. Ibid., 149.
28. Ibid., 156.
29. Ibid., 150.
30. Ibid., 151.
31. Ibid., 151–152.
32. Ibid., 151.
33. Ibid., 152.
34. Ibid., 154.
35. Paul Allen Gibb, "Wonders of the East: A Critical Edition and Commentary," (Ph.D. diss., Duke University, 1977; available through University Microfilms International, 1992). For modern English translation of the Old English text, see 100–111.
36. Ibid., 100–101.
37. Ibid., 109.
38. Ibid.
39. Ibid., 106.
40. A useful reference that updates misanthropy is Florence King, *With Charity Towards None* (New York: St. Martin's, 1992). She is a self-confessed misanthropist and gives a tongue-in-cheek account of past and present misanthropsts. More relevant for our purposes are two studies: first, R. Howard Bloch, *Medieval Misogyny* (Chicago: University of Chicago Press, 1991), in which Bloch has asserted that misogyny is a "speech act"; and Sheila Fisher and Janet E. Halley, eds., *Seeking the Woman in Late Medieval and Renaissance Writings* (Knoxville: University of Tennessee Press, 1989).
41. Gibb, "Wonders," 109.
42. Ibid., 108.
43. Ibid., 109.
44. Ibid.
45. Ibid., 102.
46. Ibid., 104.
47. Ibid.
48. Ibid.
49. Ibid., 105.
50. Bloch, *Medieval Misogyny*, 1–11.
51. Gibb, "Wonders," 101.
52. Ibid.
53. Ibid.
54. Ibid.

55. Ibid.
56. Ibid., 105.
57. Ibid.
58. Ibid., 110.
59. Ibid., 106.
60. Ibid., 107.
61. Ibid., 106.
62. Ibid., 101.
63. St. Augustine, *City of God*, trans. Henry Bettenson (Harmondsworth, England: Penguin, 1972), 664.
64. Gibbs, "Wonders," 104.
65. Ibid., 105.
66. Ibid., 111.
67. Ibid., 107.
68. Ibid., 109.
69. Ibid., 110.
70. Ibid., 102.
71. Ibid., 108.
72. Ibid.
73. Ibid., 103.
74. Ibid., 106.
75. Ibid., 110.
76. Ibid.
77. Ibid., 108.
78. An excellent in-depth treatment of Prester John is to be found in Vsevolod Slessarev, *Prester John: The Letter and the Legend* (Minneapolis: University of Minnesota Press, 1959). This book has been invaluable for providing original background information. One version of the letter is translated on pages 67–79, but see discussion of letter, 32–54; see also Olschki, *Marco Polo's Asia*, 388–391.
79. Slessarev, *Prester John*, 41.
80. Ibid., 37.
81. Bradford, *Columbus*, 41.
82. Friedrick Zarncke, *Der Priester Johannes*, 2 vols. (Leipzig: S. Hirzel, 1876 and 1879), vol. 2, 910–924; also see Slessarev, *Prester John*, 34.
83. *Spice of Life*, a four-part television documentary on The Learning Channel, dealt extensively with allspice (Jamaica), chili (Mexico), cinnamon (Sri Lanka), and cloves (Moluccas), as well as with the effect of the introduction of these spices on the European diet and world trade.
84. Leo Africanus [Johannes Leo], *A Geographical Historie of Africa* [1600], ed. John Pory (New York: De Capo, 1969). Interestingly, Pory has given Prester John's lineage and describes in scholarly detail the extent of his kingdom and power. In addition, he has utilized marginal notes and "translations" to support the "research" of other scholars.
85. Arthur Newton, *Travel and Travellers of the Middle Ages* (London: Routledge & Kegan Paul, 1926), 178.
86. Slessarev, *Prester John*, 67–79.
87. Ibid., 68.
88. Ibid., 69.

89. Ibid., 70.

90. Ibid.

91. Medina, *Discovery*, 434.

92. Slessarev, *Prester John*, 72.

93. Ibid., 75.

94. Ibid., 72.

95. Ibid., 73.

96. Ibid.

97. Ibid., 76.

98. See Hussain Khan, "Sea-Borne Horse Trade to '*Al-Sind Wa'l-Hind*,'" *Journal of the Pakistan Historical Society*, 39:4 (October 1991), 311–314. Khan has shown how, from as early as the thirteenth century, Arab ships were sturdy enough to transport large horses from the Persian Gulf to India.

99. See Nafis Ahmad, *Muslim Contribution to Geography* (Lahore, Pakistan: Sh. Muhammad Ashraf, 1972) for a good evaluation of this topic.

100. R. A Skelton, Thomas E. Marston, and George D. Painter, *The Vinland Map and the Tartar Relation* (New Haven: Yale University Press, 1965), 117–123.

101. Ahmad, *Muslim Contribution*, 157.

102. Ibid.

103. Michael Bradley, *The Black Discovery of America* (Toronto: Personal Library, 1981), 181.

104. Skelton, *Explorers' Maps*, 26.

105. T. W. Arnold, "Arab Travellers and Merchants: AD 1000–1500," in Newton, *Travel and Travellers*, 88.

106. Ahmad, *Muslim Contribution*, 23–62.

107. Thomas J. Abercrombie, "Ibn Battuta: Prince of Travelers," *National Geographic*, 180:6 (December 1991), 2–49; see especially his route map, 12–13.

108. I have made use of the exclusive quotations in a study by Ross E. Dunn, *The Adventures of Ibn Battuta* (Berkeley: University of California Press, 1986). For the section on Mali, Dunn himself used translations from N. Levtzion and J.F.P. Hopkins, eds., *Corpus of Early Arabic Sources for West African History* (Cambridge: Cambridge University Press, 1981). I have also used E. W. Bovill, *The Golden Trade with the Moors* (London: Oxford University Press, 1988).

109. Dunn, *Adventures*, 303–304.

110. Bovill, *Golden Trade*, 96–97.

111. Ibid., 97.

112. J. Devisse and S. Labib, "Africa in Inter-Continental Relations," in *General History of Africa*, 8 vols. (Paris: UNESCO, 1984), vol. 4, 635.

113. Ibid., 636.

114. Ibid.

115. Ibid., 637.

116. See map, ibid., 638.

117. Ibn Khaldun, *The Muqadimah: An Introduction to History* [1377], trans. Franz Rosenthal (Princeton: Princeton University Press, 1967), 58.

118. Ibid., 59.

119. Ibid., 63.

120. Ibid., 117.

121. Ahmad, *Muslim Contributions*, 138.

122.   Two books by Lewis Hanke are very helpful in understanding the heat generated by this debate. *Aristotle and the Indians* (Bloomington: Indiana University Press, 1959) has situated the polemical dispute within the historical context of Aristotelian principles. Second, he has placed the disputation within the larger context of its time in *All Mankind Is One* (De Kalb: Northern Illinois University Press, 1974).

123.   Newton, *Travel and Travellers*, 8.

124.   Ibid., 94.

125.   Africanus, *Geographical Historie*, 42.

126.   Ibid., 41–42.

127.   Bovill, *Golden Trade*, 133.

128.   Africanus, *Geographical Historie*, 3.

129.   Ibid., 5–6.

130.   Ibid., 20.

131.   Ibid., 29.

132.   Ibid., 37.

133.   Ibid., 284.

134.   Ibid., 288.

135.   Elkan Nathan Adler, *Jewish Travellers in the Middle Ages* (Mineola, NY: Dover, 1987). References below are made to the nineteen firsthand accounts of travelers represented in this work.

136.   Ibid., 1.

137.   Ibid., 6.

138.   Ibid., 17.

139.   Ibid., 10.

140.   Ibid., 37.

141.   Ibid., 40.

142.   Ibid., 41.

143.   Ibid., 48.

144.   Ibid., 65.

145.   Ibid., 93.

146.   Ibid., 154.

147.   Ibid., 117.

148.   Ibid., 120.

149.   Ibid., 133.

150.   Ibid., 164.

151.   Ibid., 189.

152.   Ibid., 299.

153.   Benedict, *The Marvels of Rome* [c. 1143], ed. and trans. Frances Morgan Nichols (New York: Ithaca Press, 1986), 46.

154.   Ibid., 17–18.

155.   Ibid., 28.

156.   Ibid., 26.

157.   Ibid., 35.

158.   Ibid., 38.

159.   Theoderich, *Guide to the Holy Land* [1172], trans. Aubrey Stewart, intro Ronald G. Musto (New York: Ithaca Press, 1986).

160.   Ibid., (see "Introduction" by Musto), xxxii.

161.   Ibid., 33.
162.   Ibid., 47.
163.   Ibid., 221.
164.   Ibid.
165.   See Eric Flaum, *Discovery: Exploration Through the Centuries* (New York: Gallery Books, 1990), 67–81, which provides very basic information on Carpini, Rubruck, the Polos, John of Monte Corvino, Odoric, Ibn Battuta, and Niccolo de Conti among others.
166.   For both Carpini and Rubruck, I have used John de Plano Carpini, *The Texts and Versions of John de Plano Carpini and William de Rubruquis* (London: Hakluyt Society, 1903), referred to in notes by their individual names. I have modernized the text. For William of Rubruck, I also consulted William Rubruck, *The Mission of Friar William of Rubruck*, trans. Peter Jackson (London: Hakluyt Society, 1970).
167.   Carpini, *Texts*, 110–111.
168.   Ibid., 111.
169.   Ibid., 117.
170.   Ibid., 118.
171.   Ibid., 122.
172.   Ibid., 137.
173.   Olschki, *Marco Polo's Asia*, 389.
174.   Carpini, *Texts*, 143.
175.   Campbell, *Witness*, 114.
176.   Rubruck, *Mission*, 260.
177.   Ibid., 261.
178.   Ibid., 261, n.2 and n.3; 266, n.1.
179.   Ibid., 262–263.
180.   Ibid., 122.
181.   Ibid., 146.
182.   Ibid., 158.
183.   Columbus, *Selected Documents*, vol. 1, 14.
184.   Odoric, *The Voyage and Travayle of Syr John Maundeville with the Journall of Frier Odoricus* (London: J. M. Dent, c. 1887), 232.
185.   Ibid., 234.
186.   Ibid., 236.
187.   Ibid., 238.
188.   Ibid., 239–240.
189.   Columbus, *Selected Documents*, vol. 2, 104.
190.   Winship, *Coronado*, 1–2.
191.   Ibid., 219.
192.   Odoric, *Voyage and Travayle*, 13.
193.   Ibid., 193.
194.   Ibid., 241.
195.   Ibid., 244.
196.   Ibid., 246–248.
197.   Ibid., 246.
198.   Ibid., 242.
199.   Ibid., 247.
200.   Ibid., 241.

201.   Ibid., 250.
202.   Ibid., 252–253.
203.   Ibid., 259.
204.   Ibid., 267.
205.   Ibid., 269.
206.   Ibid., 270.
207.   Ibid., 271.
208.   Quoted by Manuel Komroff, ed., *Contemporaries of Marco Polo* (New York Dorset, 1989), "Introduction," xiii. This is a useful reference that deals with some of the travelers mentioned here, particularly Carpini, Rubruck, Odoric and Rabbi Benjamin.

CHAPTER 3

1.   Bloch, *Medieval Misogyny*, 11.
2.   Some detailed treatment of Columbus' early influences is to be found in Zvi Dor-Ner, *Columbus and the Age of Discovery* (New York: William Morrow, 1991) 67–68.
3.   Ferdinand Columbus, *Admiral*, 25. Ferdinand also listed other islands, particularly Antillia and the Island of the Seven Cities; see also Sale, *Conquest of Paradise*, 64–65. Sale's book, among some 150 published in 1992, was noteworthy in that he utilized original sources to examine Columbus as man and myth. He widened this scope to examine the Columbian and post-Columbian impact on indigenous cultures and the New World environment.
4.   Samuel Eliot Morison, *Admiral of the Ocean Sea* (New York: Time, 1942), 25; also see William D. Phillips and Carla Rahn Phillips, *The Worlds of Christopher Columbus* (Cambridge: Cambridge University Press, 1992), 284, n. 28 for some additional information.
5.   For references to St. Brendan, I examined the following: for the Anglo-Norman version, E.G.R. Waters, ed., *The Anglo-Norman Voyage of St. Brendan* (Oxford: Clarendon Press, 1928); for the German version, Rolf D. Fay, ed., *Sankt Brendan: Zwei Frühneuhochdeutsche Prosafassungen* (Stuttgart: Helfant Edition, 1985); for the Italian/Latin version, Ioannes Orlandi, ed., *Navigatio Sancti Brendani* (Milan: Instituto Editoriale Cisalpino, n.d.); for the Latin version, J. P. Webb, trans., *The Age of Bede* (Harmondsworth, U.K.: Penguin, 1983).
6.   Fay, *Sankt Brendan*, x.
7.   Ibid., xi.
8.   Orlandi, *Navigatio*, 40.
9.   Waters, *Anglo-Norman Voyages*, xxii.
10.   Webb, *Age of Bede*, 213.
11.   Fay, *Sankt Brendan*, 16.
12.   See a spirited discussion by Madariaga, *Columbus*, 95.
13.   Campbell, *Witness*, 52.
14.   Waters, *Anglo-Norman Voyages*, xcviii.
15.   Orlandi, *Navigatio*, 37.
16.   Webb, *Age of Bede*, 216–217.
17.   Waters, *Anglo-Norman Voyages*, lxxxviii.
18.   Webb, *Age of Bede*, 216.

19.   Bartolomé de las Casas, *The Devastation of the Indies* [1552], trans. Herma Briffault (Baltimore: Johns Hopkins University Press, 1992), 79–80.

20.   See Magnus Magnusson and Herman Pálsson, trans. and eds., *The Vinland Sagas: Norse Discovery of America* (New York: New York University Press, 1966). This volume contains both the "Greenland Saga" and "Eirik's Saga" and is now available through Penguin.

21.   For Viking dates, see Robert Blow, ed., *Abroad in America* (London: Lennard, 1989).

22.   See two works: Skelton, Marston, and Painter, *The Vinland Map and the Tartar Relation*, 261–262; and Wilcomb E. Washburn, ed., *Proceedings of the Vinland Map Conference* (Chicago: University of Chicago Press, 1971), especially 95–103. For us, the importance of these studies lies in their providing discussion on a possible link between the Vinland map and Friar C. de Bridia's 1247 "Tartar Relation."

23.   I do not wish to enter into the debate about whether the Vinland map may be authenticated with reference to the text but merely wish to show that, even though we see the Viking *westward* movement and the Mongolian *eastward* invasion as distinct they were closely associated as a contemporary intellectual enterprise of their time. Some might even argue that the map's presence alongside the Tartar text offer a newer, and thus even more fascinating, "mythology," whereby the visual reinforces the verbal.

24.   See Skelton, Marston, and Painter, *Vinland Map*, particularly Skelton's detailed discussion, 107–240.

25.   Helge Ingstad, *Westward to Vinland* (New York: St. Martin's, 1969), 90.

26.   J.R.L. Anderson, *Vinland Voyage* (London: Eyre and Spottiswoode, 1967), 29.

27.   Magnusson and Pálsson, *Vinland Sagas*, 120.

28.   Ibid., 53.

29.   Ibid., 55.

30.   Winston Churchill, *A History of the English Speaking Peoples*, 4 vols. (New York: Dorset, 1956), vol. 1, 93.

31.   Magnusson and Pálsson, *Vinland Sagas*, 61.

32.   Ibid., 56.

33.   Ibid., 61.

34.   Ibid., 65.

35.   Ibid.

36.   Ibid.

37.   Ibid., 67.

38.   Ibid., 65.

39.   Ibid., 99.

40.   Ibid.

41.   Ibid., 98.

42.   Ibid., 69.

43.   Ibid., 66.

44.   Ibid., 82.

45.   Ibid., 94.

46.   Ibid.

47.   Ibid., 86.

48.   Ibid., 101.

49. Ibid., 100.

50. A. C. Moule and Paul Pelliot, *Marco Polo: The Description of the World*, 2 vols. (London: George Routledge & Sons, 1938), vol. 1, 41.

51. Moule and Pelliot *Marco Polo*, Vol. 1, 509.

52. Skelton, *Explorers' Maps*, 11.

53. Ibid., 13.

54. Ibid., 14.

55. Olschki, *Marco Polo's Asia*, 139.

56. Moule and Pelliot, *Marco Polo*, vol. 1, 150.

57. Friedman, *Monstrous Races*, 15.

58. Moule and Pelliot, *Marco Polo*, vol. 1, 122.

59. Ibid., 121.

60. Ibid., 432.

61. Ibid., 378. In connection with a new study on this topic, consult David Gordon White, *Myths of the Dog Man* (Chicago: University of Chicago Press, 1991), 30, 63, 242, concerning the Marco Polo connection. Also see 62–63, 201–202, concerning some of these implications for our study. White has associated the Brendan voyage with the idea of Heaven and Hell, wonders and monsters, or "the idea of purgatory as a place" (p. 11).

62. Cabeza de Vaca, *Narrative*, 21. Also see Campbell, *Witness*, 264, for additional comments.

63. Olschki, *Marco Polo's Asia*, 153.

64. Ibid., 391.

65. Moule and Pelliot, *Marco Polo*, vol. 1, 165.

66. Ibid., 167.

67. Ibid., 168.

68. Moule and Pelliot, *Marco Polo*, vol. 1, 377–378.

69. Ibid., 153.

70. Ibid., 169.

71. Friedman, *Monstrous Races*, 21.

72. Moule and Pelliot, *Marco Polo*, 154.

73. Las Casas, *Devastation of the Indies*, 80.

74. Moule and Pelliot, *Marco Polo*, vol. 1, 155.

75. Moule and Pelliot, *Marco Polo*, vol. 1, 371.

76. Ibid., 202.

77. Ibid.

78. Ibid., 251.

79. Ibid., 231.

80. Ibid., 236.

81. Ibid., 237.

82. Ibid., 222.

83. Ibid., 221.

84. Ibid.

85. Ibid.

86. Ibid., 412.

87. Ibid., 414.

88. Moule and Pelliot, *Marco Polo*, vol. 1, 129.

89. Ibid.

90.   Ibid.

91.   Columbus, *Selected Documents*, vol. 2, 38.

92.   For background material, see Mandeville, *Travels*, 10 (based on the Egerton text).

93.   Ibid., 9.

94.   Ibid., 14.

95.   Ibid., 132.

96.   Ibid., 133.

97.   Ibid., 137.

98.   Friedman, *Monstrous Races*, 9–21.

99.   Ibid., 200.

100. Ibid., 201.

101. Malcom Letts, trans., *Mandeville's Travels*, 2 vols. (London: Hakluyt Society, 1953), vol. 1, 200.

102. Ibid., 200–201.

103. Ibid., 468, modernized by me.

104. Mandeville, *Travels*, 117. See Tyrrell, *Amazons*, 64–66, for the role of Amazons in social mythmaking, and 35–39 and 75–76 for some interesting points on the role of men.

105. Mandeville, *Travels*, 169.

106. Ibid., 19. All of Mandeville's "sources" are listed in the Moseley "Introduction."

107. Columbus, *Selected Documents*, vol. 1, 116.

108. Letts, *Mandeville's Travels*, 504; Zarncke, *Priester Johannes*, 911.

109. Mandeville, *Travels*, 134.

110. Ibid., 135.

111. Ibid., 184.

112. Ibid., 182.

113. Ibid., 134.

114. Ibid., 123.

115. Martyr, *De Orbe Novo*, vol. 1, 274. Also see Speck, *Myths*, 24–25.

116. Mandeville, *Travels*, 63.

117. Ibid., 193.

118. Ibid., 184.

119. M. C. Seymour, ed., "Introduction," in *Mandeville's Travels* (Oxford: Clarendon Press, 1967), xv.

120. George Boas, *Essays on Primitivism and Related Ideas in the Middle Ages* (Baltimore: Johns Hopkins University Press, 1948), 172.

121. George P. Hammond, "The Search for the Fabulous in the Settlement of the Southwest," *Utah Historical Quarterly*, 24 (January 1956), 19.

122. Hanke, *Aristotle and the American Indians*, 4.

CHAPTER 4

1.   For the two leading authorities on Afrocentrism, see Molefi Asante, *Kemet, Afrocentricity and Knowledge* (Trenton, NJ: Africa World Press, 1990), and Maulana Karenga, *Introduction to Black Studies* (Los Angeles: University of Sankore Press, 1989).

2.   While using conventional anthropological facts, I remain particularly grateful to my wife, Hilde Dathorne, to Robert Haberstein of the University of Miami, and, of course, to Donald Johanson, especially for a lecture given on January 31, 1983, at the University of Miami and for subsequent conversation with him.

3.   See Louis S. B. Leakey, *The Progress and Evolution of Man in Africa* (Oxford: Oxford University Press, 1961) and *The Stone Age Races of Kenya* (Oxford: Oxford University Press, 1935).

4.   See Donald Johanson and Edey Maitland, *Lucy: The Beginnings of Humankind* (New York: Simon and Schuster, 1981).

5.   Johanson and Maitland, *Lucy*, 285.

6.   Donald Johanson and James Shreeve, *Lucy's Child* (New York: William Morrow, 1989), 30–31, 85–87.

7.   Richard Ardrey, *African Genesis* (New York: Dell, 1961), 181.

8.   Richard Leakey, "African Fossil Man," in UNESCO *General History of Africa*, vol. 1, ed. J. Ki-Zerbo (Paris: UNESCO, 1981), 447.

9.   Blaise Cendrars, *The African Saga*, trans. Margery Bianco [from *L'Anthologie Nègre*, 1927] (New York: Negro Universities Press, 1969), 15.

10.   Leo Frobenius and Leo Fox, *African Genesis* (Berkeley: Turtle Island Foundation, 1983), 47. Frobenius' *Der Schwarze Dekameron* appeared in Berlin in 1910 and the more extensive *Atlantis, Volkmärchen und Volkdicthtungen Afrikas*, 11 vols. (Jena: Diederichs, 1921–1928), especially vol. 10, 227. Also see "A Letter to Ezra Pound" in Nancy Cunard's *Negro* [1934] (New York: Frederick Ungar, 1970), 97, which related the important effect on American expatriates in Europe.

11.   See Mircea Eliade, *The Myth of Eternal Return* (Princeton: Princeton University Press, 1954), especially 34–48, 51–92; or Mircea Eliade, *The Quest: History and Reasoning in Religion* (Chicago: University of Chicago Press, 1969). Any one of Joseph Campbell's many works may be consulted, but I have always been especially influenced by Joseph Campbell, *The Hero with a Thousand Faces* (Princeton: Princeton University Press, 1949), 49–58, 109–120, 217–228, 349–356, where he laid out the variants of the hero monomyth — Departure, Initiation, and Return. The standard text is probably Stith Thompson, *The Folktale* (Berkeley: University of California Press, 1977). For Arthurian applications, see *The Quest of the Holy Grail*, ed. D. M. Matarasso (London: Penguin, 1969).

12.   See Marcel Griaule and Germaine Dieterlen, "Le renard pâle," in *Le mythe cosmogonique*, 1:1 (Paris: Travaux et Mémoires de l'Institut d'Ethnologie), vol. 1, xxii, 1965.

13.   Ulli Beier, *The Origin of Life and Death* (London: Heinemann Educational Books, 1966), 1–3.

14.   Asante, *Kemet*, 88.

15.   E. Bolaji Idowu, *Olódùmarè: God in Yoruba Belief* (London: Longmans, Green, 1962), 18.

16.   Herman Baumann, *Schöpfung und urzeit des menschen im mythes der afrikanischen völker* (Berlin: Reiner Steiner, 1936), 270–271.

17.   Cendrars, *African Saga*, 15.

18.   Maria Leach, *Standard Dictionary of Folklore, Mythology, and Legend* (New York: Funk & Wagnall's, 1941).

19.   Jan Vansina, *Oral Tradition: A Study in Historical Methodology* (London: Routledge & Kegan Paul, 1961), 185.

20. Placide Tempels, *Bantu Philosophy* (Paris: Présence Africaine, 1961), 64.

21. Ibid., 65.

22. Ibid., 45–46.

23. John Mbiti, *African Religions and Philosophy* (London: Heinemann, 1969), 151–152.

24. Claude Lévi-Strauss, *Structural Anthropology* (New York: Basic Books, 1963), 23, 1–27, 167–185, 188–231, dealing with history, anthropology, magic, and the link between myth and symbol.

25. Amos Tutuola, *The Palm-Wine Drinkard* (New York: Grove Weidenfeld, 1984), 19.

26. Amos Tutuola, *The Wild Hunter in the Bush of Ghosts*, intro. Bernth Lindfors (Washington, DC: Three Continents, 1982), 25.

27. Specially relevant is D. O. Fagunwa, *The Forest of a Thousand Daemons*, trans. Wole Soyinka (London: Nelson, 1968). (Tutola always stressed to me an interst in *world* oral literature.)

28. These oral accounts have been conveniently translated in Abayomi Fuja, ed., *Fourteen Hundred Cowries* (London: Oxford University Press, 1962), especially 34–36.

29. Tutuola, *World Hunter*, xv.

30. Tutuola, *Palm-Wine Drinkard*, 30.

31. Ibid., 100.

32. Noel Q. King, *African Cosmos* (Belmont, CA: Wadsworth, 1986), 8.

33. Jacques Maquet and Joan Rayfield, *Civilizations of Black Africa* (New York: Oxford University Press, 1972), 146.

34. Marcel Griaule, *Conversations with Ogotemmeli: An Introduction to Dogon Religious Ideas* (London: Oxford University Press, 1965). There has been an ongoing debate concerning this work. For some, it is an insightful account of the complex philosophy of an African people. But, since the narrative is recounted by one individual Dogon elder, others have contended that Griaule's own interests may have unduly influenced the account.

35. Maquet and Rayfield, *Civilizations of Black Africa*, 145.

36. See Ivan Van Sertima, ed., *Blacks in Science: Ancient and Modern* (New Brunswick, NJ: Transaction, 1991), 11–14 and Hunter Havelin Adams III, "African Observers of the Universe: The Sirius Question," 27–46. Other relevant material appears on 47–50.

37. Germaine Dieterlen, "A Contribution to the Study of Blacksmiths in West Africa," in *French Perspectives in African Studies*, ed. Pierre Alexander (London: Oxford University Press, 1973), 41–42.

38. Adams, "African Observers of the Universe," 29.

39. Carl Sagan, *Broca's Brain: Reflections on the romance of Science* (New York: Random House, 1979), 75.

40. Griaule, *Conversations*, 198.

41. Ibn Fadl Allah al-'Umari's account has also been entitled *al-Ta'rif bi'l-mustalah al' sharif*. An extant Arab version appeared in an 1894 Cairo edition. The present English version may be found in Devisse and Labib, "Africa in Inter-Continental Relations," 664–665.

42. M.D.W. Jeffreys, "The Arabs Discover America Before Columbus," *Muslim Digest*, 4:2 (1953), 18–26.

43.   C. L. Riley, ed., *Man Across the Sea: Problems of Pre-Columbian Contacts* (Austin: University of Texas Press, 1974).

44.   Jan Carew, "Columbus and the Origins of Racism in the Americas," *Race and Class*, Part I, 29:4 (Spring 1988), 1–19; Part 2, 30:1 (July–Sept. 1988), 33–57. Carew has contended that one reason that Martin Alonso Pinzon agreed so easily to sail with Columbus was that he knew that "sea rovers from Africa and from Europe had sailed to and from these lands," 8. See also Morison, *Great Explorers*, 364–365.

45.   D. T. Niane, *Sundiata: An Epic of Old Mali* (London: Longman, 1965), 1.

46.   Michael Bradley, *The Black Discovery of America* (Toronto: Personal Library, 1981), 5.

47.   Devisse and Labib, "Africa in Inter-Continental Relations," 665.

48.   Stewart C. Malloy, "Traditional African Watercraft: A New Look," in *Blacks in Science*, ed. Van Sertima, 162.

49.   G. E. de Zurara, *The Chronicle of the Discovery and Conquest of Guinea*, trans. C. R. Beazley and E. Prestage, 2 vols. (London: Hakluyt Society, 1899), vol. 1, 69–70.

50.   Morison, *European Discovery, Southern*, 365. Also see Samuel Eliot Morison, *The European Discovery of America: The Northern Voyages* (Oxford: Oxford University Press, 1971), 3–6.

51.   Devisse and Labib, "Africa in Inter-Continental Relations," 665.

52.   Martyr, *De Orbe Novo*, vol. 1, 286.

53,   Here I am referring to Ivan Van Sertima, *They Came Before Columbus* (New York: Random House, 1976) and to the lesser known but very thoroughly researched Leo Wiener, *Africa and the Discovery of America*, 3 vols. (Philadelphia: Innes & Sons, vol. 1, 1920, vols. 2 and 3, 1922). Wiener was well ahead of his time. He brought an encyclopedic knowledge of Meso-American food, pottery, religion, metal use, clothing, cotton, tobacco, and precious stones to examine in great detail the impact of pre-Columbian African civilization and culture on Central America and Peru.

54.   Sagan, *Cosmos*, 15.

55.   Cheikh Anta Diop, *Civilization or Barbarism: An Authentic Anthropology* (New York: Lawrence Hill, 1991), 3.

56.   Ibid., 17.

57.   Herodotus, *Histories*, 150.

58.   Ibid., 152.

59.   Ibid., 158.

60.   Ibid., 159.

61.   George G. M. James, *Stolen Legacy* (San Francisco: Julian Richardson, 1954), 265. About James, Martin Bernal (see Note 72) has added that his work was not even recognized as a "proper book." Martin Bernal, *Black Athena: The Afroasiatic Roots of Classical Civilization*, 2 vols. (New Brunswick, NJ: Rutgers University Press, 1987, 1991), vol. 1, 435.

62.   Cheikh Anta Diop, *The African Origin of Civilization* (New York: Lawrence Hill, 1974), 49.

63.   Diop, *African Origin*, 135–142. Also see Aboubacry Moussa Lam, "Égypte ancienne et Afrique noire chez Cheikh Anta Diop," *Présence Africaine*. Special Issue on Cheikh Anta Diop (New Bilingual Series 149–150, 1st and 2nd Quarterlies, 1990), 203–213.

64. Josef A. A. Ben-Jochannan. *Black Man of the Nile and His Family* (Baltimore: Black Classic, 1989), 180.

65. Josef A. A. Ben-Jochannan. *Africa: Mother of Western Civilization* (Baltimore: Black Classic, 1989), 375.

66. Chancellor Williams, *The Destruction of Black Civilization* (Chicago: Third World, 1974), 80.

67. Asante, *Kemet*, 93–94. Also see John Henrik Clarke, "Africa in the Ancient World," in *Kemet and the African Worldview*, edited by Mauliana Karenga and Jacob Carruthers (Los Angeles: University of Sankore Press, 1986), 45–54; Wade W. Nobles, "Ancient Egyptian Thought and the Renaissance of African (Black) Psychology," in *Kemet and the African Worldview*, edited by Mauliana Karenga and Jacob Carruthers (Los Angeles: University of Sankore Press, 1986), 100–118; Daina M. Clark, "Similarities Between Egyptian and Dogon Perceptions of Man, God and Nature," in *Kemet and the African Worldview*, edited by Mauliana Karenga and Jacob Carruthers (Los Angeles: University of Sankore Press, 1986), 119–130.

68. Maulana Karenga, *The Book of Coming Forth by Day* (Los Angeles: University of Sankore Press, 1974), 22.

69. Janine Bourriau and Stephen Quirke, *Pharaohs and Mortals* (Cambridge: Cambridge University Press, 1988), 84.

70. Ibid., 77–78.

71. Van Sertima and Runoko Rashidi, *African Presence in Early Asia* (New Brunswick, NJ: Transaction, 1988), 24. Also see James Edward Brunson, *Predynastic Egypt: An African-centric View* (Chapel Hill: Professional Press, n.d.), especially 67–73 for an overview and 127–131 for ancient Egyptian survivals in modern Africa.

72. Martin Bernal's first two volumes address, as their subtitles state, *The Fabrication of Ancient Greece 1785–1985* (vol. 1) and *The Archaeological and Documentary Evidence* (vol. 2). An early and sympathetic response appeared in J. Peradotto and M. Myerwitz Levine, eds., "The Challenge of *Black Athena*," [special issue of *Arethusa*]. See especially an article by G. Rendsburg, "Black Athena: an Etymological Response," 67–82.

73. Bernal, vol. 1, 178–179.

74. Ibid., vol. 2, 12. Also see vol. 1, 331, 437; and vol. 2, 274–391 and 382–390 concerning Arrotiri.

75. In addition to Bruce Williams' scholarly articles, among which I recommend "The Lost Pharaohs of Nubia," *Archaeology Journal* (Sept. 1980), 12–21, Williams has helped to popularize the subject by lending his authority to at least two "popular" guides: "A Lost Kingdom in Nubia at the Dawn of History," *News and Notes* (Chicago: Oriental Institute, 1977) and "Ancient Textiles from Nubia," written with Christa C. Mayer Thurman for an exhibition organized by the Art Institute of Chicago in 1990.

76. Timothy Kendall is Associate Curator of the Boston Museum of Fine Arts. Emily Teeter, whom I wish to thank for her assistance, is associated with the Oriental Institute in Chicago. Dr. Teeter was curator of an exhibition on Nubian archaeology, which opened at the Institute in February 1992.

77. See Bruce Williams, "Excavations Between Abu Simbel and the Sudan Frontier," Part I: "The A-Group Royal Cemetery at Qustul: Cemetery L" (Chicago: Oriental Institute of University of Chicago, 1986), 2.

78.   Beatrice Lumpkin, "The Pyramids: Ancient Showcase of African Science and Technology," in Van Sertima, *Blacks in Science*, 69.

79.   Some of the material relating to Nubia has begun to appear in the more conventional press. See, for instance, John Noble Wilford, "In Egypt's Brilliance, Nubian Roots," *International Herald Tribune*, Feb. 13, 1992, p. 9. Also "Of Pygmies and Princes: Scholars Put Ancient Nubia Back on the Map," *Newsweek*, Oct. 19, 1992, p. 60. Perhaps most importantly, an exhibition on Nubia opened in 1992 at the University of Pennsylvania's Museum of Archaeology and Anthropology, before moving on to other U.S. cities.

80.   Publicity information kindly supplied by the Oriental Institute for its exhibition Feb. 4–Dec. 31, 1992. Various fact sheets were issued under the general title, "Vanished Kingdoms of the Nile: The Rediscovery of Ancient Nubia."

81.   Various fact sheets and a newsletter (*Nubian News*) were produced by the Museum of Fine Arts in Boston for its exhibition, which opened May 10, 1992. This reference, "To help journalists better understand . . . the rich history of Nubia," is dated January 1992.

82.   Williams, *Destruction*, 86.

83.   Ivan Van Sertima, ed., *Egypt Revisited* (New Brunswick, NJ: Transaction, 1991), 49. Also note the thorough study by Gude Suckale-Redlefsen, *The Black Saint Maurice* (Austin: University of Texas Press, 1987).

84.   See E. Franklin Frazier, *The Negro in the United States* (New York: Macmillan, 1957), 334–335, for the view that the African American church and culture are not "African" but "American." See Melville J. Herskovits, *The Myth of the Negro Past* (New York: Harper and Bros., 1942) for the pro-African approach being pursued here.

85.   Zora Neale Hurston, *Moses, Man of the Mountain* [1939] (New York: Harper Collins, 1991), xxiv. The volume mentioned by Hurston is available in several German editions and in English, as *The Sixth and Seventh Books of Moses* (Arlington, TX: Dorene, n.d.). Of course, it was Sigmund Freud's *Moses and Monotheism* (New York: Alfred A. Knopf, 1939) (first published in German in 1937) that helped scholars to consider seriously the idea of Moses as Egyptian. See especially pages 4–31 and note that: "The kernel of our thesis [is] the dependence of Jewish monotheism on the monotheistic episode in Egyptian history," p. 35.

86.   For a small but well researched volume, see Arthur Huff Fauset, *Black Gods of the Metropolis* (Philadelphia: University of Pennsylvania Press, 1971). Some material on the Black church is to be found in E. Franklin Frazier, *The Negro Church in America* (New York: Schocken Books, 1964), but this should be balanced with St. Clair Drake, *The Redemption of African and Black Religion* (Chicago: Third World, 1970). Drake's view is less "conservative" and tends to include the African diaspora. A good update is C. Eric Lincoln, *The Black Church Since Frazier* (New York: Schocken Books, 1974), published with Frazier's in one volume. For a recent study on Father Divine, see Jill Watts, *God, Harlem U.S.A.* (Berkeley: University of California Press, 1992). For Albert B. Cleage's views, see his work, *The Black Messiah* (New York: Sheed and Ward, 1969)

87.   See, *inter alia*, George Eaton Simpson, *Black Religions in the New World* (New York: Columbia University Press, 1978), 270–271.

88.   Early background material on the Nation of Islam may be found in E. U. Essien-Udom, *Black Nationalism: A Search for Identity in America* (Chicago:

University of Chicago Press, 1962) and C. Eric Lincoln, *The Black Muslims in America* (Boston: Beacon, 1973).

89. Edward Ullendorff, *Ethiopia and the Bible* (London: Oxford University Press, 1968), 139.

90. *Africa and the Africans as Seen by Classical Writers: The William Leo Hansberry African History Notebook*, ed. Joseph E. Harris (Washington, DC: Howard University Press, 1977), 20. Contrast the thrust of Hansberry's opinions with Carter G. Woodson, *The Mis-Education of the Negro* [1933] (Trenton, NJ: Africa World Press, 1990) where "The Father of Black History" argued that Blacks are "mis-educated" because they are "equipped to begin the life of an Americanized or Europeanized white man," p. 5. Woodson would have taken little solace from identifying himself as the "other" in classical literature.

91. Ullendorff, *Ethiopia and the Bible*, 12.

92. Frank M. Snowden, *Blacks in Antiquity* (Cambridge, MA: Harvard University Press, 1970), 144.

93. Today, James' views would certainly not be dismissed as "radical." Although Bernal has stated that he regretted that his own work had been seized on by Afro-centric scholars, he nevertheless placed James with Cheikh Anta Diop as part of a Black scholarly continuum. See Bernal, *Black Athena*, vol. 1, 435.

94. Basic information on the Moorish presence and influence may be found in any reputable historical account. The problem, however, is that it is often very difficult, for even the most persistent scholar, to understand the extent of the Moorish contribution. Among the various works consulted, the following have been particularly useful. For general purposes, Albert Hourani, *A History of the Arab Peoples* (Cambridge, MA: Belknap Press of Harvard University Press, 1991), especially 41–43, 46–47, 84–86, 95–97, 189–198. An interesting depiction of Cross/Crescent antagonisms that continued into the seventeenth and eighteenth centuries appears in Stephen Clissold, *The Barbary Slaves* (New York: Barnes & Noble, 1977), especially 7–16. Of course, what has helped put the topic in vivid perspective was the exhibition "Al-Andalus: The Art of Islamic Spain" at New York City's Metropolitan Museum of Art, July–September, 1992, following an earlier showing in Granada, Spain.

95. Various works are available on the Moorish conquest and occupation, in particular: Elmer Bendiner, *The Rise and Fall of Paradise* (New York: Dorset, 1983), 36–39, 79–81, 228–229; Bovill, *Golden Trade*, 50–57, 60–63, 87–89; Titus Burckhardt, *Moorish Culture in Spain* (New York: McGraw-Hill, 1972), 81–92; James Burke, *The Day the Universe Changed* (Boston: Little, Brown, 1985), 36–44; Robert I. Burns, *Moors and Crusaders in Mediterranean Spain* (London: Variorum Reprints, 1978), 28–29, 96–101, 127, 385–393, 751–752; M. Florian, *History of the Moors of Spain* (New York: Harper & Brothers, 1840), 89–92, 139–147, 149–150, 164–167, 189–190, 207–218, 225; L. P. Harvey, *Islamic Spain: 1250–1500* (Chicago: University of Chicago Press, 1990), 105–106, 125–126, 226–227, 276–277, 321–322; Bernard Lewis, *The Muslim Discovery of Europe* (New York: W. W. Norton, 1982), 17–33, 59–69, 112–114, 125–126, 159–161; Jan Read, *The Moors in Spain and Portugal* (London: Faber and Faber, 1974), 53–59, 71–85, 92–96, 147–151, 174–180, 212–219; and Ivan Van Sertima, ed., *Golden Age of the Moor* (New Brunswick, NJ: Transaction, 1992), 9–26, 93–150, 248–277.

96. Read, *Moors in Spain and Portugal*, 17.

97.   Ibid., 23.

98.   Ibid., 29–30.

99.   Edward Scobie, "The Moors and Portugal's Global Expansion," in Van Sertima, *Golden Age*, 34.

100.   See Geoffroi de Villehardoun's account of the Fourth Crusade and Jean, Lord of Joinville's narrative of 1268. These are replete with the tiresome clichés, including Prester John and the Old Man of the Mountain; enemies are describedm as cowards and murderers. See Jean de Joinville and Geoffroi de Villehardoun, *Chronicles of the Crusades*, trans. M.R.B. Shaw (Harmondsworth, U.K.: Penguin, 1963).

101.   See especially Arab versions of the Crusades in Francesco Gabrieli, ed., *Arab Historians of the Crusades* (New York: Dorset, 1989).

102.   Burke, *Day the Universe Changed*, 37–38; Florian, *History of the Moors*, 138–148; Read, *Moors in Spain and Portugal*, 232–237.

103.   Joseph S. Roucek and Thomas Kiernan, *The Negro Impact on Western Civilization* (New York: Philosophical Library, 1970), 431.

104.   Quoted by John Russell, "In Spain, the 'Stuff of Paradise,'" *International Herald Tribune*, April 4–5, 1992, 7.

105.   See Paolo Emilio Taviani, *Columbus: The Great Adventure* (New York: Orion, 1991), which blames Genoese timidity in funding Columbus on the unfortunate outcome of the Vivaldis' expedition. Both Thatcher, *Columbus*, vol. 1, 505, and R. V. Tooley, Charles Bricker, and Gerald Crone, *Landmarks of Mapmaking* (Amsterdam: Elsevier, 1968), 149, refer to the brothers as the "Vivaldos."

106.   Introduction to Niane, *General History of Africa*, vol. 4, 1–12, 117–171, 174, 193–199, 614–634. A handy textbook is J. F. Ade Ajayi and Ian Espie, *A Thousand Years of West African History* (Ibadan, Nigeria: Ibadan University Press, 1965). Now that the entire UNESCO series is available, it remains essential for reference and research.

107.   Dor-Ner, *Columbus*, 58–61 and Jay A. Levinson, *Circa 1492: Art in the Age of Exploration* (New Haven: Yale University Press, 1991), 35–39.

108.   Quoted in Dor-Ner, *Columbus*, 58.

109.   Ibid., 58.

110.   Ibid.

111.   Paul Henry Kaplan, *The Rise of the Black Magus in Western Art* (Ann Arbor: University of Michigan Press, 1985) has cited these figures and used them to explain the origins of the Black magus in European art. Also see a thorough examination of this intriguing topic in Suckale-Redlefsen, *Black Saint Maurice*.

112.   Jan Albert Goris cited in Levinson, *Circa 1492*, 289.

113.   See comment on these writers in O. R. Dathorne, *The Black Mind: A History of African Literature* (Minneapolis: University of Minnesota Press, 1974). For information on Juan Latino and other Latin writers, see pp. 67–75; on Ottobah Cugoano, Olaudah Equiano, and Ignatius Sancho, see pp. 76–88.

114.   Dunzo Annette Ivory, "Blacks of Sub-Saharan African Origin in Spain: Image in the Theater" (Ph.D. diss., UCLA, 1974), 46–53.

115.   See Levinson, *Circa 1492*, 289, where Albrecht Dürer's "Portrait of a Black Man" and "Portrait of Katherina" are reproduced.

116.   For an outstanding general study, see Folarin Shyllon, *Black People in Britain 1555–1833* (London: Oxford University Press, 1977), 169–240. Two older books that make for informed reading are Kenneth Little, *Negroes in Britain* (London:

Kegan Paul, Trench, Trubner, 1947) and Wylie Sypher, *Guinea's Captive Kings* (Chapel Hill: University of North Carolina Press, 1942).

117.   Francis D. Adams and Barry Sanders, *Three Black Writers in Eighteenth Century England* (Belmont, CA: Wadsworth, 1971), 107.

118.   See Sypher, *Guinea's Captive Kings*, 144–155.

119.   Paul Edwards, "Introduction" in *Letters of the Late Ignatius Sancho* (London: Dawsons of Pall Mall, 1968), xv.

120.   Ottobah Cugoano, *Thoughts and Sentiments on the Evil and Wicked Traffic of the Slavery and Commerce of the Human Species* [1787] (London: Dawsons of Pall Mall, 1969), 81.

121.   Kwesi Kwaa Prah, *Jacobus Eliza Johannes Capitein* (Trenton, NJ: Africa World Press, 1992), 37–54.

122.   Ibid., 50.

123.   See Janheinz Jahn, *A History of Neo-African Literature* (London: Faber and Faber, 1966), 38–39; Marilyn Sephocle, "Anton Wilhelm Amo," *Journal of Black Studies*, 23:2 (December 1992), 182–187.

124.   Sephocle, "Anton Wilhelm Amo," 186.

125.   Prah, *Jacobus Eliza Johannes Capitein*, 63–66.

126.   For general reading, Joseph E. Holloway, ed., *Africanisms in American Culture* (Bloomington: Indiana University Press, 1990), especially 34–147 and 225–239.

127.   The return to Africa, truly a cyclical journey, has not received as much attention as it should have done. See relevant parts of Jacob Drachler, *Black Homeland: Black Diaspora* (Port Washington, NY: Kennikat, 1975), 43–182. See also the author's "Introduction" in Tony Martin, *The Pan-African Connection* (Dover, MA: Majority, 1984), 3–29. A good, comprehensive account is Wilson Jeremiah Moses, *The Golden Age of Black Nationalism, 1850–1925* (Oxford: Oxford University Press, 1978).

128.   Frank Tannenbaum, *Slave and Citizen* (New York: Vintage, 1946), 117.

129.   Thomas Jefferson, *Notes on the State of Virginia* [1784], in *The Portable Thomas Jefferson*, ed. Merrill D. Peterson (New York: Penguin, 1975), 192.

130.   Ibid., 188–189.

131.   Benjamin Franklin, *The Autobiography and Other Writings* (New York: Bantam, 1982), 226–227.

132.   John Blassingame, *Black New Orleans* (Chicago: University of Chicago Press, 1973), 5.

133.   See Patrick Bellegarde-Smith, *Traditional Spirituality in the African Diaspora* (Lexington, KY: A.C.S., 1992).

134.   See Joseph Murphy, *Santería: An African Religion in America* (Boston: Beacon, 1988). I am indebted to Ernesto Pichardo, a nationally known *italero* for helping me to learn much about *Santería*.

135.   I have visited Oyotunji on several occasions. Not much written material is available, although a small booklet by an Afro-Cuban priest is available. See Carlos Canet, *Oyotunji* (Miami: Editorial AIP, n.d.).

136.   Abraham Lincoln, "Address on Colonization to a Deputation of Negroes," August 14, 1862, in *Collected Works of Abraham Lincoln* (New Brunswick, NJ: Rutgers University Press, 1953), 370–375. Note how Lincoln's views on Black citizenship became part of a political tug-of-war. Also see Abraham Lincoln, *Speeches*

and Writings, 1832–1858 (New York: Library of America, 1989), 270–271, 397, 402, 478, 791–792.

137.   For a general overview, see Okon Edet Uya, *Black Brotherhood* (Lexington, MA: D.C. Heath, 1971), 41–62. Even Edward Blyden harbored no illusions. He believed that Blacks could bring to Liberia "The blessings of civilization and Christianity." See Hollis R. Lynch, ed., *Selected Published Writings of Edward Wilmot Blyden* (New York: Humanities, 1971), 82.

138.   See Lamont Thomas, *Paul Cuffee: Black Entrepreneur* (Champaign-Urbana: University of Illinois Press, 1988).

139.   Uya, *Black Brotherhood*, 63–82 for Crummell and Delany; for Turner, see Stephen Ward Angell, *Bishop Henry McNeal Turner and African Religion in the South* (Knoxville: University of Tennessee Press, 1992), 139–140, 172–173, 215–224, 264–265.

140.   Martin Delany, *Official Report of the Niger Valley Exploring Party* [1861], in M. R. Delany and Robert Campbell, *Search for a Place* (Ann Arbor: University of Michigan Press, 1971), 27–148; for references, see 38.

141.   Alexander Crummell, *The Relations and Duties of Free Colored Men in America to Africa* [1861], in Uya, *Black Brotherhood*, 65.

142.   Concerning Turner et al., also see Edwin S. Redkey, *Black Exodus: Black Nationalism and Back-to-Africa Movements, 1890–1910* (New Haven: Yale University Press, 1969), 25–32, 34–40, 43–46, 179–181, 195–199, 223–224, 248–249.

143.   A number of books have been written on this topic, but the actual court document makes the best reading. See *United States* v. *The Libelants and Claimants of the Schooner Amistad*, 518 U.S. 517 (1841).

144.   See Amy Jacques Garvey, *Garvey and Garveyism* (New York: Collier, 1970), 53, 235. For the complete works, see Marcus Garvey, *The Marcus Garvey and Universal Negro Improvement Association Papers*, ed. Robert A. Hill, 7 vols. (Berkeley: University of California Press, 1983–1990).

145.   W.E.B DuBois, *Dust of Dawn: An Essay Toward an Autobiography of a Race Concept* (New York: Harcourt, Brace, 1940), 116.

146.   Claude McKay, *Selected Poems*, intro. John Dewey. See "Africa," 40; "Outcast," 41; and "Enslaved," 42.

147.   Countee Cullen, "Heritage," *Color* (New York: Harper and Brothers, 1925), 36.

148.   Walt Whitman, *Leaves of Grass* (New York: Oxford University Press, 1990), 119.

149.   Léon Damas, *Black Label* (Paris: Gallimard, 1956), 52.

150.   Langston Hughes, "The Negro Speaks of Rivers." This poem first appeared in DuBois' *Crisis* in June 1921 and then in Hughes' first publication of poems in book form — *The Weary Blues* (New York: Knopf, 1926), 51. It is, of course, widely anthologized. An account of the poem's origin appears in Arnold Rampersad, *The Life of Langston Hughes*, 2 vols. (Oxford: Oxford University Press, 1986), vol. 1, 39–40.

151.   The toast is recounted in various versions in Roger D. Abrahams, *Deep Down in the Jungle* (New York: Aldine, 1970), 113–114, 115–119, 153–156. See also Alan Dundes, ed., *Mother Wit from the Laughing Barrell*(Englewood Cliffs, NJ: Prentice-Hall, 1973), 321–328, where the story is discussed in the context of "signifying" or verbal insult intended to provoke confrontation.

152.   For good musical background to the period considered, see Eileen Southern, *The Music of Black Americans: A History* (New York: W. W. Norton, 1971), 310–311, 318–322, 331–397.

153.   Richard Wright, *Black Power: A Record of Reactions in a Land of Pathos* (New York: Harper, 1954), 158. Michel Fabre has cited the statement "I was black" as "a refrain denoting frustration, if not anxiety. Africa turned out to be a foreign country" in his study, *The Unfinished Quest of Richard Wright* (New York: Morrow, 1973), 402.

Selected Bibliography

Abercrombie, Thomas J. "Ibn Battuta: Prince of Travelers." *National Geographic* 180:6 (December 1991): 2–49.

Abrahams, Roger D. *Deep Down in the Jungle*. New York: Aldine, 1970.

Adams, Francis D., and Barry Sanders. *Three Black Writers in Eighteenth Century England*. Belmont, CA: Wadsworth, 1971.

Adler, Elkan Nathad, ed. *Jewish Travellers in the Middle Ages*. Mineola, NY: Dover, 1987.

Africanus, Leo [Johannes Leo]. *A Geographical Historie of Africa* [1600]. Ed. by John Pory. New York: De Capo, 1969.

Agatharchides of Cnidus. *On the Erythraean Sea*. Trans. and ed. by Stanley M. Burstein. London: Hakluyt Society, 1989.

Ahmad, Nafis. *Muslim Contribution to Geography*. Lahore, Pakistan: Sh. Muhammad Ashraf, 1972.

"Alexander's Letter to Aristotle about India." See Gunderson, Lloyd L., as well as Davidson, Donald, and A. P. Campbell.

Alexander, Michael, ed. *Discovering the World*, based on the works of Theodore de Bry. New York: Harper & Row, 1976.

"The Alexander Romance." See Pseudo-Callisthenes.

Anderson, J.R.L. *Vinland Voyage*. London: Eyre & Spottiswoode, 1967.

Angell, Stephen Ward. *Bishop Henry McNeal Turner and African Religion in the South*. Knoxville: University of Tennessee Press, 1992.

Arciniegas, Germán. *Germans in the Conquest of America*. New York: MacMillan, 1943.

Ardrey, Robert. *African Genesis*. New York: Dell, 1961.

Arnold, T. W. "Arab Travellers and Merchants: AD 1000–1500." In Newton, Arthur Percival.

Asante, Molefi Kete. *Kemet, Afrocentricity, and Knowledge*. Trenton, NJ: Africa World Press, 1990.

Bagrow, Leo. *History of Cartography*. Chicago: Precedent, 1964.

Baumann, Herman. *Schöpfung und Urzeit des Menschen im Mythus der afrikanischen Völker*. Berlin: Reiner Steiner, 1936.

Beier, Ulli. *The Origin of Life and Death*. London: Heinemann Educational Books, 1966.

Bellegarde-Smith, Patrick, ed. *Traditional Spirituality in the African Diaspora.* Special
     issue of *Journal of Caribbean Studies* 9:1–2 (Winter 1992–Spring 1993).
Benedict. *The Marvels of Rome* [1143]. Trans. and ed. by Frances Morgan Nichols.
     New York: Ithaca Press, 1986.
Bendiner, Elmer. *The Rise and Fall of Paradise.* New York: Dorset, 1983.
Ben-Jochannan, Yosef A. A. *Africa: Mother of Western Civilization* [1971].
     Baltimore: Black Classic Press, 1989.
_____. *Black Man of the Nile and His Family* [1971]. Baltimore: Black Classic Press,
     1989.
Beowulf and the Finnesburg Fragment. Trans. by John R. Clark Hall, revised by C. L.
     Wrenn. London: George Allen & Unwin, 1954.
Bernal, Martin. *Black Athena: The Afroasiatic Roots of Classical Civilization.* 2 vols.
     New Brunswick, NJ: Rutgers University Press, 1987 and 1991.
Blassingame, John. *Black New Orleans.* Chicago: University of Chicago Press, 1973.
Bloch, R. Howard. *Medieval Misogyny.* Chicago: University of Chicago Press, 1991.
Boas, George. *Essays on Primitivism and Related Ideas in the Middle Ages.* Baltimore:
     Johns Hopkins University Press, 1948.
Blow, Robert, ed., *Abroad in America.* London: Lennard Publishing, 1989.
Boorstin, Daniel J. *The Discoverers.* New York: Vintage, 1985.
Bourriau, Janine, and Stephen Quirke. *Pharaohs and Mortals.* Cambridge: Cambridge
     University Press, 1988.
Bovill, E. W. *The Golden Trade of the Moors.* London: Oxford University Press,
     1958.
Bradford, Ernle. *Christopher Columbus.* New York: Viking, 1973.
Bradley, Michael. *The Black Discovery of America.* Toronto: Personal Library, 1981.
Bramont, Jules. *The Voyage and Travayle of Syr John Mandeville Knight.* London: J.
     M. Dent & Sons, 1928.
Bricker, Charles, R. V. Tooley, and Gerald Crone. *Landmarks of Mapmaking.*
     Amsterdam: Elsevier, 1968.
Brunson, James E. *Predynastic Egypt: Before the Unification, an African-centric View.*
     Chapel Hill: Professional Press, n.d.
Burckhardt, Titus. *Moorish Culture in Spain.* New York: McGraw-Hill, 1972.
Burke, James. *The Day the Universe Changed.* Boston: Little, Brown, 1985.
Burns, Robert I. *Moors and Crusaders in Mediterranean Spain.* London: Variorum
     Reprints, 1978.
Cabeza de Vaca, Alvar Núñez. *The Narrative of Cabeza de Vaca.* Barre, MA: Imprint
     Society, 1972.
Campbell, Joseph. *The Hero with a Thousand Faces.* Princeton: Princeton University
     Press, 1949.
Campbell, Mary B. *The Witness and the Other World: Exotic European Travel
     Writing, 400–1600.* Ithaca, NY: Cornell University Press, 1988.
Canet, Carlos. *Oyotunji.* Miami: Editorial AIP, n.d.
Carew, Jan. "Columbus and the Origins of Racism in the Americas." Part 1. *Race and
     Class* 29:4 (Spring 1988), 1–19; Part 2. *Race and Class* 30:1 (July–September
     1988), 33–57.
Carpenter, Rhys. *Beyond the Pillars of Heracles.* New York: Delacorte, 1966.
Carpini, John de Plano. *The Texts and Versions of John de Plano Carpini and William
     de Rubruques.* London: Hakluyt Society, 1903.

Cendrars, Blaise. *The African Saga*. Trans. by Margery Bianco from *L'Anthologie Nègre*. New York: Negro Universities Press, 1969.

Chan, Walter Albert. *The Glory and Fall of the Ming Dynasty*. Norman: University of Oklahoma Press, 1982.

Churchill, Winston. *A History of the English Speaking Peoples*. New York: Dorset, 1956.

Clark, Daina M. "Similarities Between Egyptian and Dogon Perceptions of Man, God and Nature." In Karenga and Carruthers.

Clarke, John Henrik, "Africa in the Ancient World." In Karenga and Carruthers.

Cleage, Albert B. *The Black Messiah*. New York: Sheed and Ward, 1969.

Clissold, Stephen. *The Barbary Slaves*. New York: Barnes & Noble, 1977.

Columbus, Christopher. *The "Diario" of Christopher Columbus's First Voyage to America 1492–1493*. Trans. by Oliver Dunn and James E. Kelley. Norman: University of Oklahoma Press, 1989.

____. *The Four Voyages*. Ed. and trans. by J. M. Cohen. London: Penguin, 1969.

____. *The Journal of Christopher Columbus*. Trans. by Cecil Jane. New York: Bonanza, 1960.

____. *Libro de las profecías*. Trans. with commentary by Delno C. West and August Kling. Gainesville: University of Florida Press, 1991.

____. *Selected Documents Illustrating the Four Voyages of Columbus*. Trans. and ed. by Cecil Jane. 2 vols. London: Hakluyt Society, 1930 and 1933.

Columbus, Ferdinand. *The Life of the Admiral Christopher Columbus by His Son Ferdinand*. Trans. by Benjamin Keen. New Brunswick, NJ: Rutgers University Press, 1959.

Coronado, Francisco Vasquez de. In *Journey of Coronado*, ed. by George P. Winship. New York: Allerton, 1922.

____. "The Narrative of the Expedition of Coronado by Pedro de Castañeda." In *Spanish Explorers in the United States 1528–1543*, ed. by Frederick W. Hodge, 281–387. New York: Barnes & Noble, 1965.

Cortés, Fernando. *His Five Letters of Relation to the Emperor Charles V*. Ed. by Francis Augustus MacNutt. Intro. by John Greenway. Glorieta, NM: Rio Grande Press, 1977.

Cosmas Indicopleustes. *The Christian Topography*. Trans. and ed. by J. W. McCrindle. London: Hakluyt Society, 1897.

Crummell, Alexander. *The Relations and Duties of Free Colored Men in America to Africa* [1861]. In Uya, Okot Edet.

Cugoano, Ottobah. *Thoughts and Sentiments on the Evil and Wicked Traffic of the Slavery and Commerce of the Human Species* [1787]. London: Dawsons of Pall Mall, 1969.

Cullen, Countee. *Color*. New York: Harper and Brothers, 1925.

Cumming, W. P., Skelton R. A., and Quinn, D. B. *The Discovery of North America*. New York: American Heritage, 1972.

Cunard, Nancy. *Negro* [1934]. New York: Frederick Ungar, 1970.

Cuoq, J. M., ed. *Recueil des sources arabes concernant l'Afrique occidentale du 8e au 16e siècle*. Paris: C.N.R.S., Sources d'histoire médiévale, 1973.

The Curse of Columbus. Special issue of *Race and Class* 33:3 (January–March 1992).

D'Ailly, Pierre [Petrus Aliacus]. *Tractatus de Imagine Mundi or Imago Mundi*. Trans. by Edwin F. Keever from British Library Latin photostat No. 40582.

Wilmington, NC, 1948. Typescript.

Dalché, Patrick Gautier. La "Descriptio Mappae Mundi" de Hughes de Saint-Victor. Paris: Études Augustiniennes, 1988.

Damas, Léon. Black Label. Paris: Gallimard, 1956.

Dathorne, O. R. The Black Mind: A History of African Literature. Minneapolis: University of Minnesota Press, 1974.

David, Richard, ed. Hakluyt's Voyages. Boston: Houghton Mifflin, 1981.

Davidson, Basil. The Lost Cities of Africa. Boston: Little, Brown, 1959. Also published as Old Africa Rediscovered. London: Victor Gollancz, 1965.

Davidson, Donald, and A. P. Campbell, trans. and intro. "The Letter of Alexander the Great to Aristotle." The Humanities Association Bulletin 23:3 (Summer 1972), 3–16.

De Bry, Theodore. Discovering the World. Ed. by Michael Alexander. New York: Harper & Row, 1976.

Delany, M. R., and Robert Campbell. Search for a Place. Ann Arbor: University of Michigan Press, 1971.

De Soto, Hernando. "The Narrative of the Expedition of Hernando de Soto by the Gentleman of Elvas." In Spanish Explorers in the United States 1528–1543, ed. by Theodore H. Lewis, 133–272. New York: Barnes & Noble, 1965.

Devisse, J., and S. Labib. "Africa in Inter-Continental Relations." In General History of Africa. Vol. 4: Africa from the Twelfth to the Sixteenth Century, ed. by D. T. Niane, 635–672. Paris: UNESCO, 1984.

De Zurara, G. E. The Chronicle of the Discovery of the Coast of Guinea. Trans. by C. R. Beazley and E. Presage. 2 vols. London: Hakluyt Society, 1899.

Dickins, Bruce, and R. M. Wilson. Early Middle English Texts. Cambridge: Bowes and Bowes, 1957.

Dieterlen, Germaine. "A Contribution to the Study of Blacksmiths in West Africa." In French Perspectives in African Studies, ed. by Pierre Alexander. London: Oxford University Press, 1973.

Diop, Cheikh Anta. The African Origin of Civilization: Myth or Reality. New York: Lawrence Hill, 1974.

_____. Civilization or Barbarism: An Authentic Anthropology. New York: Lawrence Hill, 1991.

Donnelly, Ignatius. Atlantis: The Antediluvian World. New York: Dover, 1976.

Dor-Ner, Zvi. Columbus and the Age of Discovery. New York: William Morrow, 1991.

Drachler, Jacob. Black Homeland: Black Diaspora. Port Washington, NY: Kennikat, 1975.

Drake, St. Clair. The Redemption of Africa and and Black Religion. Chicago: Third World, 1970.

DuBois, W.E.B. Dusk of Dawn: An Essay Toward an Autobiography of a Race Concept. New York: Harcourt, Brace, 1940.

Dudley, D. R., and D. M. Lang, eds. The Penguin Companion to Literature, 4 vols. Harmondsworth, Middlesex, U.K.: Penguin, 1969.

Dundes, Alan, ed. Mother Wit from the Laughing Barrel. Englewood Cliffs, NJ: Prentice-Hall, 1973.

Dunn, Ross E. The Adventures of Ibn Battuta. Berkeley: University of California Press, 1986.

Eden, Richard. *The First Three English Books on America*. Ed. by Edward Arber. Birmingham, U.K., 1885.

The Eighth, Ninth, and Tenth Books of Moses. New York: Original Publications, 1983.

Eliade, Mircea. *The Myth of the Eternal Return*. Princeton: Princeton University Press, 1954.

___. *The Quest: History and Reasoning in Religion*. Chicago: University of Chicago Press, 1989.

Equiano, Olaudah. *The Life of Olaudah Equiano or Gustavus Vassa the African* [1789]. 2 vols. London: Dawsons of Pall Mall, 1969.

Essien-Udom, E. U. *Black Nationalism: A Search for Identity in America*. Chicago: University of Chicago Press, 1962.

Euripides. *Plays*. Trans.by A. S. Way. 2 vols. London: J. M. Dent & Sons, 1956.

Fabre, Michel. *The Unfinished Quest of Richard Wright*. New York: William Morrow, 1973.

Fagunwa, D. O. *The Forest of a Thousand Daemons*. Trans. by Wole Soyinka. London: Nelson, 1968.

Fauset, Arthur Huff. *Black Gods of the Metropolis*. Philadelphia: University of Philadelphia Press, 1971.

Fay, Rolf D., ed. *Sankt Brendan: Zwei Fruhneuhochdeutsche Prosafassungen*. Stuttgart: Helfant Edition, 1985.

Fisher, Sheila, and Janet E. Halley, eds. *Seeking the Woman in Late Medieval and Renaissance Writings*. Knoxville: University of Tennessee Press, 1989.

Fitzgerald, C. P. *The Chinese View of Their Place in the World*. Oxford: Oxford University Press, 1966.

Flaum, Eric. *Discovery: Exploration Through the Centuries*. New York: Gallery Books, 1990.

Florian, M. *History of the Moors in Spain*. New York: Harper & Brothers, 1840.

Franklin, Benjamin. *The Autobiography and Other Writings*. New York: Bantam, 1982.

Fraser, Walter H. *The First Landing Place of Juan Ponce de Leon*. St. Augustine, FL: Walter H. Fraser, 1956.

Frazier, E. Franklin. *The Negro Church in America*. New York: Shocken, 1964.

___. *The Negro in the United States*. New York: MacMillan, 1957.

Friedman, John Block. *The Monstrous Races in Medieval Art and Thought*. Cambridge, MA: Harvard University Press, 1981.

Frobenius, Leo. *Atlantis, Volkmärchen und Volkdichtungen*. 11 vols. Jena: Diederichs, 1921–1928.

Frobenius, Leo, and Leo Fox. *African Genesis*. Berkeley: Turtle Island Foundation, 1983.

Fuja, Abayomi, ed. *Fourteen Hundred Cowries*. London: Oxford University Press, 1962.

Gabrieli, Francesco. *Arab Historians of the Crusades*. New York: Dorset, 1989.

Garvey, Amy Jacques. *Garvey and Garveyism*. New York: Collier, 1970.

Garvey, Marcus. *The Marcus Garvey and United Negro Improvement Association Papers*. Ed. by Robert A. Hill. 7 vols. Berkeley: University of California Press, 1983–90.

Gibb, Paul Allen. *"Wonders of the East*: A Critical Edition and Commentary." Ph.D. diss., Duke University Press, 1977.

Giller, Pierre. *Antiquities of Constantinople* [1544]. Trans. by John Ball. New York: Ithaca Press, 1988.

Gordon, Cyrus H. *Before Columbus: Links Between the Old World and America.* New York: Crown, 1971.

Gordon, R. K. ed. and trans. *Anglo-Saxon Poetry.* London: J. M. Dent & Sons, 1954.

Greenblatt, Stephen. *Marvelous Possessions.* Chicago: University of Chicago Press, 1991.

Griaule, Marcel. *Conversations with Ogotemmêli: An Introduction to Dogon Religious Ideas.* London: Oxford University Press, 1965.

Griaule, Marcel, and Germaine Dieterlen. "Le renard pâle." *Le mythe cosmogonique.* Paris: Travaux et Mémoires de l'Institut d'Ethnologie, 1965.

Gumiler, L. N. *Searches for an Imaginary Kingdom.* Trans. by R.E.F. Smith. Cambridge: Cambridge University Press, 1987.

Gumley, C. C. *Searches for an Imaginary Kingdom.* Cambridge: Cambridge University Press, 1987.

Gunderson, Lloyd L. *Alexander's Letter to Aristotle about India.* Meisenheim am Glan, Germany: Verlag Anton Hain, 1980.

Hakluyt, Richard. *The Principall Navigations, Voyages and Discoveries of the English Nation* [1589]. 2 vols. Cambridge, England: Hakluyt Society, 1965.

Hamidullah, M. "L'Afrique découvre l'Amérique avant Christopher Colomb." *Présence Africaine* 18–19 (1958): 173–183.

Hammond, George P. "The Search for the Fabulous in the Settlement of the Southwest." *Utah Historical Quarterly* 24 (1956), 1–20.

Hanke, Lewis. *All Mankind is One.* DeKalb: Northern Illinoins University Press, 1974.

____. *Aristotle and the American Indians: A Study in Race Prejudice in the Modern World.* Bloomington: Indiana University Press, 1959.

Harley, J. B., and David Woodward, eds. *The History of Cartography.* Chicago: University of Chicago Press, 1987.

Harris, Joseph E., ed. *Africa and Africans as Seen by Classical Writers.* Vol 2. *The William Leo Hansberry African History Notebook.* Washington, DC: Howard University Press, 1977.

Harvey, L. P. *Islamic Spain.* Chicago: University of Chicago Press, 1990.

Hayden, Robert. *Selected Poems.* New York: October House, 1966.

Henige, David. *The Search for Columbus: The Sources for the First Voyage.* Tucson: University of Arizona Press, 1991.

Herodotus. *The Histories.* Trans. by Aubrey de Sélincourt. London: Penguin, 1954.

Herskovits, Melville J. *The Myth of the Negro Past.* New York: Harper and Bros., 1942.

Holloway, Joseph E., ed. *Africanisms in American Culture.* Bloomington: Indiana University Press, 1990.

Holton, Gerald, and Duane H. D. Roller. *Foundations of Modern Physical Science.* New York: Addison-Wesley, 1958.

Homer. *Odyssey.* Trans. and ed. by Albert Cook. New York: W. W. Norton, 1974.

Horton, James Africanus Beale. *West African Countries and Peoples and a Vindication of the African Race.* London: W. J. Johnson, 1868.

Hourani, Albert. *A History of the Arab Peoples*. Cambridge, MA: Belknap Press of Harvard University Press, 1991.

Hughes, Langston. *The Weary Blues*. New York: Knopf, 1926.

Hurston, Zora Neale. *Moses, Man of the Mountain* [1939]. New York: Harper Collins, 1991.

Ibn Battuta [Mohammed Ibn Allah]. *The Travels . . . A.D. 1325–1354*. Trans. by H.A.R. Gibb. Cambridge: Hakluyt Society, 1971.

Ibn Khaldun. *The Muzadimah: An Introduction to History* [1377]. Trans. by Franz Rosenthal. Princeton: Princeton University Press, 1987.

Idowu, E. Bolaji. *Olódùmarè: God in Yoruba Belief*. London: Longmans, Green, 1962.

Ingstad, Helge. *Westward to Vinland: The Discovery of Pre-Columbian Norse House-Sites in North America*. New York: St. Martin's Press, 1969.

Ivory, Dunzo Annette. "Blacks of Sub-Saharan African Origin in Spain: Image in the Theater (1500–1700)." Ph.D. diss. UCLA, 1974.

Jackson, Peter, and David Morgan, eds. *Mission of Friar William of Rubruck*. London: Hakluyt Society, 1990.

Jahn, Janheinz. *A History of Neo-African Literature*. London: Faber and Faber, 1966.

James, George G. M. *Stolen Legacy*. San Francisco: Julian Richardson, 1954.

James, T.G.H. *An Introduction to Ancient Egypt*. New York: Harper & Row, 1979.

Jefferson, Thomas. *Notes on the State of Virginia* [1784]. In *The Portable Thomas Jefferson*. Ed. by Merrill D. Peterson. New York: Penguin, 1975.

Jeffreys, M.D.W. "The Arabs Discover America Before Columbus," *Muslim Digest* 4:2 (1953), 18–26.

Jenkins, David. *Black Zion: Africa, Imagined and Real, as Seen by Today's Blacks*. New York: Harcourt Brace Jovanovich, 1975.

Johanson, Donald, and Maitland Edey. *Lucy: The Beginnings of Humankind*. New York: Simon and Schuster, 1981.

Johanson, Donald, and James Shreeve. *Lucy's Child*. New York: William Morrow, 1989.

Joinville [Jean, Lord of] and Villehardoun [Geoffroi de]. *Chronicles of the Crusades*. Ed. by M.R.B. Shaw. Harmondsworth, U.K.: Penguin, 1963.

Josephus, Flavius. *The Complete Works of Josephus*. Grand Rapids: Kregel, 1981.

Kaplan, Paul Henry Daniel. *The Rise of the Black Magus in Western Art*. Ann Arbor: University of Michigan Press, 1985.

Karenga, Maulana. *The Book of Coming Forth By Day*. Los Angeles: University of Sankore Press, 1974.

——. *Introduction to Black Studies*. Los Angeles: University of Sankore Press, 1989.

Karenga, Maulana, and Jacob Carruthers, eds. *Kemet and the African Worldview*. Los Angeles: University of Sankore Press, 1986.

Keegan, William. *The People who Discovered Columbus*. Gainesville: University Press of Florida, 1992.

Khan, Hussain. "Sea-Borne Trade to 'Al-Sind Wa'l-Hind,'" *Journal of the Pakistan Historical Society* 39:4 (October 1991): 311–314.

Kiernan, Thomas. *The Negro Impact on Western Civilization*. New York: Philosophical Library, 1970.

King, Florence. *With Charity Towards None*. New York: St Martin's, 1992.

King, Noel Q. *African Cosmos*. Belmont, CA: Wadsworth, 1986.

Komroff, Manuel, ed. *Contemporaries of Marco Polo*. New York: Dorset, 1989.

Koran. Trans. with notes by N. J. Dawood. London: Penguin, 1990.

Kravath, Fred F. *Christopher Columbus, Cosmogrpaher*. Rancho Cordova, CA: Landmark Enterprises, 1987.

Lam, Aboubacry Moussa. "Égypte ancienne et Afrique noire chez Cheikh Anta Diop," *Présence Africaine*. Special Issue on Cheikh Anta Diop. New Bilingual Series 149–150, 1st and 2nd Quarterlies, 1990, 203–213.

Las Casas, Bartolomé de. *In Defense of the Indians* [c. 1552]. Trans. by Stafford Poole. DeKalb: Northern Illinois University Press, 1974.

_____. *The Devastation of the Indies: A Brief Account* [1552]. Trans. by Herman Briffault. Baltimore: Johns Hopkins University Press, 1992.

_____. *History of the Indies*. New York: Harper & Row, 1971.

Leach, Maria. *Standard Dictionary of Folklore, Mythology and Legend*. New York: Funk & Wagnall's, 1941.

Leakey, Louis S. B. *The Progress and Evolution of Man in Africa*. Oxford: Oxford University Press, 1961.

_____. *The Stone Age Races of Kenya*. Oxford: Oxford University Press, 1955.

Leakey, Richard. "African Fossil Man." In *General History of Africa*, ed. by J. Ki-Zerbo. 8 vols. Paris: UNESCO, 1981. vol 1, 437– 451.

Leo, Johannes. See Africanus, Leo.

Letts, Malcolm. *Sir John Mandeville: The Man and His Book*. London: Batchworth, 1949.

Levinson, Jay A., ed. *Circa 1492: Art in the Age of Exploration*. New Haven: Yale University Press, 1991.

Lévi-Strauss, C. *Structural Anthropology*. New York: Basic Books, 1963.

Levtzion, N., and J.F.P. Hopkins, eds. *Corpus of Early Arabic Sources for West African History*. Cambridge: Cambridge University Press, 1981.

Lewis, Bernard. *The Muslim Discovery of Europe*. New York: W. W. Norton, 1982.

Lincoln, Abraham. *Collected Works*. New Brunswick, NJ: Rutgers University Press, 1953.

_____. *Speeches and Writings, 1832–1858*. New York: Library of America, 1989.

Lincoln, C. Eric. *The Black Church Since Frazier*. New York: Schocken, 1974.

_____. *The Black Muslims in America*. Boston: Beacon, 1973.

Lindsay, Vachel. *The Congo and Other Poems*. New York: Macmillan, 1914.

Little, Kenneth. *Negroes in Britain*. London: Kegan Paul, Trench, Trubner, 1947.

Lumpkin, Beatrice. "The Pyramids: Ancient Showcase of African Science and Technology." See Van Sertima, Ivan.

Lynch, Hollis R. *Selected Published Writings of Edward Wilmot Blyden*. New York: Humanities Press, 1971.

MacNutt, Francis, ed. *Francisco Cortés: His Five Letters of Relation to the Emperor Charles V*. 2 vols. Glorieta, NM: Rio Grande Press, 1977.

Madariaga, Salvador de. *Christopher Columbus*. New York: Frederick Ungar, 1940.

Magnusson, Magnus, and Hermann Pálsson, eds. *The Vinland Sagas*. New York: New York University Press, 1966.

Malloy, Stewart C. "Traditional African Watercraft: A New Look." See Van Sertima, Ivan.

Mandeville, Sir John. See also Jules Bramont, Malcolm Letts, C.W.R.D. Moseley, and M. C. Seymour.

____. *Mandeville's Travels: Texts and Translations*. Ed. by Malcolm Letts. 2 vols. London: Hakluyt Society, 1953.

____. *Mandeville's Travels*. Ed. by M. C. Seymour. Oxford: Clarendon Press, 1967.

____. *The Travels of Sir John Mandeville*. Trans. and intro. by C.W.R.D. Moseley. London: Penguin, 1983.

Maquet, Jacques, and Joan Rayfield. *Civilizations of Black Africa*. New York: Oxford University Press, 1972.

Martin, Tony. *The Pan-American Connection*. Dover, MA: Majority Press, 1984.

Martyr, Peter D'Anghera. *De Orbe Novo*. Trans. by Francis Augustus MacNutt. 2 vols. New York: Burt Franklin, 1970.

Massing, Jean Michel. "Early European Images of America: The Ethnographic Approach," See Levinson, Jay A.

Matarasso, D. M., ed. *The Quest for the Holy Grail*. London: Penguin, 1969.

Mbiti, John S. *African Religions & Philosophy*. London: Heinemann, 1969.

____. *Introduction to African Religion*. London: Heinemann, 1975.

McKay, Claude. *Banjo*. New York: Harper & Brothers, 1929.

____. *Home to Harlem*. New York: Harper & Brothers, 1928.

____. *Selected Poems*. Intro. by John Dewey. New York: Bookman Associates, 1953.

Medina, José Toribio. *The Discovery of the Amazons*. Mineola, NY: Dover, 1988.

Milanich, Jerald T., and Susan Milbrath. *First Encounters: Spanish Explorations in the Caribbean and the United States, 1492–1570*. Gainesville: University Press of Florida, 1989.

Morison, Samuel Eliot. *Admiral of the Ocean Sea*. New York: Time, 1942.

____. *Christopher Columbus, Mariner*. New York: New American Library, 1955.

____. *The European Discovery of America: The Northern Voyages*. New York: Oxford University Press, 1971.

____. *The European Discovery of America: The Southern Voyages, 1492–1616*. New York: Oxford University Press, 1974.

____. *The Great Explorers*. New York: Oxford University Press, 1978.

Moseley, C.W.R.D., trans. *The Travels of Sir John Mandeville*. London: Penguin, 1983. Based on the Egerton text.

Moses, Wilson Jeremiah. *The Golden Age of Black Nationalism: 1850– 1925*. Oxford: Oxford University Press, 1978.

Moule, A. C., and Paul Pelliot. *Marco Polo: The Description of the World*. 2 vols. London: George Routledge & Sons, 1938.

Murphy, Joseph. *Santería: An African Religion in America*. Boston: Beacon, 1988.

Newton, Arthur Percival. *Travel and Travellers of the Middle Ages*. London: Routledge & Kegan Paul, 1926.

Niane, D. T., ed. *General History of Africa: Africa from the Twelfth to the Sixteenth Century*. Vol 4 of 8 vols. Paris: UNESCO, 1984.

____. *Sundiata: An Epic of Old Mali*. London: Longman, 1965.

Nobles, Wade W. "Ancient Egyptian Thought and the Renaissance of African (Black) Psychology." In Karenga and Carruthers.

Odoric. *The Voyage and Travayle of Syr John Maundeville Knight with the Journall of Frier Odoricus*. London: J. M. Dent, c. 1887.

Olschki, Leonardo. *Marco Polo's Asia*. Berkeley: University of California Press, 1960.

____. "Ponce de León's Fountain of Youth: A History of a Geographical Myth," *Hispanic American Historical Review* 21 (1941).

O'Neill, Eugene. *The Emperor Jones.* Englewood Cliffs, NJ: Prentice-Hall, 1981.

Orlandi, Ioannes, ed. *Navigatio Sancti Brendani.* Milan: Instituto Editoriale Cisalpino, n.d.

Perdotto, J., and M. Myerwitz Levine, eds. "The Challenge of Black Athena," *Arethusa*, Special Issue, 1989.

Phillips, J.R.S. *The Medieval Expansion of Europe.* Oxford: Oxford University Press, 1988.

Phillips, William D., and Carla Rahn Phillips. *The Worlds of Christopher Columbus.* Cambridge: Cambridge University Press, 1992.

Pigafetta, Antonio. See Eden, Richard.

Pius II. *Historia Rerum Ubique Gestarum* [1477]. In Thacher, John Boyd.

Plato. *The Timaeus and the Critias or Atlanticus.* New York: Pantheon, 1944.

Pliny. *Natural History.* Ed. by H. Rackham, W.H.S. Jones, and D. E. Eichholz. 10 vols. Cambridge, MA: Harvard University Press, 1967.

Plutarch. *Lives.* Ed. by Alan Wordman. Berkeley: University of California Press, 1974.

Polo, Marco. *The Description of the World.* Ed. by A. C. Moule and Paul Pelliot. 2 vols. London: George Routledge & Sons, 1938.

Prah, Kwisi Kwaa. *Jacobus Eliza Johannes Capitein.* Trenton, NJ: Africa World Press, 1992.

Prester John. "Letter of Prester John." In *Mandeville's Travels*, ed. by Malcolm Letts. 2 vols. London: Hakluyt Society, 1953.

Pseudo-Callisthenes. "The Alexander Romance." In *Collected Ancient Greek Novels*, trans. by Ken Dowden, ed. by B. P. Reardon, 650–735. Berkeley: University of California Press, 1989.

Ptolemy, Claudius. *The Geography.* New York: Dover, 1991.

____. *Cosmography: Maps from Ptolemy's Geography.* Intro. by Celio Pagani. Wigston, U.K.: Magna Books, 1990.

Purchas, Samuel. *Hakluytus Posthumus* or *Purchas His Pilgrimes.* 20 vols. Glasgow: James MacLehose & Sons, 1905.

Raleigh, Walter. *The Discoverie of the Large, Rich and Bewtiful Empyre of Guiana* [1506]. Amsterdam: DaCapo Press, 1968. Modern version in *Hakluyt's Voyages.* Ed. by Richard David. Boston: Houghton Mifflin, 1981.

Rampersad, Arnold. *The Life of Langston Hughes.* 2 vols. Oxford: Oxford University Press, 1986.

Ranger, T. O., and Isaria Kimambo. *The Historical Study of African Religion.* Berkeley: University of California Press, 1972.

Read, Jan. *The Moors in Spain and Portugal.* London: Faber and Faber, 1974.

Redkey, Edwin S. *Black Exodus: Black Nationalism and Back to Africa Movements, 1890–1910.* New Haven: Yale University Press, 1969.

Reichert, Rolf. *A Historical Regional Atlas of the Arabic World.* Bahia, Brazil: Universidade Federal de Bahia, n.d.

Riley, C. L., ed. *Man Across the Sea: Problems of Pre-Columbian Contacts.* Austin: University of Texas Press, 1971.

Roucek, Joseph S., and Thomas Kiernan. *The Negro Impact on Western Civilization.* New York: Philosophical Library, 1970.

Rouse, Irving. *The Taínos: Rise and Fall of the People Who Greeted Columbus*. New Haven: Yale University Press, 1992.

Rubruck, William. *The Mission of Friar William of Rubruck*. Trans. by Peter Jackson. London: Hakluyt Society, 1970.

Russell, John. "In Spain, the 'Stuff of Paradise,'" *International Herald Tribune*, April 4–5, 1992.

Sagan, Carl. *Broca's Brain: Reflections on the Romance of Science*. New York: Random House, 1979.

———— *Cosmos*. New York: Random House, 1980.

St. Augustine. *De civitate Dei* [City of God]. Trans. by Henry Bettenson. Harmondsworth, U.K.: Penguin, 1972.

St. Brendan. For Anglo-Norman version, see Benedict, *The Anglo Norman Voyage of St Brendan*. Ed. by E.G.R. Waters. Oxford: Clarendon Press, 1928. For German version, see Rolf D. Fay, ed. *Sankt Brendan: Zwei Fruhneuhoch-deutsche Prosafassungen*. Stuttgart: Helfant Edition, 1985. For the Italian/Latin version, see Ioannes Orlandi, ed. *Navigatio Sancti Brendani*. Milan: Instituto Editoriale Cisalpino, n.d. For Latin version, see J. P. Webb, trans. *The Age of Bede*. Harmondsworth, U.K.: Penguin, 1982.

Sale, Kirkpatrick. *The Conquest of Paradise*. New York: Alfred A. Knopf, 1990.

Sancho, Ignatius. *Letters of the Late Ignatius Sancho* [1782]. Intro. by Paul Edwards. London: Dawsons of Pall Mall, 1968.

Scobie, Edward. "The Moors and Portugal's Global Expansion." See Van Sertima, Ivan.

"Seafarer." In *Anglo-Saxon Poetry*, ed. by R. K. Gordon, 76–78. London: J. M. Dent & Sons, 1954.

Seneca. *Selections*. Ed. by Umbert Moricca. Turin, Italy: I. B. Paravia, 1947.

Sephocle, Marilyn. "Anton Wilhelm Amo," *Journal of Black Studies* 23:2 (December 1992), 182–187.

Seymour, M. C., ed. *Mandeville's Travels*. Oxford: Clarendon Press, 1967.

Shape of the World. Chicago: Rand McNally, 1991.

Sherratt, Andrew. *The Cambridge Encyclopedia of Archaeology*. New York: Crown, 1980.

Shirley, Rodney W. *The Mapping of the World*. London: Holland Press Cartographica, 1984

Shyllon, Folarin. *Black People in Britain, 1555–1833*. London: Oxford University Press, 1977.

Simpson, George Eaton. *Black Religions in the New World*. New York: Columbia University Press, 1978.

Sir Gawain and the Green Knight. Ed. by J.R.R. Tolkien and E. V. Gordon. Oxford: Clarendon Press, 1952.

The Sixth and Seventh Books of Moses. Arlington, TX: Dorene, n.d.

Skelton, R. A. *Explorers' Maps: Chapters in the Cartographic Record of Geographical Discovery*. London: Routledge and Kegan Paul, 1958.

Skelton, R. A., Thomas E. Marston, and George D. Painter. *The Vinland Map and the Tartar Relation*. New Haven: Yale University Press, 1965.

Slessarev, Ysevolod. *Prester John: The Letter and the Legend*. Minneapolis: University of Minnesota Press, 1959.

Snowden, Frank M. *Before Color Prejudice*. Cambridge, MA: Harvard University Press, 1983.

———. *Black in Antiquity*. Cambridge, MA: Harvard University Press, 1970.

Southern, Eileen. *The Music of Black America: A History*. New York: W. W. Norton, 1971.

Speck, Gordon. *Myths and New World Explorations*. Fairfield, WA: De Galleon, 1979.

Suckale-Redlefsen, Gude. *The Black Saint Maurice/Mauritius: Der Heilige Mohr*. Austin: University of Texas Press, 1987.

Sypher, Wylie. *Guinea's Captive Kings*. Chapel Hill: University of North Carolina Press, 1942.

Tannenbaum, Frank. *Slave and Citizen*. New York: Vintage, 1946.

Taviani, Paolo Emilio. *Columbus: The Great Adventure*. New York: Orion, 1991.

Tempels, Placide. *Bantu Philosophy*. Paris: Présence Africaine, 1961.

Thacher, John Boyd. *Christopher Columbus: His Life, His Work, His Remains*. 3 vols. New York: G. P. Putnam's Sons, 1903.

Theoderich. *Guide to the Holy Land* [1172]. Trans. by Aubrey Stewart. New York: Ithaca Press, 1986.

Thomas, Lamont. *Paul Cuffee, Black Entrepreneur*. Champaign-Urbana: University of Illinois Press, 1988.

Thompson, Stith. *The Folktale*. Berkeley: University of California Press, 1977.

Thorlby, Anthony, ed. *The Penguin Companion to Literature*. 4 vols. Harmondsworth, U.K.: Penguin, 1969.

Turner, Paul. *Selections from the History of the World*. Carbondale: Southern Illinois University Press, 1962.

Tutuola, Amos. *The Palm-Wine Drinkard*. New York: Grove Weidenfield, 1984.

———. *The Wild Hunter in the Bush of Ghosts*. Intro. by Bernth Lindfors. Washington, DC: Three Continents Press, 1982.

Tyrrell, William Blake. *Amazons: A Study in Athenian Mythmaking*. Baltimore: Johns Hopkins University Press, 1991.

Ullendorff, Edward. *Ethiopia and the Bible*. London: Oxford University Press, 1968.

'Umari, Ibn Fadl Allah al. Cited in J. Devisse and S. Labib, "African Inter-Continental Relations," in *General History of Africa*, 8 vols. Ed. by D. T. Niane, 644–665. Paris: UNESCO, 1984.

Uya, Okot Edet. *Black Brotherhood*. Lexington, MA: D.C. Heath, 1971.

Van Sertima, Ivan, ed. *Blacks in Science: Ancient and Modern*. New Brunswick, N.J.: Transaction, 1991.

———. *Egypt Revisited*. New Brunswick, NJ: Transaction, 1991.

———. *Golden Age of the Moors*. New Brunswick, NJ: Transaction, 1992.

———. *They Came Before Columbus*. New York: Random House, 1976.

Van Sertima, Ivan, and Runoko Rashidi, eds. *African Presence in Early Asia*. New Brunswick, NJ: Transaction, 1988.

Vansina, Jan. *Oral Tradition: A Study in Historical Methodology*. London: Routledge & Kegan Paul, 1961.

Van Vechten, Carl. *Nigger Heaven*. New York: Alfred A. Knopf, 1926.

Vespucci, Amerigo. *Letter to Piero Soderni* [1504]. Trans. by George T. Northup. 5 vols. in series. Princeton: Princeton University Press, 1916.

____. *Letters from a New World*. Ed. by Luciano Formisano. New York: Marsilio, 1992.

____. *Mundus Novus* [Letter to Lorenzo Pietro de Medici]. Trans. by George Tyler Northrop. 5 vols. Princeton: Princeton University Press, 1916.

Vico, Giambattista. *The New Science*. Ithaca: Cornell University Press, 1948.

The Vinland Sagas: Norse Discovery of America [contains "Greenland Saga" and "Erik's Saga"]. Trans. and intro. by Magnus Magnusson and Hermann Pálsson. New York: New York University Press, 1966.

Virgil. *The Aeneid*. Trans. by Robert Fitzgerald. New York: Random House, 1981.

"Wanderer." In *Anglo-Saxon Poetry*, ed. by R. K. Gordon. 73–75. London: J. M. Dent & Sons, 1954.

Washburn, Wilcomb E., ed. *Proceedings of the Vinland Map Conference*. Chicago: University of Chicago Press, 1971.

Waters, E.G.R., ed. *Anglo-Norman Voyage of St. Brendan*. Oxford: Clarendon Press, 1928.

Watts, Jill. *God, Harlem U.S.A.* Berkeley: University of California Press, 1992.

Webb, J. R., ed. *The Age of Bede*. Harmondsworth, U.K.: Penguin, 1983.

Wheatley, Phillis. *The Collected Works of Phillis Wheatley*. Ed. by John Shields. New York: Oxford University Press, 1988.

____. *Poems on Various Subjects* [London, 1773]. Chapel Hill: University of North Carolina Press, 1966.

White, David Gordon. *Myths of the Dog-Man*. Chicago: University of Chicago Press, 1991.

Whitman, Walt. *Leaves of Grass*. New York: Oxford University Press, 1990.

Wiener, Leo. *Africa and the Discovery of America*. 3 vols. Philadelphia: Innes & Sons, 1920, 1923.

Wilford, John Noble. "In Egypt's Brilliance, Nubian Roots," *International Herald Tribune*, February 13, 1992.

Williams, Bruce. "Excavations Between Abu Simbel and the Sudan Frontier." Vol 3 of the Nubian Expedition. Part 1: "The A-Group Royal Cemetery at Qustul: Cemetery L." Chicago: Oriental Institute of University of Chicago, 1986.

____. "The Lost Pharaohs of Nubia," *Archaeology Journal* (September 1980), 12–21.

Williams, Chancellor. *The Destruction of Black Civilization — Great Issues of a Race From 450 B.C. to 2000 A.D.* Chicago: Third World Press, 1974.

Winship, George P., ed. *The Journey of Coronado*. New York: Allerton, 1922.

Wood, Michael. *World Atlas of Archaeology*. Boston: G. K. Hall, 1985.

Woodson, Carter G. *The Mis-Education of the Negro* [1933]. Trenton, NJ: Africa World Press, 1990.

Wright, Richard. *Black Power: A Record of Reactions in the Land of Pathos*. New York: Harper, 1954.

Wright, Thomas, ed. *Early Travels in Palestine*. New York: A.M.S. Press, 1969.

Zarncke, Friedrich. *Der Priester Johannes*. 2 vols. Leipzig: S. Hirzel, 1876, 1879.

Index

234 Index

interpolations in letter, 58–59; and
King João II, 63; and later travel
accounts, 63; *Letter of*, 41, 56–64, 74;
and misogyny, 60–61; and monsters,
56, 60, 61, 63; New World affinities,
63; and Paradise, 56, 62; and pepper
forest, 56, 61, 63; Pope Alexander
III's reply, 56, 62; his power, 56; and
St Thomas, 57; as super text, 63; and
the "Three Indias," 56, 59; visualized,
58; his wealth, 56, 59; also see
Africanus, Carpini, Columbus,
Mandeville, Mongols, Odoric, Polo,
Rubruck and Travel, African
Prince Henry the "Navigator," 63, 172
Prophet F.S. Cherry, 187
Proto text, 41, 55, 107, 117. *See also*
Polo, subtext
Psalms, 3, 8, 39
Pseudo-Callistenes, 22. *See also*
Alexander
Ptolemy, *Guide to Geography*, 3, 14–15,
44, 68
Purchas, Samuel, 25
Pygmies, 22, 41, 42, 88. *See also*
monsters

Queen Hippolyte, 32. *See also* Amazons
Quest, 7. *See also* journey, Travel and
Travelers
Quetzlcoatl, 31, 39
Quivira, 12. *See also* Antilla, Cibola, El
Dorado, Hy Brasil, St. Brendan's,
Three Indies

Raleigh, Sir Walter, 11–12, 25, 82, 85
Reconquista, 166
Red Sea, 65
Reubeni, David, 77
Revelations, as biblical reference, 46
Robeson, Paul, 188
Rome, 38, 42, 71, 78
Rosetta Stone, 151
Rousseau, Jean Jacques, 34, 104
Rubruck, William of (or Rubrouck,
Guillaume de), 22, 81, 83–85, 91; and
barbarians, 83; and Christianity as
solution, 83; compared with Carpini,

83; and Columbus, 85; and El Dorado,
84; and epic journey, 83; and Fountain
of Youth, 84; and Gog and Magog,
83; and gold, 84; and Jews, 83–84; and
landscape, 85; negative attitude to non-
Europeans, 83; and Paradise, 84; and
Pliny, 85; and Prester John, 84
Rufus, Quintus Curtius, 46
Russworm, John, 181

Saint Damien, 5
Saint Jerome, 5
Saint Paulinus, 5
Saint-Victor, Hughes de, *Descriptio
Mappae Mundi*, 6
Sancho, Ignatius, 174, 175–176
Santería, 141, 180
Saracens, 27, 61. *See also* Muslims and
Polo
Sciopods, 22. *See also* monsters
Sciritoe, 22
"Scraelings" childlike and simplistic,
103; concept of beauty, 104; as evil,
104; and language, 104; leadership,
104; as monsters, 104; Viking battles
with, 106; and witchcraft, 105
Sea Islands, 179. *See also* DuBose
Hayward, Gershwin, Gullah
Sea monsters, 21
Sea of Darkness, 5
"Seafarer," 8
Seneca, *Medea*, 27, 30
Sepúlveda, Juan Ginés de, and 1550
debate with Bartolomé de las Casas,
18, 70, 121
Serpents, 21
Seven Cities or Island of Seven Cities,
10, 16
Signifying Monkey,185
Silk, 9, 71, 76
Silver, 31, 59, 75, 78, 86, 90
Sinbad, 65
Sir Gawain and the Green Knight, 19–20
Sixth and Seventh Books of Moses, 158
Slave narrative, 186. *See also* Bontemps,
Cleaver, Cugoano, Douglass, Equiano,
Malcolm X, Sancho, Washington
Slave Revolts, 186

Christian travelers, 75; and conquest, 75; and European mythology, 75; and Jerusalem as "home," 75, 77; and scholarship, 70. *See also* under specific names, Benjamin ben Jonah of Tudela, Jacob Ha Cohen, Meshullam ben R. Menahem, Petachia of Ratisbon, and David Reubeni

Travelers/Missionary (to the East), 65–71, 74-92. *See* Amazons; cannibals, China, India, Genghis Khan, Kublai Khan, Mongols, legendary people and places, monsters. *See also* Carpini, John of Monte Corvino, Odoric, and Rubruck

Travelers, Muslim, 67–74. *See* Travelers, Arab and under specific names including Africanus, Ibn Battuta, Ibn Khaldun

Troglodytes, 22

Turner, Henry McNeal, 181

Tutuola, Amos, *The Palm Wine Drinkard*, 138–141; death, 140; global concerns, 138, 141; landscape, 138–139; monsters,140; oral nature, 139; quest, 138; rebirth and Yoruba belief; and Yoruba writing, 139–140

U. S. Supreme Court, 182

Ulysses, 13, 30

'Umari, Ibn Fadl Allah al and account of African New World travel, 143–145

Umayyads, 161

Utopia, 75, 85, 90, 91, 98, 126. *See also* Bacon, Campanella, More, Odoric, St. Brendan,Vikings

Van Vechten, Carl, 184

Veneto, Paolino Fra, 5–6

Verbal accounts, 7–14, 101, 133–138, 185. *See also* Tutuola

Vespucci, Amerigo, 37

Viewed accounts, 2–3, 14–18

Viking Sagas ("Erik's Saga" and "Greenland Saga"), 100–106; and black color, 105; Christian propaganda, 101, 103; and conquest, 101; Winston Churchill and the Vikings, 103; cruelty of, 103; departure from North

America, 100; and "discovery," 101; literary descendants of, 104; North America as utopia, 102–103; and "otherness," 103–104; and the Vinland map, 100–101, and redrawn map of 1590 and 1670, 102; women in, 105. *See also* "Scraelings," St. Brendan

Vinland map, 100–102

Virgil, 22, 31

Visionary responses, 2–3, 18–28, 37–38, 56, 61, 87

Visual accounts, 2–3, 4–7, 58, 65–66, 100–102, 124. *See also* cartographers

Vodun, 141, 180

Voodoo. See *Vodun*

Waldseemüller, Martin, 38–39

Wallace, Alfred, 157

"Wanderer," 8

Wheatley, Phillis, and Africa, 157

Whitman, Walt, and Africa, 184

Wife-givers, 22, 88, 113. *See also* Alexander, monsters, Pliny

"Wild Man," 20, 38, 39, 125. *See also* Caliban, Charles V, Christianity, Friday, "Indian," "Noble Savage," Pliny

Williams, Chancellor, 149, 154–155

Women, 44, 53, 81, 88, 105, 113, 122; mariginalized, 25; as monstrous creatures, 23, 50, 55, 60–61; Native American women, 25; victimized, as whores, 24. *See also* Amazons, Mandeville, Polo

Wonders of the East, 41, 44, 45, 52–55, 61, 64, 89

Wonders, 41, 43. *See also* Alexander, monsters, Polo, *Wonders of the East*

Wright, Richard, *Black Power*, 188–189

Y-Hang, 18

Yoruba, 180–181. *See also* candomblé, santería and vodun. *See* Afrocentric, Afrocentricity, Afrocentrism. *See also* Asante, Karenga

Zanzibar, 65

ABOUT THE AUTHOR

O. R. DATHORNE is Professor of English at the University of Kentucky and Executive Director of the Association of Caribbean Studies. His lastest publications include two seminal studies (*Black Mind* (1974) and *Dark Ancestor* (1981)), a novel (*Dele's Child* (1986)), and a book of poems (*Songs for a New World* (1988)). Dr. Dathorne is also the editor of *Journal of Caribbean Studies*.